Revolutionary Subjectivity
in the Thought of Karl Marx

Historical Materialism Book Series

The Historical Materialism Book Series is a major publishing initiative of the radical left. The capitalist crisis of the twenty-first century has been met by a resurgence of interest in critical Marxist theory. At the same time, the publishing institutions committed to Marxism have contracted markedly since the high point of the 1970s. The Historical Materialism Book Series is dedicated to addressing this situation by making available important works of Marxist theory. The aim of the series is to publish important theoretical contributions as the basis for vigorous intellectual debate and exchange on the left.

The peer-reviewed series publishes original monographs, translated texts, and reprints of classics across the bounds of academic disciplinary agendas and across the divisions of the left. The series is particularly concerned to encourage the internationalization of Marxist debate and aims to translate significant studies from beyond the English-speaking world.

For a full list of titles in the Historical Materialism Book Series available in paperback from Haymarket Books, visit: www.haymarketbooks.org/series_collections/1-historical-materialism.

Revolutionary Subjectivity in the Thought of Karl Marx

*Exploring the Psychosocial
Dynamic of Emancipation*

Paul Elias

Haymarket Books
Chicago, IL

First published in 2024 by Brill Academic Publishers, The Netherlands
© 2025 Koninklijke Brill NV, Leiden, The Netherlands

Published in paperback in 2025 by
Haymarket Books
P.O. Box 180165
Chicago, IL 60618
773-583-7884
www.haymarketbooks.org

ISBN: 979-8-88890-574-6

Distributed to the trade in the US through Consortium Book Sales and
Distribution (www.cbsd.com) and internationally through Ingram
Publisher Services International (www.ingramcontent.com).

This book was published with the generous support of Lannan
Foundation, Wallace Action Fund, and the Marguerite Casey Foundation.

Special discounts are available for bulk purchases by organizations and
institutions. Please call 773-583-7884 or email info@haymarketbooks.org
for more information.

Cover art and design by David Mabb. Cover art is a section from
*Construct 74, After John Henry Dearle (for Morris & Co.) Sweet Briar /
Varvara Stepanova, untitled textile design*, acrylic on wallpaper mounted on
linen (2024).

Printed in the United States.

Library of Congress Cataloging-in-Publication data is available.

Andre,
Thanks for the message about my book.
This isn't the book you read, but it doesn't matter.
I'll see you in Temagami.

∴

Contents

A Confession

'It is a matter of a *confession*, and nothing more'.
MARX[1]

∴

In the midst of an intimate conversation at a time when this project was just a hazy idea of an amorphous plan for critical engagement with Marx's philosophy, I found myself in the odd position of identifying as a Marxist, supporting the central philosophical and political tenets of Marx's social theory, but simultaneously maintaining that his theory of revolutionary subjectivity – which, in my view, is a central component of his revolutionary theory – is inconsistent and full of gaps. In a way, this work has inadvertently become a recounting of the shedding of my theoretical skin – a kind of *anámnēsis*. It is not just an interpretation of Marx's writings; it is intended to be a critical engagement with his thinking. The point of interpretive work is to raise the truth of Marx's thought higher and to reanimate it for our current historical moment.

I do not attempt to solve the problem of revolutionary subjectivity as it exists in his work. A 'scientific' theory of the development of revolutionary subjectivity can only be demonstrated through self-evidence which is both 'theoretical and practical', at which point the apparent opposition between theory and practice is sublated. In other words, the 'soul' of the revolutionary subject cannot be known merely as an object in the world but fundamentally as the activity of a subject through our own collective participation in 'revolutionary practice'.

Admittedly, attempting to solve the problem was part of my initial aim as a Marxist until I went deeper into Marx's thought. Engaging with the question of revolutionary subjectivity compelled me to move beyond my Marxism and alter my theoretical orientation. I had to sublate Marx's thought and was not able to do it as a Marxist because it took me down paths that were untrodden and obstructed by Marxist interpretations of his thinking. This intellectual journey is elaborated throughout the present work.

---

1 MECW 3, p. 145.

At a Historical Materialism conference in Toronto in May 2016 I was asked why I bothered to investigate Marx's idea of revolutionary subjectivity 'theoretically'. This question had never crossed my mind in any significant way until that moment. My interlocutor argued that the revolutionary subjects are created by 'history' and that we do not need a theory because we/they just need to become revolutionary. Essentially, the question boiled down to why I even bothered to make it a philosophical problem if Marx's revolutionary social theory is ultimately about 'changing the world'. I cannot recall how I responded but I remember wanting to say that we are driven to comprehend this philosophically because of our 'material and spiritual' struggles, as Marx put it. The lives of working people are becoming more difficult and our suffering is increasing. The worker's movement around the globe is stagnating and extreme right-wing reaction is on the rise worldwide – and as the average temperature of the Earth rises at an intensified rate, it appears that the 'icy water of egotistical calculation' is only getting colder.[2] Widespread economic precarity since the Great Recession of 2008 has led to an ever deepening global political crisis after banks and corporations were bailed out and the masses of working people were met with punitive and devastating austerity. The legitimacy of the neoliberal politics of so-called centrists has collapsed. Political attitudes are rapidly polarising in this environment and the ideological conflict is becoming sharper. It is particularly troubling that the rise of extreme right-wing politics around the globe is eclipsing the organisational efforts of the disarrayed left. Indeed, nationalist, racist, xenophobic, and authoritarian trends are ascendant features in political life. As a plethora of far-right tendencies are on the rise globally among societies under immense stress from socioeconomic crises and profound inequality, the world approaches a political precipice. With the percolating instability of the global economy and anticipated destabilising effects of climate change looming on the horizon, a perfect storm for intense social conflict within nations and between nations is brewing.

It is in this time of crisis and increasing sociopolitical polarisation, in which a decidedly reactionary right is ascendant in many parts of the globe, that we find ourselves in the midst of a Marx revival. At the same time, the growing support for increasingly far-right politics among significant sections of the working class poses significant challenges to his theory about the ascendancy of the revolutionary proletariat and the movement for 'human emancipation in general'.[3] And yet Marx's work also contains the vision of counter-revolutionary

---

2   MECW 6, p. 487.

3   MECW 3, p. 155.

tendencies which mirror the contemporary working-class susceptibility to far-right politics. This situation evinces the need for a systematic re-examination of Marx's thought about revolutionary subjectivity in a way that goes further than existing literature and into the depths of his philosophy – and beyond it.

Marx claimed that humanity 'inevitably sets itself on such tasks as it is able to solve'.[4] Whether or not this is determined to be true, we cannot comprehend the solutions to the social problems and political conflicts that we face without comprehending *ourselves*, and if we seriously intend to achieve these aims, we cannot avoid becoming involved in philosophy. As Alfred North Whitehead claimed,

> Every epoch has its character determined by the way its populations react to the material events which they encounter. This reaction is determined by their basic beliefs – by their hopes, their fears, their judgments of what is worthwhile. They may rise to the greatness of an opportunity ... On the other hand, they may collapse before the perplexities confronting them. How they act depends partly on their courage, partly on their intellectual grasp. Philosophy is an attempt to clarify those fundamental beliefs which finally determine the emphasis of attention that lies at the base of character.[5]

This kind of philosophical approach shares a similar spirit with what Marx called the 'self-clarification' – or '*confession*' – of 'the present time of its struggles and desires'.[6] In his opinion it is a '*task of history*' to 'establish the *truth of this world*', and the immediate task of '*philosophy*' insofar as it 'is in the service of history' is 'to unmask human self-estrangement'.[7] However, this book demonstrates that Marx's philosophical approach is not – and indeed cannot be – oriented toward discovering the truth for others to merely 'accept, preach and put into practice'.[8] Instead, its ethos is akin to the sentiment expressed in what Socrates said, while he stood on the threshold of the Cave, about those who are not aware of their chains: 'They're like us'.

---

4   MECW 29, p. 263.
5   Whitehead 1967, p. 99.
6   MECW 3, p. 145.
7   MECW 3, p. 176.
8   MECW 23, p. 106.

Introduction

> All this nonsense. Digression.
> MARX[1]

∴

Karl Marx's idea of revolutionary subjectivity has not received the critical attention that it deserves from scholars of his work and proponents of his revolutionary theory.[2] He thought that he perceived the genesis of an emancipatory form
of individuality within the ranks of the working classes in societies shaped by
the capitalist mode of production.[3] Through a critical analysis of capitalism
Marx envisioned the initiation of a free society by the actions of revolutionary
subjects whose incipient development is evident in the 'historical movement
going on under our very eyes'.[4] In his view, the fundamental life activity of
working people in capitalist society, including the struggles that arise from it,
would shape the proletariat into a revolutionary subject. And yet he simultaneously depicts the position of the working class as though their conditions of
life undermine the development of the character and capacities required for
self-emancipation.

This problem in his thinking about working-class revolution takes on an
added layer of significance if we consider the fact that the revolution he envisioned has not taken place – even though there have been glimpses of workers'
emancipation – at which point we must wonder why his claims about the detrimental nature of working-class life have not had a more disturbing influence
on Marxist thinking. But even if we recognise, as Joseph McCarney did, that
'the failure' of the revolutionary subject to 'play its historical role' is a 'crisis'
facing Marxism, the problem with Marx's idea of revolutionary subjectivity is

---

1   MECW 28, p. 204.
2   Guido Starosta is one of the relatively few exceptions, and he claimed that 'not many works
    have explicitly put the problematic of *revolutionary subjectivity* at the center of the critique
    of political economy' (Starosta 2005, p. 162). See Chapter Five for remarks on Starosta's work.
3   In 1845 Marx thought many of these subjects had already begun to blossom in relatively
    advanced capitalist countries. He claimed that 'a large part of the English and French pro-
    letariat is already *conscious* of its historic task and is constantly working to develop that
    consciousness into complete clarity' (MECW 4, p. 37).
4   MECW 6, p. 498.

not simply 'the absence of this subject as Marx conceived it'.[5] Indeed, we might be short sighted and 'this subject' may still appear. The real problem ultimately arises from the inconsistent configuration of Marx's undertheorised idea of the revolutionary subject.

Re-examining this aspect of Marx's thought is worthwhile in periods when the working-class movement is weak and divided, and significant sections develop regressive political tendencies which hinder it from realising its inherently revolutionary interests. The global rise of the far-right and development of increasingly extreme political tendencies in our contemporary social climate makes the current historical conjecture a particularly fitting time for such reflection on Marx's thought. But while his 'materialistic conception of history' is renowned for its insightfulness into social and political life and useful for articulating the conditions which give rise to extreme politics, Marx's depiction of a fundamental subjective dimension involved in the etiology of any given form of social and political struggle is not adequately emphasised in secondary literature.[6]

Comprehending Marx's idea of revolutionary subjectivity and providing an account of it that illuminates hitherto neglected aspects of his thinking requires close examination of other key elements of his social philosophy. The critical analysis of it in this book is arrived at through exploring his ontology and 'dialectical method', his philosophical anthropology, his vision of 'communist society', and his thoughts about the historical process of human development. A chapter is devoted to each of these aspects of his thought.

Marx's idea of the 'dialectical method' is the focus of the first chapter. This is a frequently discussed aspect of his philosophy that he never elaborated at length, paving the way for a variety of misinterpretations. Its exposition in this book is treated as fundamental for the interpretation of the other aspects of his social philosophy that follow. In Marx's writing, 'dialectic' signifies a method, or mode of thought, and an ontological concept which originated in a philosophical tradition beginning with ancient Hellenic thought and sublated by Hegel. In Hegel's words, a central ontological premise of this tradition is the idea that 'Reason directs the world'.[7] Marx's writings demonstrate that Hegel's sublation of this idea into his own philosophy had a profound and enduring influence on Marx's thought. For this reason, Hegel's writings are an invalu-

---

5 McCarney 1990, pp. 163; 180. Elsewhere he claims that Marx failed to correctly identify the revolutionary subject because of 'the undeveloped state of the object of analysis', i.e., 'it has yet to reach maturity' (McCarney 1991, p. 31).

6 MECW 24, p. 305.

7 Hegel 1956, p. 12.

able source of further clarification for all key components of Marx's method. Even though there is substantial evidence found throughout the span of Marx's writing which indicates that he critically retheorised this ontological idea, it nevertheless remains largely overlooked.[8] He thought that essential features of our activity in capitalism display the work of 'Reason' in an unreasonable form because it is instrumental in the development of 'the productive forces of social labour' and 'the integral development of every individual producer' which are preconditions for a 'reasonable' form of society.[9]

Through a 'critical analysis of the actual facts' of social life-activity, Marx concluded that there is a discernable tendency for 'a higher economic form of society' to emerge.[10] If this goes unrecognised we risk making the mistake of interpreting his 'mature' critique of capitalism primarily as an attempt to merely expose the *transitory* character of the capitalist mode of production. Allen Wood, for instance, claimed that the 'ultimate aim of Marx's theory, of course, is to reveal the tendencies to change inherent in bourgeois society'.[11] This view, in which it is believed that abstract 'change' is all that Marx recognised in the historical process, is not accurate because Marx emphasised the transitory character of capitalism insofar as he claimed to see the imminent development of 'a higher form of society' from within the social life process of capitalism.[12] An indispensable aspect of Marx's 'dialectical method' was thus the comprehension of the 'positive in the negative', which is a feature of what in Hegelian terminology is a 'speculative' (or 'positively rational') form of thought.[13] The fact that Marx sublated Hegel's 'dialectical method' is widely recognised by commentators on Marx's thought but a commonly held view among them is that Marx abandoned the 'speculative' aspect of Hegel's method along with his rejection of Absolute Idealism. However, substantial evidence from Marx's writing indicates that he retained the element of 'speculative' thought. Encouraged perhaps by Marx's excessive criticism of Hegel's

---

8   See Ted Winslow's paper '"Internal relations" and Marx's "materialist conception of history"' (2015, *Capital & Class*, 39, 1: 95–110) for a notable exception.

9   MECW 3, p. 143; MECW 24, p. 200; MECW 35, p. 90.

10   MECW 35, p. 17; MECW 37, p. 763.

11   Wood 2004, p. 226.

12   MECW 37, p. 806. Cf. McCarney's claim that 'what underlies Marx's conception of the practical significance of his social theory is his allegiance to an idea of method derived ultimately from Hegel', i.e., 'the phenomenological dialectic', and that 'the central substantive insight of dialectics is' the 'idea that behind the phenomenal forms of existing society there is a more rational order struggling to be born' (McCarney 1990, pp. 114; 193).

13   Hegel 1969, p. 56. According to Hegel it is 'the most important aspect of dialectic' and 'for thinking which is as yet unpractised and unfree it is the most difficult' (Ibid.).

'dialectical method', the 'speculative' is habitually treated as one of the key features of Hegel's thought that Marx decisively discarded after his so-called materialist turn.[14] In comparison, the phenomenological character of Marx's method is recognised more readily, although a proper analysis of it further elucidates Marx's connection to Hegel's Idealism. Ultimately, the key components of Marx's 'dialectical method' form a triad: the ontological idea that 'Reason directs the world', its phenomenological character, and his 'speculative' thinking.

The second chapter examines Marx's philosophical anthropology. This involves an analysis of his writing about 'human nature' and addresses the interpretive controversy about whether he had an idea of *'universal human* nature' that is transhistorical or an idea that it is determined by transitory social relations and modes of life.[15] The apparent opposition of these apparently diametrically opposed positions is resolved by excavating the strong influence of Aristotle – for whom the 'nature' of a thing is what it is when fully developed – in Marx's writings on this topic. Clarifying this theoretical impasse overcomes many problems in the interpretive literature on Marx's work. For Marx, even though our 'essential' character (as expressed through our life activity) is such that its expression changes throughout the transitions between varying forms of what he termed the 'ensemble of the social relations', each character is a determinate gradation in our 'universal' development nonetheless.[16] Throughout his work he described various aspects of the 'human being' but his consistent description of humanity as a 'universal' being – along with his identification of us with the activity of consciousness, 'mind', and 'reason' – enables us to determine the definition that most accurately captures his idea of humanity; namely, that we are a 'free' being when our development is completed.[17] And while his articulation of 'human nature' morphs at various points throughout his work, the fundamental idea of humanity as a consciously 'rational' and ultimately 'free' being remained essential throughout.[18]

---

14 Evidence from Marx's 'mature' writings which indicates that he did not abandon or profoundly alter the ontological and epistemological foundations of his method as his thought developed will be presented throughout this chapter.

15 MECW 1, p. 191.

16 MECW 5, p. 4.

17 The notion of 'full [human] development' arises explicitly in *Capital*, wherein Marx also identifies humanity with the activity of mind, and wherein he claims that the goal of 'the education of the future' is to produce 'fully developed human beings' (MECW 35, pp. 412; 486).

18 This also bears the influence of Hegel and his association of humanity with 'self-conscious Reason'.

With the development of our '*species-powers*' we are able to feel, think and act with knowledge of the 'universal', which is 'reason', as it pertains to all aspects of our life. Thus according to Marx the 'five senses', along with our 'mental' and 'practical senses', can be more or less rational.[19] As he put it, the 'human' species has the potential to know 'how to apply everywhere the inherent standard to the object', which in his view applies to the ethical, aesthetic, and intellectual aspects of our life activity (all of which are unique to 'human' existence).[20] Taken in accordance with his ontological premises in which 'reason' is conceived as the 'substance' of the natural universe, Marx's writings put forth the idea that we can become conscious of 'reason' in the form of 'universal' laws (e.g., the 'laws of beauty') which forms the core theoretical foundation for Marx's idea of self-determination (e.g., when 'the music is good' and 'the listener understands music').[21] This concept of freedom is at the centre of Marx's sporadic definition of humanity. Aristotle's influence is also evident here and it is possible to articulate Marx's idea of our 'universality' as the development of the totality of our capacities for virtuous activity.[22]

Marx's vision of the realisation of freedom is explored in the third chapter which focuses on his idea of 'a communist organisation of society', and his idea of human nature is further elaborated in the process.[23] The 'social reason' he envisioned is a mode of life devoted to 'full [human] development', which, somewhat paradoxically, is dependent on the actions of 'universally developed individuals'.[24] In accordance with the interpretive points made in the previous chapter, such individuals are 'universal' not only because they have developed in an all-round fashion but fundamentally because they have developed virtue in the Aristotelian sense. It follows that the activities and ethical character of relations which define this society can be articulated in relation to Aristotle's idea of a life of 'living well and acting well' arising from the practice of 'complete virtue' in our relations with others.[25] Particular focus is placed on the

---

19   MECW 3, pp. 301–2.

20   MECW 3, p. 277.

21   Ibid.; MECW 31, p. 195. According to Hegel, 'if I am dependent, my being is referred to something else which I am not … I am free on the contrary, when my existence depends upon myself' (Hegel 1956, p. 17). Likewise, Marx thought that a '*being* only considers himself independent … when he owes his *existence* to himself' (MECW 3, p. 304).

22   Aristotle describes virtue as 'a being-at-work of the soul in accordance with reason' (Aristotle 2002, p. 11).

23   MECW 5, p. 394.

24   MECW 36, p. 314; MECW 28, p. 99.

25   Aristotle 2002, pp. 13; 84.

ethical character of social relations in this society – the 'universal' ethical good which is an essential feature of a free life – because revolutionary subjects must develop the ethical capacities (i.e., those capacities involved in relating to others) which are required to initiate an incipient form of these relations as part of their revolutionary practice.

The fourth chapter explores vital philosophical components of Marx's writing on history. It reconnects in a necessary way with the ontological and methodological ideas from the first chapter and puts forward what is likely to be one of the more controversial interpretations presented in this book. The method described in the first chapter is evident in his attempts at 'comprehending theoretically the historical movement as a whole'.[26] Marx presented a 'speculative' view of history which comprehends a 'dialectic' in human activity that drives human development and, more specifically, the growth of 'communist society' from within capitalism. On Marx's premises, 'reason' allegedly 'governs' our species' developmental history. This interpretation of Marx's ontology and its relation to his idea of history will likely be considered too Hegelian for most commentators on Marx's thought. But textual evidence indicates that Hegel inspired Marx to think that there is a 'dialectic of negativity' at work through 'estrangement' in the labour process, whereby the 'Reason' that 'has always existed' attains its 'reasonable' form in 'a higher phase of communist society' when 'the practical relations of every-day life offer to [humanity] none but perfectly intelligible and reasonable relations with regard to [our fellow human beings] and to Nature'.[27] Marx's idea that certain forms of human activity are motivated by irrational 'passions' that unintentionally bring about progress in the development of freedom is also reminiscent of Hegel's philosophy of history. In Hegel's philosophy these 'passions' are connected to 'world-historical individuals', whereas in Marx's thought the 'avarice' of the capitalist class plays an analogous role. He claimed that the 'historical mission' of capitalism, its 'great historical aspect' achieved via its 'unbounded lust for enrichment' and 'ceaseless striving for' surplus value production, is that it

> creates the material elements for the development of the rich individuality, which is as varied and comprehensive in its production as in its consumption, and whose labour therefore no longer appears as labour, but as the full development of activity itself, in which natural necessity

---

26   MECW 6, p. 494.
27   MECW 3, pp. 332–3; MECW 24, p. 87; MECW 35, p. 90. Elements of Kant's influential philosophy regarding our ability to discern a 'rational' movement in history will also be explored in this chapter.

has disappeared in its immediate form; because natural need has been replaced by historically produced need.[28]

The capitalist mode of production is a form of human 'estrangement' and Marx was unambiguous about his belief that it drives 'towards its transcendence through itself'.[29] It does so primarily because it gives 'the greatest impulse a once to the productive forces of social labour and to the integral development of every individual producer', and it strives ceaselessly to spread itself across the globe.[30]

Freedom as our 'nature' (which is defined as what we are when fully developed) is the *telos* of the life of our species, and there is evidence which indicates that Marx thought there has indeed been progress in the 'historical process' whereby 'the higher development of individuality' is achieved.[31] Philosophical debates about whether Marx's idea of humanity's genesis involves a concept of teleology will be addressed in this chapter, but it deserves to be said upfront that this idea does not entail that Marx conceived of the realisation of freedom, full human development, and 'communism' as inevitable.[32] Nor does this interpretation suggest that his ontology operates like a kind of secularised providential demiurge determining the course of history, as though 'reason' is a subject which consciously determines nature and humanity from beyond nature and humanity. It is evident that Marx thought human beings 'make their own history' in 'circumstances directly encountered, given and transmitted from the past', but on his premises the element of freedom in this equation of human activity throughout history is dependent on the extent to which the 'richness of [humanity's] essential being' has unfolded, and thus the extent to which 'reason' is consciously objectified in our activity.[33] Thus, while he conceived his-

---

28   MECW 28, pp. 250–1.

29   MECW 28, p. 337.

30   MECW 24, p. 200. 'The life of a people', Hegel claimed, 'ripens a certain fruit; its activity aims at the complete manifestation of the principle which it embodies. But this fruit does not fall back into the bosom of the people that produced and matured it; on the contrary, it becomes a poison-draught to it. That poison-draught it cannot let alone, for it has an insatiable thirst for it: the taste of the draught is its annihilation, though at the same time the rise of a new principle' (Hegel 1956, p. 78).

31   MECW 31, p. 348.

32   In fact, while it may seem counterintuitive at first, this ontology ultimately precludes the idea that Marx's 'historical dialectic' involves the application of 'fundamental laws of dialectics' to human history in order to demonstrate the inevitability of communism, as proposed by such systems as the Soviet 'Diamat'.

33   MECW 11, p. 103; MECW 3, p. 301.

tory as 'multilinear' with divergent paths and various possibilities for liberation, insofar as there is a '*universal human* nature' there is a necessity (connected to our level of development) operating through our particular circumstances which circumscribes our activity. To illustrate this by way of example, consider expanding the 'realm of freedom' on the basis of 'universal human emancipation': this would necessarily require, in part, a level of control over natural necessity which is dependent on a definite degree of sociohistorical development.[34]

Marx's idea of the revolutionary subjectivity that will perform the 'transcendence' of capitalism is the topic of the fifth chapter. Marx claimed that the 'proletariat goes through various stages of development' but does not elaborate this process as it pertains to subjectivity.[35] Nevertheless, we are able to determine that he thought that our initial discontent and rebelliousness will lead to '*revolutionary practice*' which transforms us in such a way that we become able to establish the 'first phase of communist society'.[36] This requires that the 'estranged' conditions of life in capitalism have also previously shaped the subjectivity of the working class for its role in this process. His idea of revolutionary subjectivity centres on the development of two particular aspects of human individuality: the productive capacities required to appropriate the knowledge objectified in the productive forces, which includes the technical skill required to use them and which also develops further in the act of appropriation; and ethical capacities, i.e., the development of a state of character required for the social relations which are necessary to initiate the revolution, including for the specific way that the working class must unite in order to carry out the revolutionary appropriation of the productive forces and reorientation of social life for the good of all on the basis of a common plan. He also thought that general intellectual development accompanies the growth of these capacities, but in the literature on Marx's theory of revolution there tends to be an overemphasis on revolutionary *consciousness*, as though revolutionary subjectivity solely entails a kind of intellectual awareness and knowledge. For Marx, the development of the class consciousness of the workers involves a transformation of what Hegel termed the 'sensuous will', along with an expansion of thought. It is more accurate to think of revolutionary subjectivity in the context of the totality of an individual's character, i.e., as a revolutionary orientation of the individual's entire personality.

---

34   MECW 37, p. 807; MECW 3, p. 280.
35   MECW 6, p. 492.
36   MECW 5, p. 4; MECW 24, p. 87.

The ethical capacities of revolutionary subjects may be more concretely described as the mental and emotional (i.e. psychological) capabilities associated with the revolutionary character. Describing them as 'ethical' maintains emphasis on their connection to the ethos of revolutionary social relations and activity for which the guiding principle and aim is 'universal human emancipation'. On Marx's premises, the recognition of every human being as an end in themselves and as inherently 'free' entails a development of the so-called 'mental' and 'practical senses' such as 'will' and 'love'.[37] At this point a distinction must be made between the developmental processes associated with 'estrangement' and *revolutionary practice* because Marx's claims about the detrimental side of 'estranged' social life in capitalist society undermine his theory. He thought that capitalism exhausts the physical and mental energies of the working class, leaving us without enough time or energy for mental culture, and that the 'material privation' of the poor and working classes 'dwarfs their moral as well as their physical stature'.[38] In particular, he claimed that the squandering of our 'nerves and brain' leads to 'physical and mental degradation', resulting in 'ignorance', 'stupidity' and 'cretinism', which contradict his claims about the positively developmental context of wage labour for the development of revolutionary class consciousness.[39] In short, his idea that the capacities required to initiate the revolution develop through 'estrangement' in capitalism is inconsistent in the form that he left it because, according to him, it also has a persistent tendency to ruin us physically and mentally.

This inconsistency does not necessarily imply that Marx's social philosophy is beset with a contradiction that simply cannot be overcome. Ultimately, his theory of revolutionary subjectivity is profoundly undertheorised. But even if this problem is the result of undertheorisation, the inconsistency inherent in Marx's theory happens to be consistent with the persistence of 'estrangement' among the working classes of the world. While it might be premature to simply maintain that it cannot be overcome, there are a plethora of relentless counter-revolutionary tendencies – observable now and throughout the years since Marx was active – which suggest that the problem in his theoretical work is mirrored in reality nonetheless. Indeed, substantial historical evidence indicates that in some circumstances working people can become reactionary instead of revolutionary, e.g., by turning against each other on the basis

---

37   MECW 3, p. 302.

38   MECW 22, p. 602.

39   MECW 37, p. 92; MECW 35, pp. 275; 640; MECW 3, p. 273.

of various prejudiced attitudes. This is something Marx witnessed and pointed out. From our vantage point in history we can include the rise of fascism
in the twentieth century and the contemporary resurgence of so-called alt-
right politics amid the rising tide of reaction worldwide as social and political
phenomena that are prefigured in the problem with his theory. In the context of Marx's social philosophy, the issues arising from the deleterious effects
of 'estrangement' in capitalism and its disrupting influence on revolutionary
politics – e.g., the tendency of the working class to become divisive and fight
among itself on the basis of reactionary attitudes – pertain to the development
of revolutionary ethical capacities.[40]

As this issue with Marx's theory remains unaddressed and revolutionary
subjectivity is predominantly conceived in a limited way as essentially class
consciousness, a vanguardist tendency which permeates the Marxist left continues to proliferate. The vanguardist principle underlies the refrain that the
absence of a revolutionary working class, especially in conditions of crisis and
mass discontent, can be attributed to a failure of the revolutionary left. This suggests that the onus for the weakness of the working-class movement is on the
most experienced and theoretically advanced layers of the left who have neglected their responsibility to guide the disaffected masses toward class struggle
and provide them with organisational structure, leadership, and the theory
required for revolutionary awareness.[41] Marx's idea of 'revolutionary practice'
is inconsistent with vanguardism and in fact precludes it. His work does not
indicate that he thought it was his task to make the working class revolutionary,

---

40   Consider Hal Draper's claim that 'Most of the problems of proletarian revolution stem
      from the massive role of divisions ... within the working classes ... The process of over-
      coming these diversities and discords is a key part of the road to proletarian revolution.
      One can view this process as one of maturation. Maturation has several sides (physical,
      intellectual, emotional, and so on)' (Draper 1978, p. 52).

41   The extent to which this tendency exists in revolutionary theory varies from those who
      openly claim that a Marxist vanguard is indispensable to those whose vanguardism is
      more subtle and perhaps not even fully conscious, dwelling under the surface of their
      theorising. But even though different perspectives tend to stress the significance of the
      role of vanguardism more or less and define the scope of activity differently, the underly-
      ing principle is essentially the same. Consider, for example, the following claims by Robert
      Brenner in the first issue of *Catalyst* which typifies a softer version of the vanguardist prin-
      ciple that has become endemic among the Marxist left: 'the fact remains that, up to now,
      in most of the world, right-wing nationalist-cum-populist forces have been able to capital-
      ise on the profound distress and disaffection of working people far more effectively than
      has the radical left'; the 'question is whether a still embryonic radical left can develop
      the capacity to exploit the implicit and explicit opportunities that are certain to present
      themselves in the coming period' (Brenner 2017).

as though he thought that the role of a revolutionary theorist involves bringing guidance to the masses about the necessary content of their revolutionary
action. Nor did Marx maintain that the proletariat needs a vanguard to compel it to engage in 'revolutionary activity', i.e., activity in which 'the changing
of oneself coincides with the changing of circumstances', because in his view
it is as a result of our fundamental life activity that we develop the needs and
capacities required for revolution.[42] Nevertheless, on his premises – as is amply
demonstrated by the record of his activity – this does not repudiate the importance of organising ourselves through the creation of groups with revolutionary
aims, participating in mass protest movements, engaging in educational activities, or participating in the construction of a party apparatus to unify and clarify
our interests and aims, influence state policy, and eventually attain state power.
The vanguardist approach to this activity is mistaken because the subjective
transformation required for a revolution cannot be attained through the guidance of a vanguard. At times when the working-class movement is waning, if
the issue is conceived as the absence of an organised revolutionary left, the left
will remain stuck in a terminal vanguardism which obfuscates the real issues.
If a substantial portion of the working class is dominated by irrationality in
their social and political life, such as being open to false narratives and harbor-
ing reactionary prejudices, it is not possible for a vanguard to rectify the lack
of revolutionary development among the workers. Marx's revolutionary theory
makes its appeal to the 'reason' of 'thinking proletarians' who have developed
the corresponding ethical powers.[43]

Even though Marx portrayed the working class as inherently revolutionary,
it is important to recognise his insinuation that there is a tendency to resist
what he considered a 'reform of consciousness'.[44] In his work he took account
of human subjectivity as a site of social and political struggle, and he described
a tendency for individuals to become mired in 'estrangement' and saturated in
various illusions that arise organically out of our conditions of life. He thought
that life in capitalism is experienced differently by the subject who perceives
it with 'sober senses' compared to the 'illusory' experience of a subject with
a 'mystical consciousness'.[45] Thus he proposed that a serious inquiry into our
subjectivity is worthwhile and described the possibility for a 'reform of consciousness' through 'analysing the mystical consciousness that is unintelligible

---

42   MECW 5, p. 214.
43   MECW 7, p. 505.
44   MECW 3, p. 144.
45   MECW 6, p. 487; MECW 3, p. 176.

to itself'.[46] This has not received the attention that it deserves in the literature on Marx's work. This lapse is concomitant with the commonplace theorisation of an abstract opposition between Marx's focus on sociomaterial practice and the subjective dimension of human life in which the latter is treated as epiphenomena. Arguably, this misreading has been encouraged in part by Marx's own statements. He claimed, for instance, that a theory of 'a so-called general development of the human mind' is not suitable for the comprehension of 'social existence' *apart from* a comprehension of 'material life conditions'.[47] But he perceived our life activity as an objectification of the developed powers of our 'mind' nonetheless, and it is evident that he thought an inquiry into the world of human life activity necessarily entails an inquiry into human subjectivity as it is sublated in social life. Even though he did not develop a robust theory of his own, his writing indicates that he had a sophisticated understanding of it nonetheless. Indeed, his work contains an incipient psychology.[48] Recognising this does not necessitate diminishing the theoretical significance of the material basis of social forms as if to privilege a psychological conceptualisation. In principle, neither material conditions nor human subjectivity are conceptually privileged in Marx's social philosophy, and despite his overemphasis on material practice in his writings, human subjectivity was an essential element in his understanding of socioeconomic phenomena.

Marx's idea of 'estrangement' is closely connected to the problem of revolutionary subjectivity. The final chapter will rearticulate 'estrangement' in Marx's social philosophy as a kind of psychosocial phenomenon and explore a fruitful starting point for elucidating his thoughts on human subjectivity with elements of Freudian psychoanalysis and Husserlian phenomenology. The work of Freud and Marx overlap in significant ways, particularly in relation to their theorisation of the struggle with natural necessity – including humanity's own 'animal spirits' – in the development of the human species.[49] However, there is a deep theoretical impasse between psychoanalysis and the philosophic tradition within which Marx's thought is situated. Particular attention is given to the limitations of Freudian psychoanalysis for coherently theorising the kind of ethical life that Marx makes a fundamental feature of a 'higher phase' of

---

46   MECW 3, p. 144. He suggests that we can 'start out from any form of theoretical and practical consciousness' (MECW 3, p. 143).

47   MECW 26, pp. 262–3.

48   To begin with we can consider, for example, his use of psychological terminology to describe the subjective basis of socioeconomic life activity, such as 'lust', 'accursed passion', etc. (MECW 28, p. 100).

49   MECW 35, p. 346.

communist society. The ontological foundation of Freud's psychological theory results in a conception of the human being and the human mind that is inconsistent with Marx's definition of humanity as a 'universal' and ultimately 'free' being. The contrast between the two also helps to elucidate Marx's thoughts about human subjectivity and it is emphasised in connection to Husserl's elaboration of an ontology of the mind that shares significant parallels with Marx's social philosophy.

While various theorists have attempted to bring Marx's thought into conversation with Freud's work, not enough attention has been given to the Kleinian version of psychoanalysis in this regard.[50] To this end, the final chapter will draw connections between Marx's social philosophy and Melanie Klein's interventions in the psychoanalytic tradition. Even though her psychoanalytic theory shares the same fundamental flaws as Freud's initial version in relation to Marx's thought, her work is more compatible with the philosophical premises of Marx's idea of 'universal human emancipation'. Ultimately, her work presents an opportunity to sublate concepts from psychoanalytic psychology which compliment a 'historical materialist' analysis of the character of progressive-revolutionary and conservative-reactionary social and political phenomena. The point of bridging Marx's social philosophy with psychoanalytic psychology is not to create yet another monstrous hybrid of the two, but rather to contribute towards sublating their insights into a coherent psychosocial theory that can address the various manifestations of 'estranged' social and political struggle.

The book concludes by reflecting on features of the inner connection between psychological and social dimensions of political 'estrangement'. The foregoing analysis of Marx's work facilitates a perspective of the distinctly psychological and social struggles that give rise to – and flow from – regressive politics as moments of the same internally related psychosocial process. Incipient psychological ideas contained in Marx's work and his rudimentary theory of subjectivity help to illuminate the central concept of 'estrangement'.[51] This functions to elucidate some fundamental elements of a philosophically coherent psychosocial perspective on the problem of revolutionary subjectivity in

---

50 Consider, for example, Fromm's claim that Klein's 'evidence and constructions have not been convincing in the opinion of most psychoanalysts, including myself' (Fromm 1970, p. 32).

51 This includes, for example, related concepts like 'illusory consciousness' and 'mind'. The inchoate theory of 'mind' in Marx's work is a good example of the necessity for a comprehensive understanding of his philosophy because it requires familiarity with other core elements of his thinking, specifically of his ontological and anthropological ideas.

Marx's work. To the extent that this aspect of his thought reflects actual social and political struggles in our contemporary world, such a perspective is necessary to address *theoretically* the immediate practical concerns arising from the manifestations of extreme right-wing politics. The conclusion is not intended to establish a complete foundation for a novel theory, but rather to develop reflections about psychosocial dynamics inspired by the interpretive analysis of key philosophical elements of Marx's social theory throughout this book, in conjunction with other complimentary psychological and sociological ideas.

CHAPTER 1

Ontology and Method

I am so far advanced that in five weeks I will be through with the whole economic shit. And that done, I will work over my Economics at home and throw myself into another science in the museum. I am beginning to tire of it.

MARX, 1851[1]

•••

There is no royal road to learning, and the only people with any chance of scaling its sunlit peaks are those who have no fear of weariness when ascending the precipitous paths that lead up to them.

MARX, 1872[2]

••
•

1 Ancient Hellenic Philosophy and the 'Exploration of the Rational'

Marx was initially exposed to the origins of the ontological idea that 'Reason directs the World' in an ancient Hellenic tradition of philosophy that he studied in university. Aside from his direct study of ancient Hellenic philosophy, he was also exposed to this tradition in a renewed form through his studies of German writers, most notably in the philosophy of Hegel. Hegel claimed it was Anaxagoras who 'was the first to enunciate the doctrine that νοῦς ... or Reason, governs the world'.[3] For Heraclitus, another notable progenitor of this tradition,

---

1 McLellan 1973, p. 283.

2 MECW 35, 23.

3 Hegel 1956, p. 11. Cf. the following passage from Hegel's *Science of Logic*: 'Anaxagoras is praised as the man who first delcared that *Nous*, thought, is the principle of the world, that the essence of the world is to be defined as thought. In so doing he laid the foundation for an intellectual view of the universe, the pure form of which must be logic. What we are dealing with in logic is not a thiking *about* something which exists independently as a base for our thinking and apart from it, nor forms which are supposed to provide mere signs or distinguishing marks

'all things come to pass in accordance with' the '*logos*'.[4] According to Hegel, the intelligible order of the cosmos is evident, for example, in the 'movement of the solar system' which 'takes place according to unchangeable laws' which are 'Reason, implicit in the phenomena in question'.[5] Thus Hegel proposed that the 'sole business of science is to make conscious' the 'work which is accomplished by the reason of the thing itself'.[6] It is within this philosophic tradition that we should locate the ontological foundations of Marx's assertion that 'the ultimate aim' of *Capital* was to 'lay bare the economic law of motion of modern society', one of 'the natural laws of its movement'.[7] On the one hand, the existence of social and political 'science' of this sort entails that we can have real insight into our social life process, enabling us to take conscious, collective, and ultimately 'free' control of it; on the other hand, it also entails that we cannot 'suggest fantastic solutions' to 'social antagonisms' in the place of such knowledge.[8]

Hegel emphasised that 'we must clearly distinguish' between Anaxagoras's principle and 'intelligence as self-conscious Reason', and he claimed that it was Socrates who 'adopted the doctrine of Anaxagoras' and radically transformed it, taking 'the first step in comprehending the union of the Concrete with the Universal'.[9] Socrates agreed with Anaxagoras that 'Mind' is a sovereign force in the world but he maintained that it was most truly active in the shared consciousness of human beings; hence the sentiment attributed to him by Plato: 'I am devoted to learning; landscapes and trees have nothing to teach me – only the people in the city can do that'.[10] Marx thought that this tradition and the philosophy of Hellenic antiquity in particular reached its zenith with Aristotle for whom the 'the work of a human being is a being-at-work of

---

of truth; on the contrary, the necessary forms and self-determinations of thought are the content and the ultimate truth itself' (Hegel 1969, p. 50).

4   Heraclitus 2001, p. 2.

5   Hegel 1956, p. 11. This will be discussed further in Chapter Five.

6   Hegel 1991, p. 60. For him, of course, this is ultimately the process of 'Spirit' or 'Mind' becoming conscious of itself: 'the aim of all genuine science is just this, that mind shall recognize itself in everything' (Hegel 1971, p. 1).

7   MECW 35, p. 10.

8   MECW 23, p. 106.

9   Hegel 1956, pp. 12–13. As A.E. Taylor put it, 'Mind, said Anaxagoras, is the cause of all natural law and order, just as mind is the cause of the orderliness and coherence of human action. To Socrates this suggested that the universe at large is the embodiment, like a properly conducted human life, of coherent rational plan' (Taylor 1952, p. 64).

10   Plato 1997, 510. Cf. Marx's claim that 'Feuerbach's aphorisms seem to me incorrect only in one respect, that he refers too much to nature and too little to politics. That, however, is the only alliance by which present-day philosophy can become truth' (MECW 1, p. 400).

the soul in accordance with reason', i.e., *'logos'*.[11] This tradition is foundational for Marx's philosophical anthropology insofar as he conceived of the human 'species being' as 'a *universal* and therefore a free being'.[12]

The idea of 'Reason' underwent further development in Hegel's philosophy. He articulated it as

> *Substance,* as well as *Infinite Power;* its own *Infinite Material* underlying all the natural and spiritual life which it originates, as also the Infinite Form, – that which sets this Material in motion. On the one hand, Reason is the *substance* of the Universe; viz. that by which and in which all reality has its being and subsistence. On the other hand, it is the *Infinite Energy* of the Universe ... It is *the infinite complex of things,* their entire Essence and Truth. It is its own material which it commits to its own Active Energy to work up; not needing, as finite action does, the conditions of an external material of given means from which it may obtain its support, and the objects of its activity. It supplies its own nourishment and is the object of its own operations. While it is exclusively its own basis of existence, and absolute final aim, it is also the energising power realising this aim; developing it not only in the phenomena of the Natural, but also of the Spiritual Universe – the History of the World. That this "Idea" or "Reason" is the True, *the Eternal,* the absolutely *powerful* essence ... is the thesis which ... has been proved in Philosophy.[13]

Textual evidence indicates that Hegel's idea of 'reason' as 'the substance of the Universe' had a profound influence on Marx in his formative years and that he 'received the inner call *to comprehend',* as Hegel put it, whereby he came to 'recognise reason as the rose in the cross of the present' which enabled him 'to delight' in it.[14] His writings also indicate that this philosophical orientation influenced his revolutionary disposition. In May 1843, he wrote to Arnold Ruge: 'You will not say that I have had too high an opinion of the present time; and

---

11   Aristotle 2002, p. 11. Hegel maintained that 'With Anaxagoras a light, if still a weak one, begins to dawn, because the understanding is now recognized as the principle. Aristotle says of Anaxagoras: "But he who said that reason (*nous*), in what lives as also in nature, is the origin of the world and of all order, is like a sober man as compared with those who came before and spoke at random"' (Hegel 1968, p. 319).

12   MECW 3, p. 275. Cf. Aristotle's view that 'the life in accord with the intellect ... most of all is a human being', and Hegel's claim that 'the *universal*' which unites all of humanity, 'man as man', is 'mind' (Aristotle 2002, p. 193; Hegel 1971, p. 1).

13   Hegel 1956, pp. 9–10.

14   Hegel 1991, p. 22.

if, nevertheless, I do not despair of it, that is only because it is precisely the desperate situation which fills me with hope'.[15] Another letter to Ruge from September 1843 suggests that this disposition of Marx's was directly associated with what Hegel termed the 'rational insight' and 'reconciliation with actuality' that 'philosophy' granted Marx's 'inner' calling.[16] Marx wrote that 'Reason has always existed, but not always in a reasonable form. The critic can therefore start out from any form of theoretical and practical consciousness and from the forms *peculiar* to existing reality develop the true reality as its obligation and its final goal'.[17] *Capital* indicates that he continued to sublate this throughout the period in which he developed his so-called 'mature' theory. Through his 'scientific' critique of capitalism and political economy he attempted to 'make conscious' the 'work' of 'reason' which is 'implicit in the phenomena' of life in capitalist society. Hegel's idea of *'reconciliation'* was for Marx an inherently revolutionary one.[18]

Insofar as Marx critically appropriated the Hegelian principle that 'philosophy is *exploration of the rational'*, his revolutionary social theory is 'for that very reason the *comprehension of the present and actual*, not the setting up of a *world beyond* which exists' only 'in the errors of a one-sided and empty ratiocination'.[19] This idea is expressed in the manuscripts posthumously published as *The German Ideology* in which Marx and Engels wrote that 'Communism is for us not a *state of affairs* which is to be established, an *ideal* to which reality [will] have to adjust itself. We call communism the *real* movement which abolishes the present state of things'.[20] In this way, Marx took up what Hegel described as the 'task of philosophy', i.e., to 'comprehend *what is*' because '*what is* is reason'.[21] This principle was vital for Marx's idea of the relationship between

---

15   MECW 3, p. 141.

16   Hegel 1991, p. 22.

17   MECW 3, p. 143.

18   Sean Sayers incorrectly identifies the Young Hegelian 'critical approach', i.e., the 'utopian and subjective wishful thinking' that abandoned the 'scientific attitude of studying what is', with Marx's idea of the activity of the 'critic' in 1843 (Sayers 1987, p. 153). While Sayers is justified in defining 'subjective wishful thinking' as utopian, it is mistaken to associate this with Marx's position in 1843 because, based on the philosophical premises which are evident in his writing at the time, 'reason' is 'what *is*' (Hegel 1991, p. 21). Thus Marx's call for an immanent critique of the present in 1843 does not entail that 'the world is judged and criticised in light of how it ought to be', as Sayers maintains (Sayers 1987, p. 153).

19   Hegel 1991, p. 20.

20   MECW 5, p. 49.

21   Hegel 1991, p. 21. Hegel states further that if 'theory does indeed transcend [its] own time, if it builds itself a world *as it ought to be*, then it certainly has an existence, but only within ... opinions, a pliant medium in which the imagination can construct anything it pleases'

theory and practice. For him, a genuinely 'scientific' theory of 'communism' depicts it as it 'emerges' from the 'womb' of capitalist society, unlike the fanciful imagination of 'utopian' reformers who have not attained sufficient insight into their contemporary circumstances and instead make fantastic plans for the future.[22]

2   'Dialectic' as the Onto-Methodological 'Higher Movement of Reason'

One of Marx's most well-known statements on the 'dialectical method' can be found in the 1873 afterword to *Capital* where he wrote that it is a process of 'inquiry' whereby we 'appropriate the material in detail', 'analyse its different forms of development' and 'trace out their inner connection. Only after this work has been done, can the actual movement be adequately described. If this is done successfully ... the life of the subject-matter is ideally reflected as in a mirror'.[23] The onto-methodological nature of 'dialectic' is difficult to discern from only this passage, although it can be pieced together from this and other sources in Marx's writing and clarified with the aid of Hegel's work.[24] It is

---

(Hegel 1991, p. 22). It follows that since every philosophy 'is a philosophy of its time', it 'provides satisfaction only for those interests which are appropriate to their time' (Hegel 1968, p. 106). 'Socrates', for example, 'did not grow like a mushroom out of the earth, for he stands in continuity with his time' (Hegel 1968, p. 384). It is evident that Marx also held a similar position. He maintained that 'philosophers do not spring up like mushrooms out of the ground; they are products of their time, of their nation, whose most subtle, valuable and invisible juices flow in the ideas of philosophy' (MECW 1, p. 195).

22   MECW 24, p. 85. Contrary to Guido Starosta's claim that 'Marx's materialist dialectical science entailed the transcendence of *all* philosophy', Marx remained philosophical in this sense (Starosta 2016, p. 52). Starosta argues that Marx abandoned 'the abstract character of idealist philosophy as present in' Hegel because 'the very essence of philosophy' is 'to be indifferent to the real movement of human practice. Within the limits of philosophical thought, no real mediation is possible between theory and practice', and 'the relation between theory and practice cannot but become inverted' (Starosta 2016, p. 14). However, the standpoint of philosophy according to Hegel as outlined above is not inconsistent with the fact that Marx turned 'his attention on the way human life is materially produced' (Starosta 2016, p. 15). It remained a necessary ontological foundation for the kind of 'science' characteristic of Marx's 'materialist dialectical science'.

23   MECW 35, p. 19.

24   As McCarney argued, 'questions of ontology' must be explored because 'no account of dialectic can be adequate without treating them' (McCarney 1987, p. 181). Cf. his claim that in 'the usual litanies ... of what is living and what is dead in Hegel, it is his ontological vision that is most readily assigned to the philosophical graveyard' (McCarney 1987, p. 162).

important to stress the ontological aspect of Marx's idea of 'dialectic' because of the increasingly common tendency to treat it simply as if it were a mere theoretical tool.[25]

The ontological meaning of 'dialectic' is conveyed in an abstract and obscure way when it is presented as the grand process of change in the cosmos or the transformative power at work in the flux of things. Hegel did in fact claim that it is 'in general the principle of all motion, of all life, and of all activation in the actual world'.[26] However, as the principle of 'all activation in the actual world', 'dialectic' does not simply denote change *per se*, although this is certainly an essential aspect of it. On the contrary, as an onto-cosmological principle, 'dialectic' is a feature of the developmental movement of 'reason' which takes place within the objective world as well as the activity of thought.[27] We can observe this, for instance, in Hegel's *Science of Logic* where he treats 'dialectic' *simultaneously* as an ontology and as a mode of thought, even within a single sentence: 'we call dialectic the higher movement of reason in which ... seemingly utterly separate terms pass over into each other spontaneously, through that which they are, a movement in which the presupposition sublates itself'.[28]

The unity of the ontological and methodological dimensions of 'dialectic' is conspicuously presented in Hegel's *Encyclopaedia Logic*. In this text we read that the form of 'the *logical*' has 'three sides': '*the side of abstraction or of the understanding*', '*the dialectical* or *negatively rational side*', and '*the speculative* or *positively rational* one'.[29] Thus the 'dialectical' is necessarily present as a form of thought corresponding to the '*negatively rational*' side of the '*logical*', hence Hegel's claim in the *Science of Logic* that 'dialectic' is 'a *necessary function of*

---

25   A clear example of this tendency can be found in Arthur Schipper's review of *Dialectics in World Politics* in which he describes 'dialectics' as consisting of 'a highly intuitive set of methodological tools', a 'sophisticated theoretical machinery', and 'a step-by-step method for applying this machinery' (Schipper 2016).

26   Hegel 1991b, pp. 128–29. 'Everything around us can be regarded as an example of dialectic. For we know that, instead of being fixed and ultimate, everything finite is alterable and perishable, and this is nothing but the dialectic of the finite, through which the latter, being implicitly the other of itself, is driven beyond what immediately is and overturns into its opposite' (Hegel 1991b, p. 130).

27   At this point it is perhaps helpful to recall Hegel's idea that 'reason' is both 'substance' and 'subject'. According to him, 'everything turns on grasping and expressing the True, not only as *Substance*, but equally as *Subject*' (Hegel 1977, p. 10). Cf. Whitehead's claim that there 'is Reason, asserting itself above the world, and there is Reason as one of many factors within the world' (Whitehead 1929, p. 10). In Marx's work it is clear that 'reason' conceived as 'subject' is humanity.

28   Hegel 1969, p. 105.

29   Hegel 1991b, p. 125.

reason.[30] The implications for methodology become clearer when we compare 'dialectical' thinking to the thought of what Hegel calls the 'understanding', i.e., thought which 'stops short at the fixed determinacy and its distinctness vis-à-vis other determinacies' and 'behaves toward its ob-jects in a way that separates and abstracts them'.[31] The moment of the 'understanding' is a necessary moment in the process of cognition, but to treat the finite abstractions of the 'understanding' as concrete or true in-themselves is a distortion of reality.[32] Thus the moment of the 'understanding' is supplanted by the *dialectical moment*' which 'is the self-sublation of these finite determinations on their own part, and their passing into their opposites'.[33] Put simply, this tendency of the finite to sublate itself constitutes the 'dialectical' nature of reality (i.e., 'the *logical*' or 'reason').[34] All finitude is ultimately a moment in an infinite pro-

---

30 Hegel 1969, p. 56.

31 Hegel 1991b, pp. 125–6. Engels described an analogous tendency in the thinking characteristic of the natural sciences: 'The analysis of nature into its individual parts' has 'left us as legacy the habit of observing natural objects and processes in their isolation, apart from their connection with the vast whole; of observing them in repose, not in motion; as constants, not as essentially variables; in their death, not in their life' (MECW 25, p. 22). Notably, Whitehead emphasised that the 'materialist' ontology of the natural sciences – which is distinct from the ontology present in Marx's social philosophy – results in a conception of a 'lifeless' nature (Whitehead 1968, p. 127). Cf. the following line from the comedic novel *Tristram Shandy* by Laurence Stern, which Marx was very fond of: 'There lies your mistake, my father would reply; – for, in *Foro Scientiae* there is no such thing as MURDER, – 'tis only DEATH, brother' (Sterne 2009, p. 56). In this context it is interesting to note Hegel's claim that an abstraction 'detached from what circumscribes it' – whereby it attains 'an existence of its own and a separate freedom' – is the result of 'the tremendous power of the negative; it is the energy of thought, of the pure "I". Death, if that is what we want to call this non-actuality, is of all things the most dreadful, and to hold fast what is dead requires the greatest strength. Lacking strength, Beauty hates the Understanding for asking of her what it cannot do. But the life of Spirit is not the life that shrinks from death and keeps itself untouched by devastation, but rather the life that endures it and maintains itself in it. It wins its truth only when, in utter dismemberment, it finds itself' (Hegel 1997, p. 19).

32 Whitehead termed this the 'Fallacy of Misplaced Concreteness' (Whitehead 1925, p. 58).

33 Hegel 1991b, p. 128. Cf. Marx's claim that 'the laws of appropriation or of private property, laws that are based on the production and circulation of commodities, by their own inner and inexorable dialectic changed into their very opposite' (MECW 35, p. 582).

34 According to Hegel, this 'is what everything finite is: its own sublation' (Hegel 1991b, p. 128). The finite 'sublates itself by virtue of its own nature, and passes over, of itself, into its opposite' (Hegel 1991b, p. 129). For Hegel 'all finite things ... are affected with untruth; they have a concept, but their existence is not adequate to it. For this reason they must go to ground. The animal as something singular has its concept in its kind, and the kind frees itself from singularity through death' (Hegel 1991b, p. 60). Cf. Marx's claim that '*Death* seems to be a harsh victory of the species over the *particular* individual and to contra-

cess, famously expressed by Heraclitus's 'πάντα ῥεῖ' ('everything flows').[35] In this view the entire cosmos is alive in the sense of being an unceasingly active process – one total cosmic process which encompasses all natural processes in an internally related web of infinite life.[36]

The ultimate nature of the finite, its 'truth', is thus 'ideality', hence the importance of the 'dialectical' for Hegel's Idealism.[37] This passing over of the finite, whereby finitude sublates itself, is the power of negativity, i.e., the ontological antithesis of finite or 'one-sided' determinations. The internal relation of antitheses makes them each a moment in the process of their self-sublation.[38]

---

dict their unity. But the particular individual is only a *particular species-being*, and as such mortal' (MECW 3, p. 299).

35   This idea is elaborated in Hegel's distinction between the '*spurious or negative* infinite' and 'true Infinity'. The 'spurious' infinite 'is nothing but the negation of the finite' whereby 'the finite arises again in the same way, so that it is no more sublated than not', i.e., when something 'becomes an other, but the other is itself a something, so it likewise becomes and other, and so on *ad infinitum*' (Hegel 1991b, p. 149). We have '*genuine Infinity*' when what something 'passes into is entirely the same as what passes into it – neither having any further determination than this identical one of being an *other* – in its passing into another, [that] something only comes together *with itself*' – i.e., when something is related 'to itself in the passing and in the other' (Hegel 1991b, p. 151). This is also known as 'the negation of the negation', i.e., when 'the Infinite is affirmative, and it is only the finite which is sublated' (Hegel 1991b, p. 152). Hegel regarded the 'genuine Infinite' as 'the basic concept of philosophy' (Ibid.). The context within which Marx applied the concept of the 'negation of the negation' in *Capital* entails the ontology elaborated here.

36   'How true', wrote Thomas Carlyle, 'that there is nothing dead in this Universe; that what we call dead is only changed, its forces working in inverse order! "The leaf that lies rotting in moist winds," says one, "has still force; else how could it rot?" ... The thing that lies isolated inactive thou shalt nowhere discover ... [Indeed], what is this Infinite of Things itself, which men name Universe, but an action, a sum-total of Actions and Activities? The living ready-made sum-total of these three, – which Calculation cannot add, cannot bring on its tablets; yet the sum, we say, is written visible: All that has been done, All that is doing, All that will be done! Understand it well, the Thing thou beholdest, that Thing is an Action, the product and expression of exerted Force: the All of Things is an infinite conjugation of the verb To do. Shoreless Fountain-Ocean of Force, of power to do; wherein Force rolls and circles, billowing, many-streamed, harmonious ... From beyond the Star-galaxies, from before the Beginning of Days, it billows and rolls, – round thee, nay thyself art of it, in this point of Space where thou now standest, in this moment which thy clock measures' (Carlyle 2002, pp. 331–2).

37   Hegel 1991b, 152–153. 'This ideality of the finite is the most important proposition of philosophy, and for that reason every genuine philosophy is *Idealism*. Everything depends on not mistaking for the Infinite that which is at once reduced in its determination to what is particular and finite' (Hegel 1991b, p. 152). In his lectures on the history of philosophy Hegel maintained that, in a word, 'Idealism' means that the finite must be sublated.

38   Cf. Marx's claim that 'What constitutes dialectical movement is the coexistence of two contradictory sides, their conflict and their fusion into a new category' (MECW 6, p. 168).

For example, the categories of 'Being' and 'Nonbeing' are negatively related to each other. The existence of one implies the existence of the other, and they cannot exist without each other. Grasped at the level of their negative unity, they pass infinitely over into each other. Their unity is unfathomable for the abstractive intellect that Hegel called 'understanding'. With 'speculative' thought, their *positive* unity – their sublation – is known as 'Becoming'.

'Dialectical' negativity is a key component of the philosophy of internal relations, also known as Process Philosophy. This mode of thought understands determinate 'things' as relations (or, to put it in other terms, as activities and processes). Bertell Ollman explains that 'the philosophy of internal relations' treats 'the relations in which anything stands as essential parts of what it is, so that a significant change in any of these relations registers as a qualitative change in the system of which it is part', and thus 'relations rather than things' are 'the fundamental building blocks of reality'.[39] Relations are internal to each 'thing' and determine the movement of identity.[40] As an ontological principle, 'dialectical' negativity is present throughout Marx's writings. For instance, he presented the relationship between wage labour and capital as an '*internal* relation' and '*contradiction*', and hence as 'a dynamic relationship driving towards resolution'.[41]

Marx's claims regarding the existence of the 'dialectic of negativity' in the production process of capitalism indicates that his idea of a 'dialectical' inquiry

---

39 Ollman 2003, p. 5. Anne F. Pomeroy writes that 'a philosophy of internal relations is one in which there is a real transmission of historical data and a constitution of each "entity" by its particular relational incorporation of that data, yielding process ... as the organic movement of inheritance and the productive relationality to, of, and by that inheritance. It is thus that any part examined can be analyzed at the multiple levels of its constitutive relations' (Pomeroy 2004, p. 25).

40 Ollman calls this 'ontological relations' (Ollman 2003, p. 25). With an ontology of internal relations, reality is conceived as a totality and as a process. As Allen Wood claimed, in Marx's eyes the world 'is a system of organically interconnected processes' (Wood 2004, p. 208). Thus, it is only an *abstract* rendering of the life-world that gives us the picture of stable 'things' with an apparent self-sustaining identity. Cf. Whitehead's claim that 'There is a conventional view of experience, never admitted when explicitly challenged, but persistently lurking in the tacit presuppositions. This view conceives conscious experience as a clear-cut knowledge of clear-cut items with clear-cut connections with each other. This is the conception of a trim, tidy, finite experience uniformly illuminated. No notion could be further from the truth. In the first place the equating of experience with clarity of knowledge is against evidence. In our own lives, and at any one moment, there is a focus of attention, a few items in clarity of awareness, but interconnected vaguely and yet insistently with other items in dim apprehension, and this dimness shading off imperceptibly into undiscriminated feeling' (Whitehead 1929, p. 78).

41 MECW 3, p. 294.

into the 'real movement' of capitalist society is premised on the idea of 'dialectic' as a 'higher movement of reason'. For example, in *The Holy Family* he wrote that it is

> not a question of what this or that proletarian, or even the whole proletariat, at the moment *regards* as its aim. It is a question of *what the proletariat is*, and what, in accordance with this *being*, it will historically be compelled to do. Its aim and historical action is visibly and irrevocably foreshadowed in its own life situation as well as in the whole organisation of bourgeois society today.[42]

It is a question of '*what the proletariat is*' because – to use Hegel's phrase – '*what is* is reason'. The 'higher movement of reason' is also invoked in Marx's assertion that the 'proletariat' is 'the *negative* side of the antithesis' between itself and 'its opposite, private property, which determines its existence, and which makes it proletariat'.[43] According to him, 'private property drives itself in its economic movement towards its own dissolution ... only inasmuch as it produces the proletariat *as* proletariat, poverty which is conscious of its spiritual and physical poverty ... and therefore self-abolishing'.[44]

3   Phenomenology and the 'Higher Dialectic of the Concept'

The phenomenological character of Marx's thought also owes much to Hegel's influence and we can derive substantial insights into it through an examination of Hegel's writings. In the process we shall see that Marx's so-called 'inversion' of Hegel's method is not what it appears, and that their methods are, in fact, essentially similar. Hegel defined phenomenology as the 'Science of Knowing in the sphere of appearance'.[45] This phenomenological 'dialectic' of 'appearance' and 'essence' is evoked, for instance, by Hegel's claim that 'nature is *rational within itself*' and that 'it is this *actual* reason present within it which knowledge must investigate and grasp conceptually – not the shapes and contingencies which are visible on the surface, but nature's eternal harmony, conceived,

---

42   MECW 4, p. 37.

43   MECW 4, p. 36.

44   Ibid. Note that in this instance Marx does not depict this 'dialectical' process as a simply mechanical one. Human subjectivity and consciousness are involved in mediating the transformation.

45   Hegel 1977, p. 493.

however, as the law and essence *immanent* within it'.[46] According to Marx, 'all science would be superfluous if the outward appearance and the essence of things directly coincided'.[47] There are various other passages in Marx's writings which demonstrate his phenomenological approach to the critique of political economy.[48] For instance, he thought that 'Surplus-value and rate of surplus-value' are 'the invisible and unknown essence that wants investigating, while rate of profit and therefore the appearance of surplus value in the form of profit are revealed on the surface of the phenomenon'.[49] This phenomenological orientation is also evident in his treatment of 'estranged' consciousness and in the course of his elaboration he evokes the ontological concepts of internal relations and 'dialectical' negativity as well. He claimed that with 'estranged outward appearances' the 'internal relationships' of phenomena 'are concealed'.[50] We see this, for example, with Lassalle's conception of wages. In his view Lassalle followed 'in the wake of the bourgeois economists and took the appearance for the essence of the matter', whereas Marx's 'scientific understanding' in this instance was 'that *wages* are not what they *appear* to be, namely the *value*, or *price, of labour*, but only a masked form for the *value*, or *price, of labour power*'.[51]

---

46   Hegel 1991, p. 12. 'For what matters', Hegel wrote, 'is to recognize in the semblance of the temporal and transient the substance which is immanent and the eternal which is present' (Hegel 1991, p. 20). Cf. Aristotle's claim regarding 'knowledge': 'We all assume that what we know is not capable of being otherwise. And with things that are capable of being otherwise, whenever they occur outside our view, it escapes our notice whether they *are* not. Therefore, a thing that is known *is* by necessity, and therefore it is everlasting, since all things that *are* simply by necessity are everlasting, and everlasting things are ungenerated and indestructible' (Aristotle 2002, p. 104).

47   MECW 37, p. 804.

48   In a discussion about the phenomenological 'dialectic of appearance' in Marx's work, Enzo Paci claimed that the 'reader of *Capital* who follows the dynamics of the analysis cannot fail to be struck by the continuous metamorphosis of appearance and reality' (Paci 1972, p. 423).

49   MECW 37, p. 47.

50   MECW 37, p. 804. He also mentioned this in a letter to Engels where he claimed that the 'vulgar economists' *manner of conceiving things* arises, namely, because the only thing that is ever reflected in their minds is the immediate *form of appearance* of relations, and not their *inner connection*. Incidentally, if the latter were the case, we would surely have no need of *science* at all' (MECW 42, p. 390).

51   MECW 24, p. 92. It thus 'was made clear that the wage-worker has permission to work for his own subsistence, that is, *to live* only insofar as he works for a certain time gratis for the capitalist'; that 'the whole capitalist system of production turns on increasing this gratis labour'; and that 'consequently, the system of wage labour is a system of slavery' (MECW 24, p. 92). Engels claimed that 'socialism became a science' with the 'discoveries' of 'the materialistic conception of history and the revelation of the secret of capitalistic production through surplus-value' (MECW 25, p. 27).

There are numerous instances in Hegel's writings in which he makes the phenomenological distinction between 'that which is only *appearance*, transient and insignificant' from 'that which truly and in itself merits the name of *actuality*'.[52] 'Actual knowledge', he claimed, 'insofar as it does not remain outside the object but in fact occupies itself with it, must be immanent to the object, the proper movement of its nature, only expressed in the form of thought and taken up into consciousness'.[53] This 'dialectical' relationship of subject and object inherent in the process of cognition is present throughout Hegel's work and coupled with it is an idea of consciousness which is also present in Marx's writings.[54] According to Hegel, 'consciousness is, on the one hand, consciousness of the object, and on the other, consciousness of itself ... Since both are *for* the same consciousness, this consciousness is itself their comparison'.[55] The significance of this idea is expressed in Hegel's claim that 'in the alteration' of our 'knowledge, the object itself alters for [us] too, for the knowledge that was present was essentially a knowledge of the object'.[56] This view of experience can be elaborated in conjunction with the idea of 'intentionality'. Franz Brentano described 'intentionality' as 'the fact that something is an object for the mentally active subject, and, as such, is present in some manner in his consciousness, whether it is merely thought of or also desired, shunned, etc.'.[57] Marx's writings indicate the existence of an incipient idea of 'intentionality' in his thought. He claimed, for instance, that 'my object can only' exist 'for me insofar as my essential power exists for itself as a subjective capacity; because

---

52   Hegel 1991b, p. 29. Cf. his discussion about 'the conscious insight into the untruth of phenomenal knowledge' in the *Phenomenology* (Hegel 1977, p. 50).

53   Hegel 2007b, p. 43.

54   Hegel thought that subjectivity and objectivity are 'thoroughly dialectical' and that it is 'absurd' to consider them 'as a fixed and abstract antithesis' (Hegel 1991b, p. 273). He claimed that 'the task of science, and more precisely of philosophy, is nothing but the overcoming of this antithesis [between subjectivity and objectivity] through thinking. In cognition, what has to be done is all a matter of stripping away the alien character of the objective world that confronts us' (Ibid.).

55   Hegel 1997, p. 54.

56   In other words, 'as the knowledge changes, so too does the object, for it essentially belonged to this knowledge' (Hegel 1977, p. 54). He referred to this 'dialectical movement which consciousness exercises on itself and which affects both its knowledge and its object' as 'precisely what is called experience' (Hegel 1977, p. 55). This conception of experience is inherent in Marx's thought as well. As Paci claimed, 'in his analysis [in *Capital*], Marx does not talk about dialectics: *he is in the dialectic*' (Paci 1972, p. 423).

57   Brentano 2015, p. 189. It can be described further as 'reference to a content, direction toward an object ... or immanent objectivity. Every mental phenomenon includes something as object [intentionally] within itself' (Brentano 2015, p. 92).

the meaning of an object for me goes only so far as *my* sense goes'.[58] This aspect of Marx's thought also bears the influence of Aristotle whose *On The Soul* contains a nascent theory of 'intentionality'.[59]

In Brentano's wake, Edmund Husserl reinvigorated the idea of 'intentional experiences'. He described this as the 'being directed' to objects which is 'an immanent essential feature of the respective experiences involved', and maintained that 'in the experiences of consciousness themselves, that of which we are conscious is included *as such'*.[60] The phenomenological character of Marx's method is congruent with Husserl's treatment of phenomenology as a science which grounds experience in 'the world as the universal horizon, common to all men, of actually existing things'.[61] Consider, for instance, the way in which Marx makes the commodity into a phenomenon at the outset of *Capital*. He claims that it 'appears, at first sight, a very trivial thing, and easily understood', but that 'analysis shows that it is, in reality, a very queer thing, abounding in metaphysical subtleties and theological niceties'.[62] This moment in the process of Marx's

---

58   MECW 3, p. 301.

59   Marx was closely familiar with this work of Aristotle and even translated it into German. Hegel's claim that the 'books of Aristotle on the Soul' are 'still by far the most admirable, perhaps even the sole, work of philosophical value on this topic' is noteworthy (Hegel 1971, 3). Aristotle claimed that 'the perceptive being is, in potency, such as the perceived thing already is in full activity ... So it is acted upon when it is not like the perceived thing, but when it is the state that results from being acted upon, it has become likened to it, and is such as that is' (Aristotle 2004, p. 99). He claimed further that 'If thinking works the same way perceiving does, it would either be some way of being acted upon by the intelligible thing, or something else of that sort. Therefore it must be without attributes but receptive of the form and in potency not to be the form but to be such as it is'; 'the intellect, in its being-[at]-work, *is* the things it thinks' (Aristotle 2004, pp. 138–9; 148). Put another way: 'what thinks and what is thought are the same thing, for contemplative knowing and what is known in that way are the same thing'; 'Knowledge, in its being-at-work, is the same as the thing it knows' (Aristotle 2004, pp. 142; 145).

60   Husserl 1999, pp. 323–24. Cf. Whitehead's claim that 'thought is a factor in the fact of experience', and thus 'the immediate fact is what it is, partly by reason of the thought involved in it. The quality of an act of experience is largely determined by the factor of the thinking which it contains' (Whitehead 1929, p. 80).

61   Husserl 1970, p. 164. Husserl locates his phenomenology within essentially the same tradition as Marx's thinking is rooted: 'Phenomenological philosophy regards itself in its whole method as a pure outcome of methodical intentions which already animated Greek philosophy from its beginnings; above all, however, [it continues] the still vital intentions which reach, in the two lines of rationalism and empiricism, from Descartes through Kant and German idealism into our confused present day' (Husserl 1999, p. 335).

62   MECW 35, p. 81. Cf. Paci's claim that 'Marx has brought to light what political economy as a science has hidden. He began from the "data" and discovered what the data were hiding. His analysis is phenomenological, since it has transformed the data into *phenomena*.

method parallels Husserl's 'phenomenological reflection', which he also called 'epoché'. In short, this denotes the act of placing in question all 'hitherto existing convictions' and forbidding 'in advance any judgemental use of them'.[63] According to Husserl 'phenomenological reflection leads to a multiple and yet synthetically unified intentionality. There are continually varying differences in the modes of appearing of objects, which are caused by the changing of our "orientation" ... with the consequent differences in perspective involved'.[64] He claimed further that

> If one attends to the distinction between things as 'originally one's own' and as 'empathized' from others, in respect to the *how* of the manners of appearance, and if one attends to the possibility of discrepancies between one's own and empathised views, then what one actually experiences *originaliter* as a perceptual thing is transformed, for each of us, into a mere 'representation of', 'appearance of', the one objectively existing thing ... 'The' thing itself is actually that which no one experiences as really seen, since it is always in motion, always, and for everyone, a unity for consciousness of the openly endless multiplicity of changing experiences and experienced things, one's own and those of others.[65]

Husserl's meaning here is not that 'things' cannot be truly known or universally experienced as actually existing, and it would be a mistake to think that his phenomenological 'epoché' results in a radical skepticism. The same principle stands for the philosophy underlying Marx's motto, as recorded in a 'Confessions' questionnaire in 1865: '*De omnibus dubitandum*'. Hegel's writing is useful for articulating this aspect of Marx's philosophy as well.

Hegel claimed that 'everything must be doubted, all presuppositions given up, to reach the truth as created through the [Concept]'.[66] He infamously articulated the realisation of actual knowledge as the union of the 'Concept' – which for him is subjective – and objectivity, and he called this unity the 'Idea':

The same thing happens when an ideology is examined: the reality hidden beyond the ideological construction is eventually discovered' (Paci 1972, p. 391). The 'trinity formula' is an example of 'a mystery that Marx wants to bring to light and phenomenologically transform into a *phenomenon*' (Paci 1972, p. 428).

63   Husserl 1970, p. 76.
64   Husserl 1999, p. 324.
65   Husserl 1970, p. 164.
66   Hegel 1968, p. 406.

For since the rational, which is synonymous with the Idea, becomes actual by entering into external existence, it emerges in an infinite wealth of forms, appearances, and shapes and surrounds its core with a brightly coloured covering in which consciousness at first resides, but which only the concept can penetrate in order to find the inner pulse,[67] and detect its continued beat even within the external shapes.[68]

It is generally agreed among scholars of Marx's work that his thinking diverges from Hegel's at this point. Upon further examination, however, it becomes evident that Marx remained a lot closer to Hegel's Idealism than is commonly believed. For instance, in his analysis of a form of thought in which '*everything appears reversed*', Marx used a manner of expression that parallels Hegel's phenomenological description of the 'external existence' of 'the rational':

The final pattern of economic relations as seen on the surface, in their real existence and consequently in the conceptions by which the bearers and agents of these relations seek to understand them, is very much different from, and indeed quite the reverse of, their inner but concealed essential pattern and the conception corresponding to it.[69]

In Hegelian terms, comprehending what Marx described as 'the conception corresponding to' the object of thought is achieved via the 'higher dialectic of the concept' (the concept's 'moving principle'):

The higher dialectic of the concept consists not merely in producing and apprehending the determination as an opposite and limiting factor, but in producing and apprehending the *positive* content and result which it contains; and it is this alone which makes it a *development* and immanent progression. This dialectic, then, is not an *external* activity of subjective thought, but the *very soul* of the content which puts forth its branches and fruit organically.[70]

---

67   Cf. Heraclitus: 'One thunderbolt strikes root through everything' (Heraclitus 2001, p. 19).

68   Hegel 1991, pp. 20–1. According to Hegel, this 'development of the Idea as the activity of its own rationality is something which thought, since it is subjective, merely observes, without for its part adding anything extra to it' (Hegel 1991, p. 60). Cf. Ian Fraser's claim that 'When the objective reality ... corresponds with the universal concept ... then the Idea ... is realised as reason and truth. When they are not in correspondence then the result is untruth or "mere *Appearance*"' (Fraser 1997, p. 87).

69   MECW 37, pp. 206–7.

70   Hegel 1991, p. 60. Engels described this as 'the Hegelian "inner purpose" – i.e., a purpose

Sayers claimed that Marx 'essentially agrees with Hegel's view' in this passage and Ian Fraser claimed that, in general, 'Marx is talking about the concept and its actualisation just as Hegel is despite Marx's attempt to confine Hegel's dialectic to the realm of thought'.[71] After all, Marx identified 'the nature of capital' with 'the essential character of its very concept'.[72] The implication of this relationship to Hegel's philosophy is that Marx also practiced a form of 'speculative' philosophy.

4   Marx's 'Speculative' Thought and Undue Criticism of Hegel

Marx's critical comments about Hegel's 'dialectical method' complicates the interpretation of his own. It is well known that Marx took issue with the way in which Hegel attributed a kind of mystical agency to the 'Idea', treating it as a form of alienation whereby rational thought is attributed to the 'Concept' existing independently from the minds of human individuals. Commentators on Marx's work generally agree that it was this move, according to Marx, which resulted in Hegel's mystification of the 'dialectical method'. For example, Hegel claimed that the

> Concept, which is initially only subjective proceeds to objectify itself by virtue of its own activity and without the help of an external material or stuff. And likewise the object is not rigid and without process; instead, its process consists in its proving itself to be that which is at the same time subjective, and this forms the advance to the *Idea*.[73]

This is indeed a key issue that prompted Marx's divergence from Hegel's Idealism.[74] In 1873 Marx articulated his criticism as follows:

---

which is not imported into nature by some third party acting purposively, such as the wisdom of providence, but lies in the necessity of the thing itself' (MECW 25, p. 62).

71   Sayers 1987, p. 158; Fraser 1997, p. 99.

72   MECW 28, 342. Cf. his claim in the third volume of *Capital* that in 'a general analysis of this kind it is usually always assumed that the actual conditions correspond to their conception, or, what is the same, that actual conditions are represented only to the extent that they are typical of their own general case' (MECW 37, p. 142).

73   Hegel 1991b, p. 273.

74   Engels claimed that 'in its Hegelian form', the 'dialectical method' was 'was no use' because for Hegel 'dialectics is the self-development of the concept', whereby 'the dialectical development apparent in nature and history ... is only a copy of the self-movement of the concept going on from eternity, no one knows where, but at all events independently

My dialectic method is not only different from the Hegelian, but is its direct opposite. To Hegel, the life process of the human brain, i.e., the process of thinking, which, under the name of 'the Idea,' he even transforms into an independent subject, is the demiurgos of the real world, and the real world is only the external, phenomenal form of 'the Idea.' With me, on the contrary, the ideal is nothing else than the material world reflected by the human mind, and translated into forms of thought.[75]

Hegel did in fact write that the 'developed, authentic actuality' of the Idea 'is to be as *subject* and so as spirit'.[76] However, insofar as it is 'subject' as 'spirit', it is arguable that humanity is the 'subject' within which Hegel's 'Idea' is realised. According to Hegel, the 'Idea' is the unity of the 'Concept' and objectivity – hence his assertion that we must 'base science ... on the development of thought and the concept' – but from the perspective of his philosophy this unity is only achieved in the thinking mind, the 'Spirit', of humanity.[77] Hegel's identification of the human being with 'Reason' means that we are the ultimate subject to the extent that 'self-conscious Reason' has developed. After all, he wrote that overcoming the 'alien character of the objective world that confronts us' requires 'tracing ... what is objective back to the Concept, which is our innermost self'.[78] The point at which mysticism appears to arise most strongly, however, is with the *Absolute* Idea: 'the Idea that thinks itself' and 'is [present] *as* thinking' – the 'Idea' which, according to Engels, 'is only absolute in so far as [Hegel] has absolutely nothing to say about it'.[79]

At the end of his *Encyclopaedia Logic*, Hegel wrote that 'Up to this point the Idea in its development through its various stages has been *our* ob-ject; but from now on, the Idea is its own ob-ject'.[80] He associated the 'Absolute Idea' with the 'νοήσεως νόησις' of Aristotle, i.e., 'the thought of thought' ('God' conceived as pure contemplative activity).[81] And yet for Hegel this could also be a

---

of any thinking human brain. This ideological perversion had to be done away with' (MECW 26, p. 384).

75 MECW 35, p. 19.

76 Hegel 1991b, p. 287.

77 Hegel 1991, p. 15; Hegel 1991b, p. 286. He wrote that the 'Idea is what is true *in and for itself, the absolute unity* of Concept and Objectivity ... The Idea is the *Truth*; for this means that objectivity corresponds with the Concept' (ibid.).

78 Hegel 1991b, p. 273.

79 Hegel 1991b, p. 303; MECW 26, p. 360.

80 Hegel 1991b, p. 303.

81 According to Hegel, 'God alone is the genuine agreement between Concept and reality' (Hegel 1991b, p. 60).

comment on the 'divine' nature of rational thought itself – and of humanity as the self-consciously rational being – rather than the 'Absolute Idea' *per se*.[82] In fact, Hegel's definition of 'God' as 'Unity of the Universal and Individual' is consistent with the way he describes fully developed humanity as self-consciously rational individuals.[83]

Even though Marx was adamant that his 'dialectical method' was the 'direct opposite' of Hegel's, textual evidence indicates that Marx's 'method' was essentially Hegelian insofar as he sublated the ontological idea that 'Reason directs the world', adopted a phenomenological orientation, and conveyed the activity of 'speculative' thought in his writing. Marx's disparaging remarks about Hegel's 'speculative' philosophy are misleading for interpreters of his 'materialist' inversion of Hegel's method. The fact that Marx charged Hegel with mysticism has encouraged readers who are sympathetic to his thought to write off Hegel as an Idealist whose 'speculative' philosophy was of no importance for Marx's method because it is dissociated from consideration of the 'material' world.[84] And yet abundant textual evidence indicates that Marx thought 'speculatively'.

In the manuscript that became the third volume of *Capital*, Marx wrote that uncovering 'the actual intrinsic relations of the capitalist process of production is a very complicated matter and a very extensive work; if it is a work of science to resolve the visible, merely external movement into the true intrinsic movement'.[85] Marx's recognition of the 'intrinsic relations' of the capitalist mode of production is 'dialectical' ('negatively rational') in Hegel's sense of the 'dialectic' as 'the *immanent* transcending' which overcomes the 'one-sidedness

---

82   As Geraets et al. claim, 'Hegel ... is clearly claiming that *our* thinking has at this stage become "divine"' (Hegel 1991b, p. 335).

83   Hegel 1956, p. 50. Cf. Husserl's claim that 'Along with [our] growing, more and more perfect cognitive power over the universe, [we] also [gain] an ever more perfect mastery over [our] practical surrounding world, one which expands in an unending progression. This also involves a mastery over humankind as belonging to the real surrounding world, i.e., mastery over [ourselves] and [each other], an ever greater power over [our] fate, and thus an ever fuller "happiness" – "happiness" as rationally conceivable for [us]. For [we] can also know what is true in itself about values and goods. All this lies within the horizon of this rationalism as its obvious consequence for humanity. Humanity is thus truly an image of God. In a sense analogous to that in which mathematics speaks of infinitely distant points, straight lines, etc., one can say metaphorically that God is the "infinitely distant human"' (Husserl 1970, p. 66).

84   Norman Levine, for instance, claims that 'Marx retained many forms of the Hegelian Method after they were shed of their Speculative content' and that he 'confined the Hegelian System within the Speculative, which he rejected' (Levine 2012, pp. 12; 72).

85   MECW 37, p. 311.

and restrictedness of the determinations of the understanding'.[86] However, the manner in which Marx comprehended what he believed to be the 'actual' movement of the social life process of capitalism in *Capital* also involved 'speculative' thought because in that text he 'apprehends the unity of the determinations in their opposition, the *affirmative* that is contained in their dissolution and in their transition'.[87] Thus it is more accurate to describe Marx's method as 'speculative' because the 'dialectical' moment is sublated within the 'positive' moment. If Marx's cognition had stopped at the 'negatively rational' moment he would be stuck positing the mere transience of capitalism.

The significance of 'speculative' thought for Marx's revolutionary social theory is evident, for example, in his recognition of the 'intrinsic relations' between economic conditions of 'rent (landed property), *profit* (capital) and wages (wage labour)', which he thought are 'conditions of struggle and antagonism' that contain the potential for revolutionary social transformation.[88] The activity of the 'critic' that he described in his letter to Ruge, presented in his own theoretical activity in *Capital* and elsewhere, displays the birth process of 'communist society' as the 'true reality'.[89] Thus while his analysis of the capitalist mode of production and criticism of the way it appears to classical and 'vulgar' political economists operates in accordance with the principle of 'dialectical' negativity, his thought is 'speculative' nonetheless. We see this, for instance, in a letter to Engels:

> At last we have arrived at the *forms of manifestation* which serve as the starting point in the vulgar conception: rent ...; profit ... from capital; wages, from labour. But from our standpoint things now look different. The apparent movement is explained. Furthermore, A. Smith's nonsense, which has become the *main pillar* of all political economy hitherto ... is overthrown. The entire movement in this apparent form. Finally, since

---

86   Hegel 1991b, p. 128. This is why 'the dialectical', according to Hegel, 'constitutes the moving soul of scientific progression' and 'is the principle through which alone *immanent coherence and necessity* enter into the content of science' (Hegel 1991b, p. 128).

87   Hegel 1991b, p. 131. Cf. Hegel's claim that 'the essential character of the rational' is 'just to bring together what is separated' (Hegel 1971, p. 49).

88   MECW 39, p. 62. Cf. Marx's critical remark about utopian socialists in *The Poverty of Philosophy* who 'see in poverty nothing but poverty, without seeing in it the revolutionary, subversive side, which will overthrow the old society' (MECW 6, p. 178).

89   Hence Engels's claim that the 'task of economic science' is to indicate the 'approaching dissolution' of the capitalist system 'and to reveal, within the already dissolving economic form of motion, the elements of the future new organisation of production and exchange' (MECW 25, p. 138).

those 3 items (wages, rent, profit (interest)) constitute the sources of income of the 3 classes of landowners, capitalists and wage labourers, we have the *class struggle*, as the conclusion in which the movement and disintegration of the whole shit resolves itself.[90]

This kind of 'speculative' thinking is present in the infamous passage on the 'negation of the negation' in chapter thirty-two of the first volume of *Capital*:

> capitalist production begets, with the inexorability of a law of Nature, its own negation. It is the negation of negation. This does not re-establish private property for the producer, but gives him individual property based on the acquisitions of the capitalist era: i.e., on co-operation and the possession in common of the land and of the means of production.[91]

5   The 'Concrete' Nature of 'Speculative' Thought and Clarification of Marx's 'Empiricism'

Rather than providing clarity on the matter, it appears that Marx's excessively strong distinction between Hegel's method and his own has for the most part encouraged a range of misinterpretations.[92] A common misinterpretation is the tendency to think that Marx was a kind of materialist-Empiricist who diverges fundamentally from the 'speculative' nature of Hegel's method.[93] Marx claimed, after all, that 'Hegel ... arrived at the illusion that the real was

---

90   MECW 43, p. 25.

91   MECW 35, p. 751.

92   Theorists whose work contributes to the New Dialectic school, for instance, interpret Marx's 'dialectical method' in an excessively formal and schematic way. In this tradition, Marx's so-called 'systematic dialectic' is understood as 'a method of exhibiting the inner articulation of a given whole' (Arthur 2014, p. 269). Caligaris and Starosta explain that 'most contributors [to the New Dialectic school] agree that the structure of the argument in *Capital* is organised in a dialectical form which, at the very least, can be said to draw formal inspiration from the general form of movement of categories that Hegel deploys in his *Logic*' (Caligaris and Starosta 2014, p. 89). This approach is severely limited, however. With regard to Lassalle, who intended 'to expound political economy in the manner of Hegel', Marx claimed that he 'will discover to his cost that it is one thing for a critique to take a science to the point at which it admits of a dialectical presentation, and quite another to apply an abstract, ready-made system of logic to vague presentiments of just such a system' (MECW 40, p. 261).

93   H.T. Wilson, for example, claimed that 'Marx endorsed an empirical method in explicit opposition to the speculative method of Hegel' (Wilson 1991, p. 61).

the result of thinking synthesising itself within itself ...; actually, the method of advancing from the abstract to the concrete is simply the way in which thinking assimilates the concrete and reproduces it as a mental concrete'.[94] And yet what Marx described as 'concrete' implies the activity of 'speculative' thought and not simply the so-called material world that we perceive sensuously.[95]

Hegel maintained that 'the speculative ... expressly contains the very [abstract] antitheses at which the understanding stops short ... sublated within itself; and precisely for this reason it proves to be concrete and a totality'.[96] This is because the speculatively 'rational', 'positive result' of 'dialectic', 'although it is something-thought and something-abstract, is at the same time ... a *unity of distinct determinations'*.[97] Marx made an essentially similar claim in the *Grundrisse*:

> The concrete is concrete because it is a synthesis of many determinations, thus a unity of the diverse. In thinking, it therefore appears as a process of summing-up, as a result, not as the starting point, although it is the real starting point.[98]

---

94   MECW 28, p. 38.
95   Cf. Hegel's claim that 'In order to find things out, Empiricism makes use, especially, of the form of *analysis*. In perception we have something multifariously concrete, whose determinations must be pulled apart from one another, like an onion whose skins we peel off. So this dismembering means that we loosen up, and take apart, the determinations that have coalesced, and we add nothing except the subjective activity of taking them apart. Analysis, however, is the advance from the immediacy of perception to thought, inasmuch as the determinations that the analysed ob-ject contains united within it acquire the form of universality by being separated. Empiricism falls into error in analysing ob-jects if it supposes that it leaves them as they are, for, in fact, it transforms what is concrete into someting abstract. As a result it also happens that the living thing is killed, for only what is concrete, what is One, is alive. Nevertheless, the division has to hapen in order for comprehension to take place, and spirit itself is inward division. But this is only one side, and the main issue is the unification of what has been divided ... Analysis starts with the concrete, and in this material it has a great advantage over the abstract thinking of the older metaphysics. Analysis itself fixes the distinctions and this is of great importance; but these distinctions are themselves only abstract determinations once more, i.e., *thoughts*. And since these thoughts count as what the ob-jects are in-themselves, we meet again the presupposition of the older metaphsics, namely, that what is genuine in things lies in thought' (Hegel 1991b, pp. 78–9).
96   Hegel 1991b, p. 132. In fact, according to Hegel, speculative 'philosophy does not deal with mere abstractions or formal thoughts at all, but only with concrete thoughts' (Hegel 1991b, p. 131). He states further that 'Philosophy does not waste time with ... empty and otherworldly stuff. What philosophy has to do with is always something concrete and strictly present' (Hegel 1991b, p. 150).
97   Hegel 1991b, p. 131.
98   MECW 28, p. 38. Cf. the following claim in Hegel's *Encyclopaedia Logic*: 'As for ... concrete-

It would thus be a mistake to interpret Marx's 'materialism' as another form of Empiricism which alleges that the 'concrete' is simply the so-called material world that we perceive sensuously. Hegel claimed that the issue with *this* kind of 'Materialism', i.e., 'the view in which matter as such counts as what is genuinely objective', is that it overlooks the fact that

> matter is itself already something abstract, something which cannot be perceived as such. We can therefore say that there is no "matter"; for whenever it exists it is always something determinate and concrete. Yet this abstract "matter" is supposed to be the foundation of everything sensible.[99]

Marx's 'materialist' epistemology is not consistent with *this* kind of 'materialist' Empiricism; on the contrary, his description of what counts as 'concrete' is the 'result' of 'thinking' and it is consistent with Hegel's 'speculative' claim that '"Matter" is an abstraction precisely because form is present in it, to be sure, but only as an indifferent and external determination'.[100]

Ultimately, Marx's claim that the 'premises' he starts out with are 'real premises' that can 'be verified in a purely empirical way' must be interpreted in accordance with the ontological and phenomenological nature of his method.[101] His idea that '*Sense-perception* ... must be the basis of all science' presupposes that our senses have 'become *human*', and '*senses* capable of human gratification' – 'the human nature of the senses' – have a 'rational' character which entails the 'intentionality' of a self-consciously rational subject.[102] Marx claimed that

---

ness of content, it simply means that the ob-jects of consciousness are known as inwardly determined, and as a unity of distinct determinations' (Hegel, 1991b, p. 76).

99   Hegel 1991b, p. 79.
100 Hegel 1991b, p. 159.
101 MECW 5, p. 31. In the context of his 'materialist conception of history' these premises are 'the real individuals, their activity and the material conditions of their life, both those which they find already existing and those produced by their activity' (Ibid.). Cf. Husserl's claim that '*Empiricism* can only be overcome by the most universal and consistent empiricism, which puts in place of the restricted [term] "experience" of the empiricists the necessarily broadened concept of experience [inclusive] of intuition which offers original data, an intuition which in all its forms ... shows the manner and form of its legitimation through phenomenological clarification' (Husserl 1999, p. 335).
102 MECW 3, pp. 303; 296; 301; 302. Cf. McCarney's claim that 'Marx's dialectic presupposes from the start a subject meeting minimal conditions of rationality and capable of developing through the dialectical process so as to meet more exacting ones', and thus 'the

If [humanity] draws all [its] knowledge, sensation, etc., from the world of the senses and the experience gained in it, then what has to be done is to arrange the empirical world in such a way that [humanity] experiences and becomes accustomed to what is truly human in it and that [we become] aware of [ourselves] as [human beings].[103]

Thus his claim that the 'question whether objective truth can be attributed to human thinking is not a question of theory' but 'a *practical* question' is not a sufficient basis for identifying him as a conventional Empiricist.[104] After all, he associates sense experience with the moment of *appearance* in the process of cognition involved in a 'scientific analysis'. He claimed, for instance, that the

general and necessary tendencies of capital must be distinguished from their forms of manifestation.

It is not our intention to consider, here, the way in which the laws, immanent in capitalist production, manifest themselves in the movement of the individual masses of capital, where they assert themselves as coercive laws of competition, and are brought home to the mind and consciousness of the individual capitalist as directing motives of his operations. But this much is clear; a scientific analysis of competition is not possible, before we have a conception of the inner nature of capital, just as the apparent motions of the heavenly bodies are not intelligible to any but him, who is acquainted with their real motions, which are not directly perceptible by the senses.[105]

---

possibility arises that a vindication of dialectics may have at its core not an empirical regularity but a movement of reason' (McCarney 1990, pp. 118; 14).

103   MECW 4, p. 130.

104   MECW 5, p. 3. Cf. Whitehead's idea that 'there is progress from thought to practice, and regress from practice to the same thought. This interplay of thought and practice is the supreme authority' (Whitehead 1929, p. 81).

105   MECW 35, p. 321. Cf. Whitehead's claim that 'sense perception for all its practical importance is very superficial in its disclosure of the nature of things. This conclusion is supported by the character of delusiveness – that is, of illusion – which persistently clings to sense perception. For example, our perception of stars which years ago may have vanished ... My quarrel with modern epistemology concerns its exclusive stress upon sense perception for the provision of data respecting nature. Sense perception does not provide the data in terms of which we interpret it' (Whitehead 1968, p. 133).

6   A Note on the Relationship between Hegel's Philosophy and Marx's Thought, and Its Significance for Marxism

There are indeed substantial grounds for Fraser's claim that 'Hegel's and Marx's dialectic are not opposites' but 'are instead intrinsically similar'.[106] The similarity suggests that the 'essential task' of a Marxist social theory is, as McCarney claimed, 'to discover and express the rational potentiality' within the capitalist order which 'accords with the midwife role of theory in dialectical tradition'.[107] 'What is required to make such a role viable', he continued, 'is the assumption that the present really is pregnant with a more rational future, that, in Hegelian terminology, the rational is the actual' – an 'assumption' in 'pressing need of justification'.[108] Regardless of whether this can be justified – and whether we agree with Hegel that it 'has been proved in Philosophy' – it is not possible to critically appropriate Marx's 'dialectical method' without the sublation of the ontological idea that 'Reason directs the world'. This ontological principle is ultimately indispensable for his interest in the 'dialectical immanent nature' – to use Hegel's phrase – of capitalism while he sought to 'scientifically' comprehend the 'real movement' of its genesis, life, and death as it engenders the possibility of a 'free' life.[109]

To treat 'reason' as the substance of everything, however, is to go against the 'materialism' that many Marxists define themselves by. As McCarney claimed, the 'real problem is whether one needs the assumption that reason is the substance not just of "spiritual" but also of "external" things'.[110] But Marx's writings indicate that his critical appropriation of Hegel's philosophy avoided this problem. Ultimately, Hegel's claim that 'the supreme and ultimate purpose of science' is 'to bring about the reconciliation of the reason that is conscious of itself with the reason that *is*, or actuality, through cognition of' its 'accord with actuality and experience' is consistent with the revolutionary orientation of Marx's social philosophy.[111] This general principle manifests in his writings as part of the philosophical basis for revolutionary discord within the prevailing social order. After all, Marx did not interpret Hegel's infamous claim that 'What is rational is actual; and what is actual is rational' as a conservative statement or

---

106   Fraser 1997, p. 82.
107   McCarney 1990, p. 129.
108   Ibid.
109   Hegel 1969, p. 105; MECW 5, p. 49.
110   McCarney 2000, p. 74.
111   Hegel 1991b, p. 29. According to Hegel, philosophy's 'accord with actuality and experience' is 'an outward touchstone' for 'the truth of philosophy' (Ibid.).

some kind of philosophical vindication of the existing order.[112] It was instead a vital source of philosophical inspiration for Marx's attempt at a *ruthless criticism of all that exists*' in the service of human emancipation.[113]

---

112   Hegel 1991, p. 20. Mészáros misleadingly claimed that the 'function' of philosophy in the Hegelian sense is 'reconciliatory resignation' to 'the false positivity of the established world' which 'could only result in an essentially pessimistic worldview of unavoidable reconciliation and inward-oriented resignation' (Mészáros 2011, p. 38). Cf. Fraser's claim that this statement 'does not mean that what currently exists is rational in its observable form and that Hegel is therefore justifying existing institutions and conditions. It is rather that the rational is present even within an imperfect world and the Speculative philosopher's task is to comprehend this rationality' (Fraser 1997, p. 90). Engels thought that Hegel's statement is revolutionary because it carries the meaning that 'All that exists deserves to perish' (MECW 26, p. 359).

113   MECW 3, p. 142.

Philosophical Anthropology

By the sea, by the desolate nocturnal sea,
Stands a youthful man,
His breast full of sadness, his head full of doubt.
And with bitter lips he questions the waves:

"Oh, solve me the riddle of life!
The cruel, world-old riddle,
Concerning which already many a head hath been racked.
Heads in hieroglyphic hats,
Heads in turbans and in black caps,
Periwigged heads, and a thousand other
Poor, sweating human heads.
Tell me, what signifies man?
Whence does he come? Whither does he go?
Who dwells yonder above the golden stars?"

The waves murmur their eternal murmur,
The winds blow, the clouds flow past.
Cold and indifferent twinkle the stars,
And a fool awaits an answer.

> Heinrich Heine[1]

∴

1   'Nihil humani a me alienum puto'

Marx's idea of 'human nature' owes much to his Aristotelianism and the En-
lightenment thinkers who were also influenced by the Hellenic tradition. Aristotle maintained that 'life in accord with the intellect … is a human being'.[2] The

---

1   Heine 1982, p. 21.
2   Aristotle 2002, p. 193. Cf. Marx's claim that 'human beings … would imply thinking beings'
     (MECW 3, p. 134).

original ancient Greek word which is often translated as 'intellect' or 'reason' is '*logos*', although its meaning cannot be adequately expressed by a single word in the English language. The idea of *logos* evokes the dual character of 'Reason' as both the intelligible law of phenomena but also as a subjective capacity for thought and activity. Our inherent potential to develop this 'rationality' is the basis for Aristotle's claim that 'the good and the doing it well' is 'in the work' of 'a human being', i.e., 'a being-at-work of the soul in accordance with reason [*logos*]'.[3] In other words, 'human good' in Aristotle's philosophy is 'a being-at-work of the soul in accordance with virtue, and if the virtues are more than one, in accordance with the best and most complete virtue'.[4] A 'eudaimonic' life can be described as a flourishing life because it involves the development and enjoyment of the virtues required for actualising 'reason' in our life activity, in common with others who have also developed these capacities.[5]

An examination of Marx's philosophical anthropology demonstrates that he had an idea of 'virtuosity' akin to the conception of virtue in Aristotle's philosophy.[6] In his view, a 'free' life requires the development of the capacities required for knowing and actualising 'universal' intellectual, ethical, and aesthetic principles (e.g., the 'laws of beauty') in our life activity, which entails the ability to act in accordance with a standard of 'excellence'. Marx's conception of the 'free' life activity characteristic of 'the communist organisation of society', which will be taken up in the next chapter, rests on this idea of the uniquely human capacity for virtuous activity. A fundamental basis for distinguishing between humans and animals is the 'free' character of our life activity which depends upon the development of our '*species-powers*'. 'The whole character of a species', Marx claimed, 'is contained in the character of its life activity'.[7] It is commonly argued that Marx thought our *productive* character is essential to his distinction of human activity, but this is only partly accurate.[8] It is evident that Marx thought human beings 'begin to distinguish themselves from

---

3 Aristotle 2002, pp. 10–11.

4 Aristotle 2002, p. 12.

5 For Aristotle, 'virtue is an active condition that makes one apt at choosing ... which is determined by a proportion and by the means by which a person with practical judgment would determine it' (Aristotle 2002, p. 29). He wrote that 'the virtues come to be present neither by nature nor contrary to nature, but in us who are of such a nature as to take them on, and to be brought to completion in them by means of habit' (Aristotle 2002, p. 22).

6 MECW 29, p. 82.

7 MECW 3, p. 276.

8 Karsten Struhl, for instance, claimed that 'For Marx, the distinguishing feature of the human species is our unique form of production' (Struhl 2016, p. 83).

animals as soon as they begin to *produce* their means of subsistence', but this is because of the '*universal*' character of human labour.[9] 'Admittedly animals also produce', Marx thought, but the human species is unique insofar as it 'produces universally', and we also have the potential to participate 'universally' in other activities.[10] Thus even though the way we produce is a unique form of life-activity, we are more accurately distinguished from animals by our potential for 'universality' and the freedom that flows from it. As Marx claimed, 'free, conscious activity is [humanity's] species character', and the *essential* difference between human beings and animals is that we are a '*universal* and therefore a free being'.[11]

There is not a firm consensus about the meaning of Marx's idea of 'universality'. One of the more prevalent tendencies is to interpret it as a kind of all-roundedness of human capacities. Sayers's writing provides a typical example:

> According to Marx, human beings are 'universal' beings, endowed with universal capacities and powers. To develop fully as human beings they must exercise these capacities and powers in an all-round way. Other animals, by contrast, are governed by particular drives and instincts; they have only limited powers and are capable of engaging only in limited and particular activities for particular purposes.[12]

As Marx claimed, 'the more universal [humanity] (or the animal) is, the more universal is the sphere of inorganic nature on which [we live] ... The universality of [humanity] appears in practice precisely in the universality which makes all nature [our] *inorganic* body'.[13] Thus Marx did in fact describe 'universality' in the colloquial sense of all-round development, but what is here a matter of emphasis should not overshadow the richness of Marx's meaning.[14] As a basis

---

9   MECW 5, p. 31.

10   MECW 3, p. 276.

11   MECW 3, pp. 275–6.

12   Sayers 2011, p. 143. In short, 'Human production is universal in its scope' (Sayers 2011, p. 145). Sayers also defined the concept of 'universality' as a kind of generality or common characteristic: 'It is quite evident that there are certain needs and other characteristics which are common to all human beings, pretty well regardless of their particular social or historical situation, and it is equally evident that Marx recognises this. For example, the need for food is clearly a human universal ... This basic need for food is not a historical phenomenon, it is a universal and relatively unchanging feature of the human condition due to our biological constitution' (Sayers 1998, p. 151).

13   MECW 3, p. 275.

14   This sense of the term 'universality' also enters into Marx's social critique. For example: 'If

for freedom, 'universality' must be understood as that which is 'universal' in the sense of 'reason' or '*logos*', although the 'universality' that Marx associates with humanity is connected to the idea of all-round development nonetheless. Insofar as 'the universality of the individual's needs [and] capacities' are capabilities unique to the human species, they are 'rational', and 'the fully developed individual' is an individual that is both virtuous and developed in an all-sided way.[15] Marx also referred to this individuality as 'the rich individuality, which is as varied and comprehensive in its production as it is in its consumption'.[16]

This two-fold meaning of 'universality' as 'rational' and 'total' development is evident in the following passage from Marx's 1844 Paris Manuscripts. He claimed that an animal

> produces one-sidedly, whilst [humanity] produces universally ... An animal produces only itself, whilst [humanity] reproduces the whole of nature ... An animal forms only in accordance with the standard and the need of the species to which it belongs, whilst [humanity] knows how to produce in accordance with the standard of every species, and knows how to apply everywhere the inherent standard to the object.[17]

Acting and producing with knowledge of the 'inherent standard' evokes the idea of our 'nature' as a 'rational' being, and as Marx's work matured there was no break from this idea that the essentially 'human' character of our product-

---

the circumstances in which the individual lives allow him only the [one]-sided development of one quality at the expense of all the rest, [if] they give him the material and time to develop only that one quality, then this individual achieves only a one-sided, crippled development' (MECW 5, p. 262).

15   MECW 28, p. 411; MECW 35, p. 490.

16   MECW 28, p. 251.

17   MECW 3, pp. 276–7. Compare Hegel's claim that 'Animals find what they need for the satisfaction of their wants immediately before them; human beings, by contrast, relate to the means for the satisfaction of their wants as something that they themselves bring forth and shape. Thus, even in what is here external, [humanity] is related to [itself]' (Hegel 1991b, p. 62). Kant also shared a similar view: 'Reason is the ability of a creature to extend the rules and ends of the use of all its powers far beyond its natural instincts, and reason knows no limits in the scope of its projects. Reason itself does not function according to instinct, but rather requires experimentation, practice and, instruction in order to advance gradually from one stage of insight to the next' (Kant 2006, p. 5). Cf. Rousseau's claim that 'Man, dispersed among the beasts, would observe and imitate their activities and so assimilate their instincts, with this added advantage that while every other species has only its own instinct, man, having perhaps none which is peculiar to himself, appropriates every instinct' (Rousseau 1984, pp. 81–2).

ive activity – and our life activity generally – is our ability to direct ourselves in accordance with 'logos'.[18] In *Capital*, for instance, Marx defined human labour as activity involving mind, and the way he elaborates our purposefulness is more clearly associated with the activity of 'self-conscious reason':

> We presuppose labour in a form that stamps it as exclusively human. A spider conducts operations that resemble those of a weaver, and a bee puts to shame many an architect in the construction of her cells. But what distinguishes the worst architect from the best of bees is this, that the architect raises his structure in imagination before he erects it in reality. At the end of every labour process, we get a result that already existed in the imagination of the labourer at its commencement. He not only effects a change of form in the material on which he works, but he also realises a purpose of his own that gives the law to his *modus operandi*, and to which he must subordinate his will. And this subordination is no mere moment-ary act ... [The] process demands that, during the whole operation, the workman's will be steadily in consonance with his purpose.[19]

> An instrument of labour is a thing, or a complex of things, which the labourer interposes between himself and the subject of his labour, and which serves as the conductor of his activity. He makes use of the mech-anical, physical, and chemical properties of some substances in order to make other substances subservient to his aims.[20]

In a footnote to the second passage cited above, Marx invokes Hegel's idea that 'Reason is as *cunning* as it is *mighty*'.[21] This indicates that Marx wanted to express, as Hegel put it, the 'fact that the subjective purpose, as the power over these processes (in which the *objective* gets used up through mutual friction and sublates itself), keeps itself *outside of them* and *preserves itself* in them'.[22]

---

18   'To consider something rationally', Hegel claimed, 'means not to bring reason to bear on the object from outside in order to work upon it, for the object is itself rational for itself; it is the spirit in its freedom, the highest apex of self-conscious reason, which here gives itself actuality and engenders itself as an existing world' (Hegel 1991, p. 60).

19   MECW 35, p. 188.

20   MECW 35, p. 189.

21   Hegel 1991b, p. 284. 'Its cunning', according to Hegel, 'generally consists in the mediating activity which, while it lets objects act upon one another according to their own nature, and wear each other out, executes only *its* purpose without itself mingling in the process' (Ibid.).

22   Ibid.

In other words, Marx was claiming that it is potentially free insofar as our subjective purpose is 'universal' or 'rational' and we have developed the knowledge
and ability to carry it out.[23]

The 'universal' character of human production is thus not specifically its
social character, although this is nevertheless a fundamental aspect of it in
Marx's work. He makes this distinction in what became the third volume of
Capital under Engels's editorship. He argues that 'a distinction should be made
between universal labour and co-operative labour' because both

> kinds play their role in the process of production, both flow one into the
> other, but both are also differentiated. Universal labour is all scientific
> labour, all discovery and all invention. This labour depends partly on the
> co-operation of the living, and partly on the utilisation of the labours of
> those who have gone before. Co-operative labour, on the other hand, is
> the direct co-operation of individuals.[24]

However, Marx's emphasis on 'scientific labour' (i.e., predominantly *intellectual* activity) is somewhat misleading because our 'universal' character encompasses our 'practical' capacities as well. As he claimed, we are 'affirmed in the
objective world not only in the act of thinking, but with *all* [our] senses'.[25] His
idea of the 'human nature of the senses' includes the 'mental' and 'practical
senses' associated with aesthetic objects and ethical experience and practice.[26]
Thus unlike other animals we are able to produce in accordance with the 'laws
of beauty' and direct ourselves in accordance with a principle of 'justice'.

Marx's idea of the 'mental' and 'practical senses' is one of many indications
that he believed we have ethical capacities that can be 'universally developed'.

---

23 Knowledge of Kant's work is also relevant for interpreting these passages in *Capital*. In his
    Critique of Judgement he defined 'art' (and human 'labour') in essentially the same way
    (and he also used the analogy of a bee): 'By right it is only production through freedom, i.e.
    through an act of will that places reason at the basis of its action, that should be termed
    art. For, although we are pleased to call what bees produce (their regularly constructed
    cells) a work of art, we only do so on the strength of an analogy with art; that is to say, as
    soon as we call to mind that no rational deliberation forms the basis of their labour, we
    say at once that it is the product of their nature (of instinct), and it is only to their creator
    that we ascribe it as art' (Kant 2007, p. 132).

24 MECW 37, p. 106.

25 MECW 3, p. 301.

26 MECW 3, p. 302. 'It is obvious', Marx wrote, 'that the *human* eye enjoys things in a way dif-
    ferent from the crude, non-human eye; the human *ear* different from the crude ear, etc.'.
    (MECW 3, p. 301).

For instance, he claimed that 'Insofar as man, and hence also his feeling, etc., is *human*, the affirmation of the object by another is likewise his own gratification'.[27] Marx's work indicates that he thought there is a 'universal' standard ('reason') for ethical activity and experience that we can know, feel, and act in accordance with once we develop the capacity for it.[28] Aristotle's influence on Marx in this respect is also evident and familiarity with the idea of 'moral virtue' is helpful for interpreting the philosophical basis of Marx's idea of developed 'practical senses' like 'will' and 'love'. Aristotle distinguished between 'intellect fused with desire' and 'desire fused with thinking'. For the sake of clarity it is worth quoting Aristotle at length:

> [What] affirming and denying are in thinking, pursuing and avoiding are in desiring, so that, since virtue of character is an active condition of the soul that determines choice, while choice is deliberate desire, for these reasons the rational understanding must be true and the desire right if the choice is of serious worth, and what the one affirms, the other pursues. Now this is the sort of thinking and truth that pertains to action; in thinking that is contemplative, and not pertaining to action or to making anything, truth and falsity mark it as working well or badly, since this is the work of the whole thinking activity, but of the activity of thinking that pertains to action, what marks it as working well is truth that stands in agreement with right desire.
>
> The source of action, then, is choice – the origin of motion rather than the cause for the sake of which it takes place – while the source of choice is desire combined with a rational understanding which is for the sake of something. Hence there is no choice without intellect and thinking, or without an active condition of character, since in action there is no such thing as doing well or the opposite without thinking and character. Thinking itself moves nothing, but thinking that is for the sake of something and pertains to action does cause motion, for this is also what originates the capacity to make something, since one who makes something always

---

27 MECW 3, p. 322. Cf. Hegel's claim that 'If feelings are of the right sort it is because of their quality or content – which is right only so far as it is intrinsically universal or has its source in the thinking mind' (Hegel 1971, p. 231).

28 Hegel elaborated a similar idea in a discussion on 'Law' and 'Morality'. He described them as 'universal existences, objects and aims' which 'are discovered only by the activity of thought, separating itself from the merely sensuous, and developing itself, in opposition thereto; and which must on the other hand, be introduced into and incorporated with the originally sensuous will, and that contrarily to its natural inclination' (Hegel 1956, p. 41).

makes it for the sake of something and the thing made is not simply an end (but it is relative to something and aims at something), though a thing done is. For good action is an end, and desire aims at this. For this reason choice is either intellect fused with desire or desire fused with thinking, and such a source is a human being.[29]

For Marx, truly 'human' purposes express what Aristotle here describes as 'intellect fused with desire' and 'desire fused with thinking'. In the next chapter it will be shown that, in Marx's view, the potentially 'free' character of our social life activity depends on the development of 'moral virtue' for the realisation of 'justice' which is a 'universal' ethical 'principle', defined by Aristotle as the practice of 'complete virtue' in relations with others; and Chapter Five will show that Marx's idea of revolutionary subjectivity is an individuality which is advanced in the development of 'moral virtue', and that this is integral for initiating the establishment of a 'free' society.

2   Human Self-Creation and the Role of Labour in Our
        Transformative Relationship with Nature

Marx depicts revolutionary subjectivity as a form of individuality which emerges amid the activities and relations rooted in the productive process in capitalist society. A successful revolution which marks the transition to truly 'human' life is the result of a broader historical process of 'human' development out of our bestial origin in nature, from which we emerge with only the potential to become free.[30] In Marx's view the labour process is the locus of the dialectic between human activity as natural activity and the natural activity of humanity in which nature is turning into humanity as humanity is transforming nature and becoming consciously free.[31]

We participate in this fundamentally social life activity initially only to satisfy immediate 'natural necessity', and according to Marx the growth of our

---

29   Aristotle 2002, pp. 103–4.

30   'Freedom', Hegel claimed, 'as the *ideal* of that which is original and natural, does not exist *as original and natural*. Rather it must be first sought out and won; and that by an incalculable medial discipline of the intellectual and moral powers. The state of Nature is, therefore, predominantly that of injustice and violence, of untamed natural impulses, of inhuman deeds and feelings' (Hegel 1956, pp. 40–1).

31   Cf. Engels's claim that humanity is 'that vertebrate in which nature attains consciousness of itself' (MECW 25, p. 330.).

'*species-powers*' is an unintended result of it.[32] Through labour we alter the natural world – as we find it altered by sociohistorical activity – and ourselves as well. As Marx claimed in *Capital*,

> Labour is ... a process in which both [humanity] and Nature participate, and in which [humanity] of [its] own accord starts, regulates, and controls the material reactions between [itself] and Nature. [Humanity] opposes [itself] to Nature as one of [its] own forces, setting in motion arms and legs, head and hands, the natural forces of [our] body, in order to appropriate Nature's productions in a form adapted to [our] own wants. By thus acting on the external world and changing it, [we] at the same time [change our] own nature. [Humanity] develops [its] slumbering powers and compels them to act in obedience to [its] sway.[33]

A fundamental aspect of Marx's notion of humanity is that we are self-created.[34] From his perspective, real self-determination essentially involves self-creation.[35] Humanity is able to have a free relationship with nature – in which we are self-determined but not independent of nature *per se* – insofar as we develop our '*species-powers*' because nature is governed by laws which are 'reason'.[36] In this way the human being – as 'self-conscious reason' – is fully

---

32   He thought that the initial impetus for the growth of our consciousness (and language) was the necessity of working collectively to satisfy the material needs associated with our natural-physical life. Cf. his claim in the *Grundrisse* that 'In the act of reproduction itself are changed not only the objective conditions ... but also the producers, who transform themselves in that they evolve new qualities from within themselves, develop through production new powers and new ideas, new modes of intercourse, new needs, and new speech' (MECW 28, p. 418).

33   MECW 35, p. 187.

34   He claimed that 'the *entire so-called history of the world* is nothing but the creation of [humanity] through human labour' (MECW 3, p. 305).

35   'A *being* only considers himself independent when he stands on his own feet; and he only stands on his own feet when he owes his *existence* to himself' (MECW 3, p. 304). Cf. Engels's claim that humanity 'is the sole animal capable of working [its] way out of the merely animal state – [its] normal state is one appropriate to [its] consciousness, *one that has to be created by [itself]*' (MECW 25, p. 476). McCarney attempted to elaborate this aspect of Marx's work in relation to Hegel's philosophy: 'Freedom, [Hegel] tells us, is "self-sufficient being," and so "If I am self-sufficient, I am also free." Thus, the basic idea of freedom is of a life which is at the subject's own disposal, determined by self and not by whatever is external to and other than self. Such a conception of freedom as self-determination is not only in keeping with everyday thinking but also captures the basis for the mainstream treatment of the topic by philosophers since the Greeks' (McCarney 1991, p. 23).

36   Cf. Hegel's claim that 'Nature is an embodiment of Reason', and it is therefore 'unchangeably subordinate to universal laws' (Hegel 1956, p. 12).

developed nature. Marx articulated this dialectic of nature and humanity in the following passage:

> The *human* aspect of nature exists only for *social* man; for only then does nature exist for him as a *bond* with *man* – as his existence for the other and the other's existence for him – and as the life-element of human reality. Only then does nature exist as the *foundation* of his own human existence. Only here has what is to him his *natural* existence become his *human* existence, and nature become man for him. Thus *society* is the complete unity of man with nature – the true resurrection of nature – the accomplished naturalism of man and the accomplished humanism of nature.[37]

With the growth of our inherent capacity for 'universally' conscious labour and the development of productive technology and organisation along with it, we are able to overcome the alien and dominating character of nature overtime.[38] As Marx put it, labour 'no longer appears so much as included in the production process, but rather man relates himself to that process as its overseer and regulator'; e.g., humanity 'interposes the natural process, which [we transform] into an industrial one, as an intermediary between [ourselves] and inorganic nature, which [we make ourselves] master of'.[39] Marx does not suggest that we will be entirely independent from the necessity for instrumental activity associated with our organic body, although this does not necessarily entail activity determined by something other than the human 'self'. Instead, freedom – in a 'higher phase of communist society' – can be characterised as being in tune with nature and adapting it as much as possible to our 'universal' life-activity rather than being subjected to its unconquered might, but the 'natural necessity' associated with the maintenance of our life at a desirable standard (or at all) will remain because we are always internally related to nature.[40]

This transformation and control over forces of the natural world through labour involves the modification of features of our own natural-physical being

---

37   MECW 3, p. 298.
38   Cf. his claim that 'Nature becomes one of the organs of [humanity's] activity, one that [we annex] to [our] own bodily organs, adding stature to [ourselves] in spite of the Bible' (MECW 35, p. 189).
39   MECW 29, p. 91.
40   Hence Marx's claim that 'communism, as fully developed naturalism, equals humanism, and as fully developed humanism equals naturalism; it is the *genuine* resolution of the conflict between man and nature and between man and man' (MECW 3, p. 296).

throughout the historical process. Marx imagined 'the full development of human control over the forces of nature – over the forces of so-called Nature, as well as those of [our] own nature'.[41] Hegel's philosophy was an important influence on Marx in this regard.[42] However, this Hegelian view of the 'self-creation' of humanity comes with a terrible catch. 'At the same pace that mankind masters nature', Marx claimed, 'man seems to become enslaved to other men or to his own infamy'.[43] Appropriating Hegel, Marx made 'estrangement' a key feature of the social labour process throughout the 'prehistory of human society'.[44] Our 'estrangement' provides the dynamism whereby 'reason' becomes increasingly conscious and we create the objective and subjective conditions for a life in which the full development of humanity is consciously pursued as an end in itself. Marx's idea of the role of 'estrangement' in human development will be explored further in Chapter Four.

3   Marx's Aristotelian Idea of 'Nature' and the Paradox of Humanity's Historical Genesis

The question as to whether an idea of 'human nature' exists in Marx's work is controversial. Some interpreters claim that it does not exist while those who claim it does often differ in what it supposedly is, and the different approaches in the literature on the topic tend to emphasise various elements abstracted from Marx's general idea. Those who claim that Marx did not have an idea of human nature tend to invoke his emphasis on the historical diversity and determination of definite cultural forms of social character which is contrasted to the idea of a 'universal human nature'. From the outset this view is inconsistent because it nevertheless proposes an idea of human nature, i.e., something intrinsically 'human'. As Norman Geras argued, 'if diversity in the character of human beings is in large measure set down by Marx to historical variation',

---

41   MECW 28, p. 411. Cf. Fromm's claim that humanity, 'while like all other creatures is subject to forces which determine [it], is the only creature endowed with reason, the only being who is capable of understanding the very forces which [it] is subjected to and who by [its] understanding can take an active part in [its] own fate and strengthen those elements which strive for the good' (Fromm 1947, p. 234).

42   In the *Phenomenology*, for instance, Hegel claims that in the labour process we rid ourselves of our 'attachment to natural existence in every single detail' by 'working on it' (Hegel 1977, p. 117).

43   MECW 14, p. 655.

44   MECW 29, p. 264.

the fact that they 'have a history' is explained 'in turn by some of their general and constant, intrinsic, constitutional characteristics; in short by their human nature'.[45]

Indeed, Marx distinguished between 'human nature in general' and 'human nature as historically modified in each historical epoch'.[46] This is relatively well recognised in contemporary literature.[47] However, the distinction continues to be a source of difficulty because Marx also evidently thought that 'all history is nothing but a continuous transformation of human nature'.[48] The paradoxical character of Marx's philosophical position on this matter has contributed to the interpretation that he thought 'human nature' is ultimately determined by historically fluid 'social relations'. Sayers's writing provides a typical illustration here as well: 'Human nature necessarily exists in a specific social and historical context, and social relations are always the result of specific and historically determined forms of human nature ... Human beings are social and historical beings through and through'.[49]

This is a misrepresentation of Marx's idea that 'human nature' is 'trans-historical' and yet takes on a diversity of forms through the historical process. The key to his idea of 'nature' in this instance is Aristotle's idea of 'each thing's nature' as 'the character it has when its coming-into-being has been completed'.[50] On the basis of Marx's ontology, social relations (i.e., the 'ensemble of social relations' at any given moment in history) are conceived as *internal* relations. On this basis the paradoxical character of Marx's claim that the 'nature which develops in human history – the genesis of human society – is [humanity's] *real* nature' is coherent.[51] Thus although it is evident that Marx thought sociohistorical life is uniquely 'human' and that these processes are involved

---

45   Geras 1983, p. 67.

46   MECW 35, p. 605.

47   Karsten Struhl, for example, claimed that 'Marx's *historical* concept of human nature is grounded in a robust *trans-historical* concept of human nature' (Struhl 2016, p. 81).

48   MECW 6, p. 192.

49   Sayers 1998, p. 150. 'Marx's approach', he claims, 'is historical and relative, not trans-historical and absolute' (Sayers 1998, p. 137). Sayers associated 'the notion of a universal "human essence"' with the idea of 'an unchanging set of human potentialities' and contrasted it to the idea that 'not only needs but also powers and potentialities are in a process of social and historical development' (Ibid.). He ultimately maintains an inconsistent view: 'it is clear that there are universal and trans-historical, relatively unchanging human characteristics and, in that sense, a universal human nature' (Sayers 1998, p. 151).

50   Aristotle 1998, p. 3.

51   MECW 3, 303. This becoming of 'human nature' is a problem for the abstractive intellect that Hegel called the 'understanding' because to this consciousness it is as though we are positing the non-existence of humanity while simultaneously positing its existence – as

in determining our identity, in light of what the present analysis has demonstrated it is also evident that he did not reduce 'human nature' to the fluctuating idiosyncrasies of character arising from shifting sociohistorical relations.

From Marx's perspective, our 'nature' is not begun anew in each era. In his view, all historical variations are definite expressions of the development of our 'universal human nature'. For example, he considered different 'religions are no more than *different stages in the development of the human mind*, different snake skins cast off by *history*' (and humanity is 'the snake who sloughed them').[52] This bears the influence of Hegel's notion of gradations in 'Spirit's consciousness of freedom' which he thought expressed itself in all moments of social life in each definite historical period, giving a particular character to art, science, politics, and so on.[53] The 'ensemble of social relationships' is thus also a manifestation of the 'human spirit' and the collective 'universal' powers of human beings at a definite stage of development. Indeed, in Marx's view all products of our activity are an objectification of the degree to which our 'essential powers' have developed; e.g., the productive forces are 'the objectified power of knowledge'.[54]

---

if a grapevine is not a grapevine until it has grown grapes. Cf. the following passage from Marx's 1844 Manuscripts:

'*Generatio aequivoca* is the only practical refutation of the theory of creation ... You will ... ask: Who begot the first man, and nature as a whole? I can only answer you: Your question is itself a product of abstraction. Ask yourself how you arrived at that question. Ask yourself whether your question is not posed from a standpoint to which I cannot reply, because it is wrongly put. Ask yourself whether that progression as such exists for a reasonable mind. When you ask about the creation of nature and man, you are abstracting, in so doing, from man and nature. You postulate them as *non-existent*, and yet you want me to prove them to you as *existing*. Now I say to you: Give up your abstraction and you will also give up your question. Or if you want to hold on to your abstraction, then be consistent, and if you think of man and nature as *non-existent*, then think of yourself as non-existent, for you too are surely nature and man. Don't think, don't ask me, for as soon as you think and ask, your *abstraction* from the existence of nature and man has no meaning. Or are you such an egotist that you conceive everything as nothing, and yet want yourself to exist? ... [For] the socialist man the *entire so-called history of the world* is nothing but the creation of man through human labour, nothing but the emergence of nature for man, so he has the visible, irrefutable proof of his *birth* through himself, of his *genesis*' (MECW 3, p. 305).

52   MECW 3, p. 148.

53   Cf. Marx's claim that 'In the case of an individual ... whose life embraces a wide circle of varied activities and practical relations to the world, and who, therefore, lives a many-sided life, thought has the same character of universality as every other manifestation of his life' (MECW 5, p. 263).

54   MECW 29, p. 92. Marx claimed that the 'history' of the 'development of the productive

The 'state power is not suspended in mid air', as it were, and neither are the individuals who the state rests on.[55] In secondary literature it is generally accepted that Marx thought our existence is determined in a substantial way by the conditions and relations associated with our fundamental life activity in each definite form of society.[56] The 'course' that a merchant 'shall follow', for example, 'depends wholly on the degree of development of the capitalist mode of production and, not on the merchant's goodwill.'[57] But Marx's perspective is often misunderstood and it is not uncommon to encounter misinterpretations of his idea of the relationship between the socioeconomic 'base' and cultural 'superstructure' which excessively emphasise the determination of human life by the 'economic structure of society' at the expense of his idea of human subjectivity, reducing the 'human mind' to the status of an epiphenomenon.[58] To do so is to discard what Marx thought 'human nature' is. Alan Wood summed up the prevailing view succinctly (in relation to the question of 'moral beliefs'):

> According to historical materialism, people's moral beliefs and the motives to adhere to them are part of the "ideological superstructure" of society ... Historical materialism proposes to explain the social influence of moral beliefs by the way in which they contribute to the basic economic tendencies in the society in which they are found. And it proposes

---

forces' corresponds 'at every stage' with 'the history of the development of the forces of the individuals themselves' (MECW 5, p. 82).

55 MECW 11, p. 186. Cf. Aristotle's claim that the 'city-state is excellent' because 'the citizens who participate in the constitution are excellent' (Aristotle 1998, p. 213).

56 Cf. Marx's claim from 1845 when he and Engels were attempting to articulate the premises of what became known as the 'materialist conception of history': 'By producing their means of subsistence men are indirectly producing their material life ... This mode of production must not be considered simply as being the reproduction of the physical existence of the individuals. Rather it is a definite form of activity of these individuals ... a definite *mode of life* on their part. As individuals express their life, so they are. What they are, therefore, coincides with their production, both with *what* they produce and with *how* they produce. Hence what individuals are depends on the material conditions of their production' (MECW 5, pp. 31–2).

57 MECW 37, p. 305.

58 He claimed that the 'totality of these relations of production constitutes the economic structure of society, the real foundation, on which arises a legal and political superstructure and to which correspond definite forms of social consciousness. The mode of production of material life conditions the general process of social, political and intellectual life. It is not the consciousness of men that determines their existence, but their social existence that determines their consciousness' (MECW 29, p. 263).

to account for the content of these beliefs by the way it helps to stabilise a social system or promote class interest.[59]

Wood's interpretation leaves out the fact that from Marx's perspective the 'social system', 'class interests', and the social relations of production are always an expression of the collective '*universal*' powers of human beings at a definite stage of development. Marx emphasised the definite character of historically specific forms of society because it is necessary for social analysis and critique. Thus Wood's claim that 'Marx proposes to explain the character of a society's legal system, politics and moral or religious beliefs by showing how they serve to sanction its social relations' only partially captures Marx's meaning.[60]

The excessive emphasis which is often placed on the economic 'base' is associated with the erroneous opinion that his idea of the establishment of moral/ethical values is based on a kind of economic determinism. If this were the case, his idea that we can actualise self-determined 'universal' values would be meaningless because these values would always be given. Marx's writing indicates that, in his view, there are moral and ethical values which we can know through our life activity as 'universally developed individuals', and that they are a vital component of the free life which is the fulfilment of our nature.

Marx thought that one of our defining characteristics is our self-creation, but this aspect of our 'nature' is only substantially achieved in a 'rational state of society', when 'reason' *consciously* directs the world.[61] He perceived a time 'when the objective world becomes everywhere for [humanity] in society the world of [humanity's] essential powers – human reality'.[62] In his view the realisation of 'human nature' is achieved in the life lived in an 'higher phase of communist society'. An analysis of his vision of this life is essential for comprehending his idea of revolutionary subjectivity because revolutionary subjects are going to initiate the establishment of it. Even though these individuals will not experience the flourishing of our 'human nature', Marx thought that their life activity and experience in capitalism would develop their consciousness of it nonetheless. He claimed, for example, that 'English and French workers have formed associations in which they exchange opinions not only on their immediate needs as *workers*, but as *human beings*'.[63]

---

59   Wood 2004, p. 132.
60   Wood 2004, p. 105.
61   MECW 20, p. 188.
62   MECW 3, p. 301.
63   MECW 4, p. 52.

'Communist Society'

I dream'd that was the new city of Friends,
Nothing was greater there than the quality of robust love,
    it led the rest,
It was seen every hour in the actions of the people of that city,
All in their looks and words.
    WALT WHITMAN[1]

∴

1   **'Universally Developed Individuals' and the General Character of Freedom in 'Communist Society'**

Marx's idea of 'human nature' is often expressed in conjunction with his state-ments about the 'communist organization of society', of which there is rel-atively little in his work. This society is a manifestation of our full develop-ment, although it is not an end to our development in the sense of a static state of being. It is rather the active life of our 'universal nature' – 'the abso-lute movement of becoming' – which is self-conscious 'reason'.[2] As his thought developed, Marx articulated a more concrete vision of how 'reason' consciously 'directs the world': when 'the associated producers, rationally regulating their interchange with Nature', bring 'it under their common control' in 'conditions most favourable to, and worthy of, their human nature'.[3] Indeed, he described a 'higher phase of communist society' as a mode of life in which 'the prac-tical relations of everyday life' between individuals and between humanity and nature are 'perfectly intelligible and reasonable'.[4] In this kind of life 'the cohe-sion of the aggregate production' is a law which, 'being understood and hence controlled by' the 'common mind' of 'the agents of production', 'brings the pro-

---

1   Whitman 1975, p. 164.
2   MECW 28, p. 412.
3   MECW 37, p. 807.
4   MECW 35, p. 90.

duction process under their joint control'.[5] Put another way, it is 'a community of free individuals, carrying on their work with the means of production in common, in which the labour power of all the different individuals is consciously applied as the combined labour power of the community'.[6] Aristotle's idea of 'a being-at-work of the soul in accordance with reason' is perceptible here.[7] In Marx's writing it is expressed through reference to activity which actualises 'universal' principles such as 'beauty' and 'truth'. His work suggests that a vital component of a 'free' life is the uniquely 'human' experience of ethical life in which the 'inherent standard' is the principle of 'love'.

'Universally developed individuals' would populate this society and experience truly 'free activity' which, according to Marx, is 'for the communists the creative manifestation of life arising from the free development of all abilities'.[8] It must be reemphasised that Marx meant 'universal' not merely in the sense of all-round development, but more fundamentally as 'rational'.[9] It is in

---

5   MECW 37, p. 256. Cf. Hegel's claim that 'it is the nature of humanity to press onward to agreement with others; human nature only really exists in an achieved community of minds' (Hegel 1977, p. 43).

6   MECW 35, p. 89.

7   Aristotle 2002, p. 11. Cf. Aristotle's claim that 'political communities must be taken to exist for the sake of [beautiful] actions' (Aristotle 1998, p. 81). In a word, it is a 'eudemonic' existence.

8   MECW 28, p. 99; MECW 5, p. 225.

9   The idea of all-around development is present in Marx's notion of 'universally developed individuals', nonetheless. Thus, he imagined 'communist society' as a social order 'where nobody has one exclusive sphere of activity but each can become accomplished in any branch he wishes' because 'society regulates the general production and thus makes it possible for me to do one thing today and another tomorrow' (MECW 5, p. 47). He claimed further that 'with a communist organisation of society, there disappears the subordination of the artist to local and national narrowness, which arises entirely from division of labour, and also the subordination of the individual to some definite art, making him exclusively a painter, sculptor, etc.; the very name amply expresses the narrowness of his professional development and his dependence on division of labour. In a communist society, there are no painters but only people who engage in painting among other activities' (MECW 5, p. 394). Engels, too, maintained that life in what Marx described as 'a higher phase of communist society' presupposes the all-round development of individuals: 'Industry carried on in common and according to plan by the whole of society presupposes moreover people of all-round development, capable of surveying the entire system of production ... [The] communist organisation of society will give its members the chance of an all-round exercise of abilities that have received all-round development' (MECW 6, p. 353). According to Marx and Engels, the desire for such a life was already manifesting in capitalist society. They claimed that 'workers assert in their communist propaganda that' the 'task of every person is to achieve all-round development of all his abilities, including, for example, the ability to think' (MECW 5, p. 292). 'The all-round realisation of the individual will only cease to be conceived as an ideal ... when the impact of the world which stimulates the real development of the abilities of the individual is under the control of the individuals themselves, as the communists desire' (MECW 5, p. 292.).

this sense that he claimed that the 'communist' mode of production aims at the 'free development of all abilities' of the whole person.[10] As he articulated it, the 'free and full development' of the individual is 'based on the universal development of [all] individuals', i.e., on fostering their 'universal relations, universal requirements and universal capacities'.[11] This 'free' and 'universal' character of their capacities and relations can also be articulated as 'virtuous'. As Marx claimed, in such conditions we would be 'excellent' at our all-round activity.[12]

2　Realms of Life Activity and the Character of Social Relations in 'Communist Society'

Attaining the stable social harmony that Marx thought would characterise a 'higher phase of communist society' depends on the 'full development of human control over the forces of' our 'own nature'.[13] Marx distinguished between two essential realms of activity within this society: the 'realm of necessity' and the 'true realm of freedom'.[14] His language may be misleading because both of these realms are moments of a 'free' life at this level of human development insofar as they are determined by the collective 'reason' of humanity.

The 'realm of necessity' involves all instrumental activity, i.e., for needs arising from the natural-biological aspect of our being, including the means for this activity itself, as well as for the needs arising from the 'true realm of freedom'. The social relations which determine the economic organisation of society are such that socially produced goods are distributed in accordance with a common plan that aims at the all-round cultivation of the abilities and talents of all individuals.[15] The 'realm of necessity' would be carried out with the least possible amount of time and energy expenditure with the aim of making it *'travail attractif* [attractive work]'.[16] We would also minimise the amount of time and energy required for it in order to maximise time and energy for fully 'free', 'end in itself' activity in the 'realm of freedom'. Even though the 'realm

---

10 　MECW 5, p. 225.

11 　MECW 28, pp. 411; 95.

12 　MECW 5, p. 394.

13 　MECW 28, p. 411.

14 　MECW 37, p. 807.

15 　Cf. Aristotle's claim that "if they all competed for the beautiful, and strained to the utmost to perform the most beautiful actions, then for all in common there would be what is needful, and for each in particular there would be the greatest of goods, if indeed virtue is that" (Aristotle 2002, p. 173).

16 　MECW 28, p. 530.

of physical necessity expands' with our development, we would continue to develop the productive powers of society to avoid burdening human beings with instrumental labour.[17] This is because Marx considered 'the development of the individual disposition' as 'a productive power' and thought 'communist society' is premised on the 'saving of labour time' which is 'equivalent to the increase of free time, i.e. time for the full development of the individual', and which 'in turn reacts upon the productive power of labour' as 'the greatest productive force'.[18] In other words, it would be a time 'after the productive forces have also increased with the all-round development of the individual, and all the springs of common wealth flow more abundantly'.[19] Thus in this mode of life 'necessary labour time will be measured by the needs of the social individual' and

> society's productive power will develop so rapidly that, although production will now be calculated to provide wealth for all, the disposable time of all will increase. For real wealth is the developed productive power of all individuals. Then wealth is no longer measured by labour time but by disposable time.[20]

'Free time' in 'communist society' is 'both leisure and time for higher activity'.[21] Such 'higher activity' is the time spent engaging in and enjoying the activities associated with the actualisation of 'universal' aesthetic and intellectual principles in 'the true realm of freedom'. The 'Free development of individualities' and the general 'reduction of the necessary labour of society to a minimum' is integral for 'that development of human energy which is an end in itself' because it corresponds to 'the artistic, scientific, etc., development of individuals, made possible by the time thus set free and the means produced for all of them'.[22] The influence of Aristotle is still perceptible here; he

---

17   MECW 37, p. 807.
18   MECW 29, p. 97.
19   MECW 24, p. 87.
20   MECW 29, p. 94.
21   MECW 29, p. 97.
22   MECW 29, p. 91; MECW 37, p. 807. As he put it elsewhere, disposable time 'will not be absorbed in direct productive labour, but will be available for enjoyment, for leisure, thus giving scope for free activity and development. Time is *scope* for the development of man's faculties, etc.'; 'free time, *disposable time*, is wealth itself, partly for the enjoyment of the product, partly for free activity which ... is not dominated by the pressure of an extraneous purpose which must be fulfilled, and the fulfillment of which is regarded as a natural necessity or social duty, according to one's inclination' (MECW 32, pp. 390–1).

claimed that 'those activities are chosen for their own sake from which noth-ing is sought beyond the being-at-work; and actions in accord with virtue seem to be of this sort, since performing actions that are beautiful and serious is something chosen for its own sake'.[23] This 'higher activity' is an end-in-itself and its 'rational' character is the basis for Marx's claim that really free labour 'cannot become a game'.[24] As Marx claimed, truly 'free work, e.g. the com-position of music, is also the most damnably difficult, demanding the most intensive effort', because the activity requires producing in accordance with the 'inherent standard [of] the object'.[25] Compare Kant's claim that

> in all free arts something of a compulsory character is still required ... (e.g., in the poetic art there must be correctness and wealth of language, like-wise, prosody and metre). For not a few leaders of a newer school believe that the best way to promote a free art is to sweep away all restraint and convert it from labour into mere play.[26]

Ultimately, Marx thought that 'Our products would be so many mirrors in which we saw reflected our essential nature' because they would involve an objectification of the 'universal' which is 'reason'.[27]

The 'realm of natural necessity' has a liberating character in such circum-stances because it is determined by 'reason'. Herbert Marcuse denied this. 'No matter how justly and rationally the material production may be organized', he claimed, 'it can never be a realm of freedom and gratification'.[28] Insofar as the working day 'would remain a day of unfreedom, rational but not free', Mar-cuse thought that 'real human freedom would prevail only outside the entire sphere of socially necessary labour'.[29] For Marx, on the contrary, even though the 'realm of natural necessity' remains a realm of instrumental necessity and does not become an end in itself, i.e., even though we would not spend unne-cessary time labouring in this realm because of its instrumental nature, this is not enough to qualify it as unfree. It can be carried out 'universally' – in both senses of this term – and undertaken within a 'free association' of individu-

---

23   Aristotle 2002, p. 190.
24   MECW 29, p. 97.
25   MECW 28, p. 530.
26   Kant 2007, pp. 133–4.
27   MECW 3, p. 228.
28   Marcuse 1962, p. 142.
29   Marcuse 1969, p. 21. He did however claim that 'the development of the productive forces beyond their capitalist organization suggests the possibility of freedom *within* the realm of necessity' (Ibid.).

als. In such a society we could all achieve 'rational' self-determination because as 'associated producers' we would consciously provide ourselves with what we need to develop 'universally'. The material means for a life oriented toward the 'absolute movement' of the development of our 'species powers' would be provided for the benefit of everyone by the collective power of all individuals united as a conscious social force.[30]

In step with the growth of scientific knowledge and technical aptitude as it relates to the production process, production requires less of our direct involvement as we develop the technological basis of production and discover new and better ways of carrying it out rationally, in harmony with the cosmic flow of life. It would also be carried out in accordance with the 'laws of beauty'. Food, for example, can be made to taste good with the practice of culinary arts.[31] In short, instrumental labour that cannot be overcome would be done 'rationally' and thus as freely as possible.

In these conditions 'work would be a *free manifestation of life*' and 'an *enjoyment* of *life*'.[32] As Marx put it, labour becomes 'life's prime want' because 'the external aims are stripped of their character as merely external natural necessity, and become posited as aims which only the individual himself posits, that they are therefore posited as self-realisation, objectification of the subject, and thus real freedom, whose action is precisely work'.[33] Engels elaborated this vision in his claim that 'productive labour, instead of being a means of subjugating men, will become a means of their emancipation, by offering each individual the opportunity to develop all his faculties, physical and mental, in all directions and exercise them to the full – in which, therefore, productive labour will become a pleasure instead of being a burden'.[34]

The ethical character of social relations in 'communist society' is an essential reason why Marx described it as a 'free association'. Aside from the fact that the two realms of life activity are determined by 'reason', they are 'free' fundamentally because of the social relations that Marx envisioned. In the words of Percy Bysshe Shelley, they can be described as '*Realms where the air we breathe is love*'.[35] The freedom embodied in the activity of instrumental social labour is premised on conscious 'reciprocal love'.[36] This can be elaborated in conjunc-

---

30   MECW 28, p. 412.
31   Marcuse claimed that a new aesthetic ethos would permeate a liberated society, but in his view art should also become mere play.
32   MECW 3, p. 228.
33   MECW 24, p. 87; MECW 28, p. 530.
34   MECW 25, p. 280.
35   Shelley 1956, p. 146.
36   MECW 3, p. 326.

tion with Aristotle's idea of 'justice', which is the practice of 'complete virtue' in relations with others.[37] This ethical character of social relations is vital for the functioning of the society 'in which the free development of each is the condition for the free development of all'.[38]

From the outset, activity in the 'realm of natural necessity' actualises a 'just' distribution principle: 'From each according to [their] ability, to each according to [their] needs'.[39] However, aside from being an instrumental necessity, 'justice' is also an end in itself and it is therefore essential for freedom in a twofold sense: firstly, it is indispensable for self-realisation in an instrumental way because everyone is provided with what they need to become 'universally developed', and, secondly, it is desirable for 'universally developed individuals' as an end in itself and therefore an integral component of activity in 'the true realm of freedom'.[40] In conditions that are intimate enough for mutual recognition, Marx thought that

> I would have been for you the *mediator* between you and the species, and therefore would become recognised and felt by you yourself as a completion of your own essential nature and as a necessary part of yourself, and consequently would know myself to be confirmed both in your thought and your love ... This relationship would moreover be reciprocal; what occurs on my side has also to occur on yours.[41]

---

37 According to Aristotle, 'This sort of justice ... is complete virtue, though not simply but in relation to someone else. And for this reason, it often seems that justice is the greatest of the virtues, and "neither evening's nor dawn's light is so wondrous," and we say proverbially "in justice all virtue is together in one." And it especially is complete virtue because it is the putting to use of complete virtue, and is complete because the one who has it is also capable of putting it to use in relation to someone else, and not just by oneself, for many people are able to put virtue to use among those at home but unable to do so in situations that involve someone else' (Aristotle 2002, p. 81). Of course, Marx's social theory is consistent with the politics of 'universal human emancipation', which is a principle that Aristotle did not attain, hence his position on 'natural' slaves, his xenophobia and his sexism which are diametrically opposed to Marx's position.

38 MECW 6, p. 506.

39 MECW 24, p. 87.

40 According to Marx, 'the genuine and free development of individuals' that takes place in 'communist society' is 'determined precisely by the connection of individuals ... which consists partly in the economic prerequisites and partly in the necessary solidarity of the free development of all', and 'in the universal character of the activity of individuals' (MECW 5, p. 439).

41 MECW 3, p. 228. Thus it is not sufficiently accurate to claim, as Richard Miller did, that this society 'is held together by mutual caring', although it is a valuable description of this ethos (Miller 1981, p. 327).

Freedom is thus fundamentally intersubjective in the dual sense that its content is *universal* (e.g., 'the laws of beauty') and that the free experience of others is necessary to complete the free experience of everyone.

Marx's fragmentary writing on this matter can be elaborated in conjunction with a similar account of freedom in Hegel's philosophy. According to Hegel 'true freedom … consists in my identity with the other' whereby 'I am only truly free when the other is also free and is recognized by me as free'.[42] Marx's vision of 'communist' social relations indicates that individuals would have developed what Hegel called 'Universal self-consciousness' which is 'the affirmative awareness of self in an other self' whereby 'each has "real" universality in the shape of reciprocity, so far as each knows itself recognized in the other freeman, and is aware of this in so far as it recognizes the other and knows him to be free'.[43] Hegel claimed further that 'the mutually related self-conscious subjects, by setting aside their unequal particular individuality, have risen to the consciousness of their real universality, of the freedom belonging to all, and hence the intuition of their specific identity with each other'.[44] This kind of relationship is consonant with the interpersonal basis of the independence of 'universally developed individuals' in Marx's idea of 'a rational state of society'. 'In this state of universal freedom', Hegel claimed, 'in being reflected into myself, I am immediately reflected into the other person, and, conversely, in relating myself to the other I am immediately *self*-related'.[45]

When relations are intimate enough for what Marx described as 'reciprocal love' to be mutually recognised, the relationship is akin to what Aristotle called true 'friendship'. It is based on the mutually recognised and reciprocated practice of virtue between 'universally developed individuals' whereby the eudaimonic experience of the other is the purpose of the relationship for both individuals.[46] Aristotle claimed that 'loving in return involves choice, and choice comes from an active condition', and in relations intimate enough, individuals

---

42   Hegel 1971, p. 171.

43   Hegel 1971, p. 176.

44   Ibid. Cf. Hegel's claim that 'Spirit is the knowledge of oneself in the externalization of oneself; the being that is the movement of retaining its self-identity in its otherness' (Hegel 1977, p. 459).

45   Hegel 1971, pp. 176–7.

46   Cf. Ollman's claim – which omits the idea of the practice of virtue – that the 'desire to please is not associated with any sense of duty, but with the satisfaction one gets at this time in helping others … We can approximate what takes place here if we view each person as loving all others such that he or she can get pleasure from the pleasure they derive from his or her efforts … Marx is universalizing this emotion … to the point where each

wish for good things for those they love for those others' own sake, not as a result of feeling but as a result of an active condition. And by loving the friend, they love what is good for themselves, for when a good person becomes a friend, he becomes good for the one to whom he is a friend.[47]

Such individuals are 'sharing a single soul', as Aristotle put it, and are therefore 'in a certain way the same, in separate selves'.[48]

Marx's depiction of this intersubjective experience of 'reciprocal loving' in a 'higher phase of communist society' indicates that what he called the '*human need*' for 'the *other* person as a person' would become ubiquitous.[49] This notion of an individual 'person' can be elaborated in Hegelian terms as an individual in their 'single existence as possessing universality' and, 'therefore, as inherently infinite'.[50] In such relations we would recognise this 'infinite' worth of all other human beings as ends in themselves and act toward each other in ways that affirm our shared 'universal' freedom by practicing 'complete virtue'. 'Infinity' also manifests for our consciousness in another way because love, as it were, increases in amount when it is shared. In the words of Dante,

the more souls there above who are in love
the more there are worth loving; love grows more,
each soul a mirror mutually mirroring.[51]

As Hegel claimed, love

is a mutual giving and taking ... The lover who takes is not thereby made richer than the other; he is enriched indeed, but only so much as the other is. So too the giver does not make himself poorer; by giving to the other he has at the same time and to the same extent enhanced his own treasure.[52]

---

person is able to feel it for everyone whom his/her actions effect, which in communism is the whole of society ... [People] at this time also engage in communal activities for the sheer pleasure of being with others. Human togetherness has become its own justification' (Ollman 1978, pp. 72–3).

47   Aristotle 2002, p. 150.
48   Aristotle 2011, p. 127; Aristotle 2002, p. 158. Aristotle thought that 'being a friend amounts to being a separate self. Perceiving a friend, then, must be in a manner perceiving oneself, and in a manner knowing oneself' (Aristotle 2011, p. 138).
49   Aristotle 2002, p. 146; MECW 3, p. 296.
50   Hegel 1971, p. 70.
51   Alighieri 1985, p. 163.
52   Hegel 1961, p. 307.

In the words of Shelley,

> True Love in this differs from gold and clay,
> That to divide is not to take away.[53]

Ultimately, Marx's vision of the character of social relations in 'communist society' is relevant for our understanding of his idea of revolutionary subjectivity because an incipient form of these relations, and thus also the ethical capacities corresponding to it, must develop among revolutionary subjects in capitalism as a conditional necessity for the initiation of the transition to 'communist society'.[54]

> For now we see in a mirror dimly, but then face to face; now I know in part, but then I will know fully just as I also have been fully known.[55]

3   A Note on the 'First Phase of Communist Society'

Marx imagined a period of transition between capitalism and a 'higher phase of communist society' which is relevant for understanding revolutionary subjectivity. He described this initial phase of the revolutionary transformation of capitalism as 'the first phase of communist society'.[56] He claimed there is a 'a political transition period in which the state can be nothing but *the revolutionary dictatorship of the proletariat*'.[57] It is during this period of the 'self-government of the communities' of producers that we initiate the reorganisation of social life into conditions in which our 'essential powers' flourish.[58] 'What the proletariat has [to] do', Marx maintained, 'is to transform the present capitalist character of ... organized labour and ... centralized means of labour, transform them from the means of class rule and class exploitation into forms of free associated labour and social means of production'.[59]

---

53   Shelley 1956, p. 232.
54   In other words, these revolutionary ethical capacities must develop in a society in which human beings are 'mere means of production, not an end in themselves and not the aim of production' (MECW 32, p. 175).
55   Corinthians 13:12.
56   MECW 24, p. 87.
57   MECW 24, p. 95.
58   MECW 24, p. 519.
59   MECW 22, p. 494.

This transitory period is not what Marx described, in 1844, as *'crude communism'* in his critical comments directed toward various utopian socialists (e.g. Babouvists), although there are some similarities between this and his discussion in the *Critique of the Gotha Program*. For example, in 1844 he claimed that

> The community is only a community of *labour*, and equality of *wages* paid out by communal capital – by the *community* as the universal capitalist. Both sides of the relationship are raised to an *imagined* universality – *labour* as the category in which every person is placed, and *capital* as the acknowledged universality and power of the community.[60]

In the *Critique of the Gotha Program* he wrote that in this transitory period 'everyone is only a worker like everyone else', i.e., individuals 'are regarded *only as workers* and nothing more is seen in them, everything else being ignored'.[61] However, as he claimed in *The Civil War in France*, this is qualified by the fact that even in situations when the 'Commune does not [do] away with the class struggles, through which the working classes strive to the abolition of all classes and, therefore, of all class rule', it nevertheless 'affords the rational medium in which that class struggle can run through its different phases in the most rational and human way'.[62] On Marx's premises, 'crude communism' is an early manifestation of the 'socialist principle' which is maintained by 'crude and thoughtless' individuals who have not developed within sufficient conditions in the womb of capitalist society – it is a 'still immature communism'.[63] Premature attempts at social reform or revolution (e.g., Robert Owen's New Lanark or Soviet Russia) have immature results.

Marx claimed that the 'first phase' of 'communist society' is still circumscribed by *'bourgeois right'* and 'bourgeois limitation' because it has just emerged from capitalist society.[64] It is inevitable that this phase is in 'every respect, economically, morally and intellectually, still stamped with the birthmarks of the old society from whose womb it emerges'.[65] After all, the indi-

---

60   MECW 3, p. 295.

61   MECW 24, pp. 86–7.

62   MECW 22, p. 491.

63   MECW 3, pp. 143; 294; 297. Consider, for example, Marx's claim that 'crude communism is only the culmination' of 'General *envy* constituting itself as a power', i.e., 'the disguise in which *greed* re-establishes itself and satisfies itself' (MECW 3, p. 295).

64   MECW 24, p. 86.

65   MECW 24, p. 85.

viduals creating it are raised in the 'estrangement' of capitalist society. And yet a progressive development of human capacities preceding the revolution is required to establish a new and better society nonetheless. The subjective capacities, including and especially ethical capacities, which are required to *initiate* the revolutionary transition must begin to develop within capitalist society, and subsequent development must take place amid the presence of any 'defects' in the 'the first phase of communist society'.[66] This is significant for the concept of revolutionary subjectivity because an incipient form of the desire for the social relations of 'communist society' must develop within capitalism. Marx refers to such development in his claim that working people experience a kind of 'association' through 'revolutionary practice' which leads to the development of a new, higher need of an ethical kind: 'the need for society'.[67]

4   The 'Universal' Nature of Freedom and the Principle of 'Justice' in Marx's Writings

After what has preceded, we are in a better position to take into account two distinct yet interrelated points of potential philosophical contention and debate regarding Marx's thought. These are firstly, the idea of freedom as 'universal' in an objective/intersubjective sense, and, secondly, the idea of an 'independent and transcendent' standard of 'justice'.[68] These ideas, of course, are points of contention in themselves even beyond any consideration of Marx's work.

From the perspective of Marx's social philosophy, the idea that the meaning of 'freedom' is only relative to particular groups or individuals – and thus that there are only incommensurable freedoms – is an expression of 'estrangement'.[69] This idea of freedom is closely associated with the cynical and misanthropic opinion that there exists an unresolvable antithesis between individual

---

66   MECW 24, p. 87.
67   MECW 3, p. 313.
68   Geras 1984, p. 18.
69   Hegel described this as the 'atomistic principle' of Liberalism which 'insists upon the sway of individual wills', and he claimed that its ascension in the modern world is the 'problem ... with which history is now occupied, whose solution it has to work out in the future' (Hegel 1956, p. 452). The rise of this principle has brought with it what he called the 'perpetually recurring misapprehension of Freedom' which 'consists in regarding that term only in its *formal*, subjective sense, abstracted from its essential objects and aims' (Hegel 1956, p. 41).

freedom and social existence and that we are, as a result, doomed to speak longingly of a good life, as though we can imagine it in an ideal world but believe it is impossible to experience in any actually conceivable society. In the philosophical tradition to which Marx belongs, this view of freedom is one-sided and deficient of substance in comparison to the idea that freedom is achieved through the intersubjective unity of the 'universal' wills of individuals.[70] This is expressed, for example, in Marx's idea that 'universal human emancipation' can only be attained in a society based on 'production by freely associated' individuals which is 'consciously regulated by them in accordance with a settled plan'.[71] This is a key reason why Marx thought that 'personal freedom becomes possible only within the community'.[72] Indeed, his writing indicates that in his view this would begin to arise out of necessity in the revolutionary situation:

> With the community of revolutionary proletarians ... who take their conditions of existence and those of all members of society under their control ... it is as individuals that the individuals participate in it. For it is the association of individuals (assuming the advanced stage of modern productive forces, of course) which puts the conditions of the free development of movement of individuals under their control.[73]

In Marx's vision of an emancipated society, our individuality is not lost in a dull, abstract homogeneity of subjectivities; instead, it exists as a vibrant moment in the total 'movement of becoming' of distinct individuals developing themselves 'universally'.[74] On Marx's premises every human being has the potential to develop the 'rational' capacities required to actualise this freedom, and in

---

70   This is what Hegel termed the 'rational Will' (Hegel 1956, p. 38).

71   MECW 3, p. 280; MECW 35, p. 90.

72   MECW 5, p. 78. 'Only within the community', he claimed, 'has each individual the means of cultivating his gifts in all directions ... In the real community the individuals obtain their freedom in and through their association' (MECW 5, p. 78).

73   MECW 5, p. 80.

74   As Shlomo Avineri claimed, Marx's idea of communism 'is not a collectivism which subsumes the individual under an abstract whole; it is rather an attempt to break down the barriers between the individual and society and to try to find the key to the reunion of these two aspects of human existence' (Avineri 1968, p. 89). Cf. Hegel's idea that the 'substance of the Spirit is freedom. From this, we can infer that its end in the historical process is the freedom of the subject to follow its own conscience and morality, and to pursue and implement its own universal ends; it also implies that the subject has infinite value and that it must become conscious of its supremacy. The end of the world Spirit is realised in substance through the freedom of each individual' (Hegel 1956, p. 55).

the event that the development of an individual is stunted or they are disabled in some way, they do not cease to be an end in themselves, and their wellbeing would remain an integral aspect of a 'rational' social order nonetheless.[75]

These issues concerning Marx's idea of freedom overlap with the controversy over the idea of 'justice' in his work. In the literature on his thought there is a disagreement about whether his writing puts forth the idea of 'universal' ethical values which exist independently of a given set of social relations and the definite conditions of social production to which they correspond.[76] In the previous chapter we encountered the prevalent view that Marx espoused a principle of sociohistorical relativism for the determination of ethical values. In this view – which rests upon a misconception of his view of the socioeconomic 'base' and 'superstructure' – since the values arise in sociohistorical conditions of life that are ultimately transient and fleeting, the values cannot have an 'inherent standard' that can be judged 'universally'. Sayers, for instance, maintains that 'Marxism does not involve a moral approach to history; but rather a historical approach to morality. It cannot and does not appeal to universal moral principles or values; for the essential insight of Marxism is that morality is a social and historical phenomenon'.[77] This mistakenly conflates Marx's anti-moralism with an ethical relativism rooted in fluctuations of historically determinate forms of social life activity. Marx espoused a 'universal' principle of justice in connection with his idea of a 'free' society predicated on full human development, and this is not inconsistent with the idea that, as Geras put it, 'Standards of justice ... are relative or internal to specific historical modes of

---

75   According to Marx, in these conditions 'that portion of the product' of 'labour which passes over into the individual consumption of the labourer' is relived from 'its capitalist limit' and extended 'to that volume of consumption' which 'the full development of the individuality requires'; 'surplus labour and surplus product' are also reduced 'to create an insurance and reserve fund', and 'to constantly expand reproduction to the extent dictated by social needs'; and both 'the necessary labour' and 'the surplus labour' are taken to include 'the quantity of labour which must always be performed by the able-bodied in behalf of the immature or incapacitated members of society' (MECW 37, pp. 862–3).

76   Cf. Hegel's claim that 'the State is the externally existing, genuinely moral life. It is the union of the universal and essential with the subjective will, and as such it is *Morality*. The individual who lives in this unity has a moral life, a value which consists in this substantiality alone. Sophocles' Antigone says: "The divine commands are not of yesterday nor of today; no, they have an infinite existence, and no one can say whence they came." The laws of ethics are not accidental, but are rationality itself. It is the end of the State to make the substantial prevail and maintain itself in the actual doings of men and in their convictions. It is the absolute interest of Reason that this moral whole exist' (Hegel 1956, p. 40).

77   Sayers 1998, p. 116.

production'.[78] On Marx's premises, all historically specific standards of justice can be compared in their approximation to the 'universal' principle of justice associated with a society of 'fully developed human beings'. But he was not moralistic as a result. Throughout their lives Marx and Engels maintained the perspective that

> communists do not oppose egoism to selflessness or selflessness to ego-ism ... The communists do not preach *morality* at all. They do not put to people the moral demand: love one another, do not be egoists, etc.; on the contrary, they are very well aware that egoism, just as much selfless-ness, *is* in definite circumstances a necessary form of the self-assertion of individuals. Hence, the communists by no means want ... to do away with the 'private individual' for the sake of the 'general', selfless man. That is a figment of the imagination.[79]

Ultimately, from the perspective of Marx's social philosophy, our conception of what is 'just' or morally 'right' and 'good' reflects our level of development which coincides with the definite conditions of social life activity of which we are creatures.[80] Hence his claim that

> If correctly understood interest is the principle of all morality, man's private interest must be made to coincide with the interest of humanity. If man is unfree in the materialistic sense, i.e., is free not through the neg-ative power to avoid this or that, but through the positive power to assert his true individuality, crime must not be punished in the individual, but the anti-social sources of crime must be destroyed, and each man must be given social scope for the vital manifestation of his being. If man is shaped by environment, his environment must be made human. If man is social by nature, he will develop his true nature only in society, and the

---

78   Geras 1984, p. 8. Cf. Wood's claim that 'When Marx and Engels say that people at differ-ent times and places have held diverse views about the nature of 'eternal justice', they are not espousing relativism; they are rather arguing that there are no "eternal" rational principles or formal criteria of justice, applicable irrespective of time and circumstances' (Wood 2004, pp. 133–4).

79   MECW 5, p. 247. Cf. Hegel's claim that 'a person is a specific existence; not man in general (a term to which no real existence corresponds)' (Hegel 1956, p. 24).

80   'My standpoint', Marx wrote, 'from which the development of the economic formation of society is viewed as a process of natural history, can less than any other make the indi-vidual responsible for relations whose creature he remains, socially speaking, however much he may subjectively raise himself above them' (MECW 35, p. 10).

power of his nature must be measured not by the power of the separate individual but by the power of society.[81]

In short, from Marx's perspective our moral ideas shift historically in accordance with the movement of our 'universal' development and the corresponding life activity. The ethical orientation of 'free' social relations is therefore valid for individuals who have developed 'reason' to the extent required for it. On Marx's premises, human 'self-realization' entails the development of the ability to freely determine our relations in accordance with the 'universal' ethical good that we pursue through 'desire fused with thinking'.

An accurate grasp of the ontological and anthropological premises of Marx's social philosophy is required to reconcile the paradoxical position that moral/ethical values are historically specific while simultaneously asserting the existence of a 'universal' principle of 'justice' that transcends the transient historical expressions of human life activity.[82] Otherwise, we cannot recognise that these two apparently contradictory positions are coherently united in Marx's thinking. Consider, for example, Sayers' inaccurate claim that Marx 'does not appeal to transcendent standards' but rather to those that are 'immanent, historical and relative in character'.[83] The interpretative lapse underlying this view is expressed in Sayers' claim that 'principles of justice are not eternally self-evident or rational; they are historical and relative'.[84] As we have seen, Marx

---

81   MECW 4, pp. 130–1.

82   This is why Geras, for instance, claims that there is 'an inconsistency – or paradox' in Marx's 'attitude to normative questions' (Geras 1984, p. 84). Cf. Tony Burns who agrees 'with Geras that Marx's pronouncements on justice are contradictory' (Burns 2005, p. 153). Geras attempts to get around this by claiming that Marx's apparent relativism is actually a kind of realism: 'Marx's seemingly relativist statements in this area are not, in fact, what many have taken them to be. They are statements not of moral relativism but rather, as we may call this, of moral realism. That standards of right are, for him, sociologically grounded or determined means that the norms people believe in and live by will be powerfully influenced by the nature of their society, their class position in it, and so on. It means, more particularly, that what standards of right can actually be implemented effectively and secured – this is constrained by the economic structure and resources of the given society. It does not mean that the standards to be used in evaluating or assessing a society must necessarily also be constrained by the same economic configuration; that the only valid criteria of assessment are those actually prevalent, those harmonious with the mode of production. Marx's assertion that right cannot be "higher than the economic structure" is a case in point. Its context makes clear that it is a realist, not a relativist, one' (Geras 1984, p. 19).

83   Sayers 1998, p. 131.

84   Sayers 1998, p. 144. In a more recent work Sayers claims that Marx's 'criticism of capitalism implied in the concept of alienation does not appeal to universal moral standards ... it is

explicitly identified a 'higher phase of communist society' – including this society's ethical values and the relations embodying them – with 'reason'. An analysis of some statements from Engels's polemic against Eugen Dühring can help to further illustrate this matter. In Engels's criticism of Owen's New Lanark it is evident that he shared core philosophical premises with Marx: 'The relatively favourable conditions in which [Owen] had placed them were still far from allowing them a rational development of the character and of the intellect in all directions, and much less of the free exercise of all their faculties'.[85] In the same book he wrote: 'Are there ... *eternal* truths, final and ultimate truths? Certainly there are'.[86] And yet he also claimed, in that same text, that the 'idea of equality, both in its bourgeois and in its proletarian form, is ... itself a historical product, the creation of which required definite historical conditions that in turn themselves presuppose a long previous history. It is therefore anything but an eternal truth'.[87]

5   Questioning the Possibility of Knowledge about 'Communist Society'

In the literature on Marx's work it is not uncommon to come across the idea that Marx thought we cannot attain substantial knowledge about the freedom that would be actualised in a social form that has yet to be created. For instance, in his book *Philosophy and Revolution*, Stathis Kouvelakis claims that, for Marx, communism is 'a radically open-ended political form that is yet to come', and that in his writings he 'consistently avoids ... anything resembling a ... positive representation' of it.[88] But while Marx left behind relatively few and fragmentary writings about his vision of 'communist society', he described its essential features with clarity and in definite terms nonetheless. He thought that we must know about the fundamental elements of 'communist society' before we bring it into being, even though much of its actual details will necessarily be discovered in the course of its creation. After all, one of the results of the experience of the Paris Commune was that 'the political form ... under which to work

---

historical and relative. Overcoming alienation must also be conceived in historical terms, not as the realisation of a timeless, universal moral ideal, but as the dialectical supersession of capitalist conditions achieved in communism' (Sayers 2011, pp. xii–xiii).

85   MECW 25, p. 250.
86   MECW 25, p. 81.
87   MECW 25, p. 99.
88   Kouvelakis 2003, pp. 313–14.

out the economical emancipation of Labour' was 'at last discovered' through the act of bringing it into existence.[89]

There is a world of difference between 'writing receipts' for 'the cook-shops of the future' and knowing the potentialities of our present circumstances through a 'critical analysis of actual facts'.[90] The 'speculative' nature of Marx's 'dialectical method' of critique involves comprehending the work of 'reason' in the 'actual facts' in order 'to find the new world through criticism of the old one'.[91] Marx did not write about a guaranteed 'sexual minimum' like Fourier or plans as precise as other so-called Utopian Socialists who designed elaborate schemes that at times even included instructions on how to organise the cutlery on the dinner table.[92] Marx was not interested in laying out such intricate details or attempting his own social experiment, but he thought that the fundamental elements of a 'free' life and the general character of the social organisation that it requires must be understood and consciously desired in order to bring it into being.

Ultimately, Marx wrote about 'communist society' because he thought its foundations were already in the process of creation – and not only its 'material' foundation. He wrote with conviction about the kind of social relations of production that he thought would exist in an emancipated society because he maintained that he was able to perceive – amid the flux of phenomena associated with the living movement of the capitalist system – that the germ of this new social ethos was already present.[93] He thought he had recognised a tendency for cultures of revolutionary solidarity to arise out of the life experience of working people and his writing indicates that he thought he had direct experience of the transformative potential of working-class life. Consider, for example, Marx's claim that

> When communist *artisans* associate with one another, theory, propaganda, etc., is their first end. But at the same time, as a result of this association, they acquire a new need – the need for society – and what

---

89   MECW 22, p. 334.

90   MECW 35, p. 17.

91   MECW 3, p. 142. Even though Whitehead's idea of 'speculative' thought is somewhat different from the Hegelian version that Marx critically appropriated, his idea that 'speculative Reason works' to 'submit itself to the authority of facts without loss of its mission to transcend the existing analysis of facts' is instructive in this instance (Whitehead 1929, p. 85).

92   Hunt 2009, p. 68.

93   'Cooperative factories', for example, 'furnish proof that the capitalist has become ... redundant as a functionary in production' (MECW 37, p. 385).

appears as a means becomes an end. In this practical process the most splendid results are to be observed whenever French socialist workers are seen together. Such things as smoking, drinking, eating, etc., are no longer means of contact or means that bring together. Company, association, and conversation, which again has society as its end, are enough for them; the brotherhood of man is no mere phrase with them, but a fact of life, and the nobility of man shines upon us from their work-hardened bodies.[94]

His work suggests that this lured him onward in the struggle for proletarian revolution and human emancipation, contributing to what Whitehead termed 'noble discontent', the 'value' of which laid 'in the hope' that 'never deserted' his 'glimpses of perfection'.[95]

---

94   MECW 3, p. 313.
95   Whitehead 1967, p. 12. 'The factor in human life provocative of a noble discontent is the gradual emergence into prominence of a sense of criticism, founded upon appreciations of beauty, and of intellectual distinction, and of duty' (Whitehead 1967, p. 11).

CHAPTER 4

History

To think of time – of all that retrospection.
To think of to-day, and the ages continued henceforward.
Have you guess'd you yourself would not continue?
Have you dreaded these earth-beetles?
Have you fear'd the future would be nothing to you?
Is to-day nothing? is the beginningless past nothing?
If the future is nothing they are just as surely nothing.

To think that the sun rose in the east – that men and women were
    flexible, real, alive – that everything was real and alive,
To think that you and I did not see, feel, think, nor bear our part,
To think that we are now here and bear our part.

    WALT WHITMAN[1]

∴

1   'Reason Nevertheless Prevails'

Marx did not develop a formal theory of history but he wrote a considerable amount that elucidates his thinking on the topic. As with other components of his thought, an adequate grasp of it requires an understanding of the relationship between various aspects of his philosophy, particularly his ontology, method, and anthropological ideas. From the outset, the interpretations made here are likely to be met with criticism because of the role attributed to his ontology – and to his sublation of the idea that 'Reason directs the world', in particular – in his theorisation of the historical process. We encounter Marx's sublation of the ontological idea that 'Reason directs the world' and, as a matter of course, the 'speculative' character of his thought, in the various instances in which he presented 'estrangement' in capitalist society as positive because of its developmental consequences. There is a substantial amount of evidence to

---

1   Whitman 1975, pp. 449–50.

support this interpretation of Marx's thought. In 1877, for instance, he maintained that *Capital* shows how the capitalist mode of production 'has itself created the elements of a new economic order' because its 'historical tendency' is to beget 'its own negation with the inexorability which governs the metamorphoses of nature' and give 'the greatest impulse at once to the productive forces of social labour and to the integral development of every individual producer'.[2] Similar claims are found elsewhere. For example, in the manuscripts posthumously published as the third volume of *Capital* he claims that the 'Development of the productive forces of social labour is the historical task and justification of capital', and thus it 'unconsciously creates the material conditions for a higher mode of production'.[3] In the first volume of *Capital* he claims that 'the capitalist mode of production presents itself to us historically, as a necessary condition to the transformation of the labour process into a social process'.[4] Alongside these developments in the material forces of production, capitalist society creates the subjectivity that will carry out the revolution and become the agents of the initial phases of the transitory process through which this 'new society is springing up'.[5]

As Hegel put it, 'there is Reason in history'.[6] Comprehending the form that this idea takes in Marx's thought requires understanding not only what he critically appropriated from Hegel's philosophy of history but also how he diverges from it while retaining fundamental ontological and methodological principles. McCarney, for instance, claims that Hegel thought 'History' is 'rational because reason is present in it as substance and subject. It is plain that a doctrine which presupposes rational subjectivity in this form', i.e., 'reason as an autonomous creative subject', is 'not available to Marx'.[7] This statement is only partly true in relation to Marx because while he did not think of 'reason as an

---

2   MECW 24, p. 200. In this way, capitalism is 'instrumental, *malgré lui* [despite itself], in creating the means of social disposable time ... and of thus setting free the time of all [members of society] for their own development' (MECW 29, p. 94).

3   MECW 37, p. 258.

4   MECW 35, p. 340. Marx described capitalist production as a 'transiently necessary' form 'for the development of the social productive powers of labour and the transformation of labour into social labour' (MECW 31, p. 83).

5   MECW 22, p. 7. Cf. Marx's claims about the 'great historical mission' of the trade unions and 'the class that bear in their hands the regeneration of mankind' (MECW 22, p. 191; MECW 21, p. 17). In his view it is only 'in present capitalist society' that 'the material, etc., conditions have at last been created which enable and compel the workers to lift this historical curse' (MECW 24, p. 83).

6   Hegel 1971, p. 277.

7   McCarney 1990, p. 130.

autonomous creative subject', he did sublate the idea of 'reason' as both 'substance and subject'. For Marx, 'reason' takes on a subjective form in history with us; in other words, we are the 'rational' subject. There is no otherworldly, all-powerful subject or Providence guiding history, but from his perspective 'Reason has always existed'. We cannot arbitrarily discard the ontological idea of 'reason' as 'substance' from Marx's thought about history, but it is neither thereby necessary to posit 'Reason' at work as a 'subject' separate from humanity, nor to reify rational human activity into a mystical, independent agency. Our 'reason' is initially only an implicit potential and it becomes subjectively conscious along with the development of our species – a development governed by 'universal' laws, which are 'reason', that regulate our life activity. Thus it is not entirely accurate to maintain that 'Reason is actual in history in so far as it is embodied in a subject which is the vital force of the movement of objective reality' as McCarney did, because the 'reason' implicit in the activity which leads to our development – e.g., 'the continual tendency and law of development of the capitalist mode of production' – is also a force in the movement of history.[8] To illustrate this by way of analogy, consider the lawful movements of the solar system or the movements of the molecules in our bodies; the 'reason' involved in the natural laws of this movement, which are observable and intelligible, is not a subjective entity. 'Reason' is 'at work' as the 'substance' of things, as a 'power' which determines the course of things in an ontological sense, but in this instance it is not a subjective being.

Marx did not articulate his thoughts about 'reason' and the development of freedom with obscure philosophical jargon or in the quasi-theological way that Hegel did. In his treatment of our development he emphasised the definite character of human activity in capitalism that he thought was 'indispensable' for the emergence of rational subjectivity and the corresponding progressive transformation of our life-world. For example, in an article about the victory of the Union forces in Maryland during the American Civil War on 17 September 1862, he claimed that 'Reason nevertheless prevails in world history'.[9] His writings from this period indicate that he thought wage labour in capitalism has greater positive consequences for human development than slave labour. The victory of Northern capitalism over the slave mode of production in the South thus represented a historical advance in the process of the development of the 'human spirit'. He compared the developmental potentials of slavery and 'free' wage workers and claimed that the difference between the 'activity of the free

---

8   McCarney 1990, p. 168; MECW 37, pp. 870–1.
9   MECW 19, p. 249.

worker' and the work of the slave functions to 'fit' the wage worker 'to under-take historical actions of an entirely different nature'.[10] He thought that North America was where these advantages of wage labour are 'shown particularly strongly' in 'contrast' to the 'character of *slave labour*'.[11]

It is evident that Marx thought history had provided evidence for his views. Karl Löwith was therefore mistaken, from Marx's perspective at least, to think that history is 'meaningful only by indicating some transcendent purpose bey-ond the actual facts'.[12] On the contrary, as Marx claimed, 'if we did not find lat-ent in society as it is, the material conditions of production and the correspond-ing relationships of exchange for a classless society, all attempts to explode it would be quixotic'.[13] Thus he attempted to explain how the 'capital-relation' is 'itself produced' along with 'the material conditions for its dissolution ... thereby removing its *historical justification* as a *necessary form* of economic development, of the production of social wealth'.[14] After all, Marx thought that 'scientific' insight into the genesis of 'the communist organisation of society' entails being able to comprehend it as it emerges from the 'womb' of capitalist society. 'A great mind', Hegel argued, 'has great experiences, when it looks into nature or history; it sees what is rational and expresses it'.[15]

2   The Development of Humanity through 'Estrangement' in History

The idea that Hegel had some influence on Marx's view of history is gener-ally accepted, but the extent of his influence is not adequately represented in the commentary on his work. In particular, there exists a relatively widespread misunderstanding of Marx's theoretical rift with German Idealism which has led many to overlook or deny the essential role of the development of 'the human mind' in Marx's view of human history and his overall social the-ory, aside from revolutionary class-consciousness. Marx's youthful criticism of Hegel took aim at his articulation of the struggle for freedom in terms of

---

10   MECW 34, p. 437.
11   MECW 34, p. 438.
12   Löwith 1949, p. 5. For Löwith, the 'claim that history has an ultimate meaning implies a final purpose or goal transcending the actual events', so that to 'ask earnestly the question of the ultimate meaning of history takes one's breath away; it transports us into a vacuum which only hope and faith can fulfil' (Löwith 1949, pp. 6; 4).
13   MECW 28, p. 97.
14   MECW 34, p. 466.
15   Hegel 1991b, p. 60.

'Spirit's' self-estrangement and diremption in nature, and the eventual return to itself with consciousness of its own essential freedom. In the process of clarifying his own thoughts he claimed that

> *Hegel's* conception of history presupposes an *Abstract* or *Absolute Spirit* which develops in such a way that mankind is a mere *mass* that bears the Spirit with a varying degree of consciousness or unconsciousness. Within *empirical*, exoteric history, therefore, Hegel makes a speculative, esoteric history, develop. The history of mankind becomes the history of the *Abstract Spirit* of mankind, hence a *spirit far removed* from the real man.[16]

However, rather than simply abandoning Hegel's perspective, Marx sublated his idea of the 'human spirit'. In his work he opted to avoid Hegelian terms that emphasise Spirit's consciousness of freedom, but the development of the human 'mind' and realisation of 'free, conscious activity' were an essential focus of Marx's 'materialist conception of history' nonetheless. In his view, a theory of the 'so-called general development of the human mind' is not suitable for the comprehension of 'social existence' *apart from* a comprehension of 'the material life conditions'.[17] Marx's 'materialist' emphasis on our corporeality is entirely consistent with the idea that the human species is developing its cognitive abilities throughout history; after all, he perceived every feature of our sociohistorical life activity as an objectification of the powers of our mind.[18] In his view, the sociomaterial modes of production which satisfy our needs as corporeal beings are expressions of the degree to which 'the human mind' has developed. In short, Marx did not treat the activity of mind as an epiphenomenon even though he maintained that this development is also conditioned by developments in our physical constitution and life. 'We see how the history of *industry* and the established *objective* existence of industry', he claimed, 'are the *open* book of [*humanity's*] *essential powers*, the perceptibly

---

16   MECW 4, p. 85. He described *'Hegel's conception of history'* as 'nothing but the *speculative* expression of the *Christian-Germanic* dogma of the antithesis between *Spirit* and *Matter*, *God* and the *world*' (MECW 5, p. 85.).

17   MECW 29, pp. 262–3. According to Engels, with Marx's work 'idealism was driven from this last refuge, the philosophy of history; now a materialistic treatment of history was propounded, and a method found of explaining man's "knowing" by his "being", instead of, as heretofore, his "being" by his "knowing"' (MECW 24, p. 305).

18   He claimed that 'products of human industry' are *'organs of the human mind which are created by the human hand, the objectified power of knowledge'* (MECW 29, p. 92).

existing human *psychology*.[19] The development of mind is thus a causal influence which determines the development of our sociomaterial conditions. This is evident, for example, in his claim that 'the productive power of the means of labour developed to an automatic process presupposes the subjection of the natural forces to the social intelligence'.[20] It is a principle in Marx's social philosophy that human 'intelligence' is a precondition in this way. He spoke, for example, of the 'development of the material (and therefore also of the mental) forces of production'.[21]

Marx reformulated the abstract Idealist conception of the manifestation of mind through history by critically appropriating Hegel's idea of the 'dialectic of negativity' at work through 'estrangement' in the 'material conditions' of the social labour process. Marx's ontology is expressed through the various instances in which he articulates this process in his writings. It is through this process that 'reason' is 'at work' and the powers of the 'human mind' manifest historically. This 'dialectical' component of his 'materialist conception of history' invariably displays a 'speculative' conception of 'positive' development. He claimed, for instance, that 'it is only by dint of the most extravagant waste of individual development that the development of the human race is at all safeguarded and maintained in the epoch of history immediately preceding the conscious reorganisation of society'.[22] In Marx's writing he depicts the 'estrangement' at the basis of our 'long and painful process of development' as a 'necessary' phase in the development of our 'universality' and a social order characterised by an ethos of collective harmony, including the specific form of 'estrangement' experienced in capitalism.[23] As he maintained, the

> *most extreme form of estrangement* in which – in the relationship of capital to wage labour – labour, productive activity, appears to its own conditions and its own product, is a necessary transitional stage. This form therefore already contains *in itself*, but as yet only in inverted form, the dissolution of all *conditions restricting production*, and creates and produces the unconditional premises for production, and hence all the material conditions for the total, universal development of the productive powers of the individual.[24]

---

19   MECW 3, p. 302.
20   MECW 29, p. 95.
21   MECW 28, p. 426.
22   MECW 37, p. 92.
23   MECW 35, p. 91.
24   MECW 28, p. 439.

These claims are reiterated throughout Marx's writings. For instance, he claimed that

> the ultimate development of capitalist production is a necessary trans-
> itional phase towards the reconversion of capital into the property of
> producers, although no longer as the private property of the individual
> producers, but rather as the property of associated producers, as direct
> social property. On the other hand, the stock company is a transition
> toward the conversion of all functions in the reproduction process which
> still remain linked with capitalist property, into mere functions of associ-
> ated producers, into social functions.[25]

And elsewhere he maintained that

> in the sphere of material production, in the real social life process ... [we
> find] the inversion of the subject into the object and *vice versa*. Looked at
> *historically* this inversion appears as the point of entry necessary in order
> to enforce, at the expense of the majority, the creation of wealth as such,
> i.e. the ruthless productive powers of social labour, which alone can form
> the material basis for a free human society. It is necessary to pass through
> this antagonistic form ... It is the *alienation process* of [humanity's] own
> labour.[26]

In a word, 'estrangement' is a process whereby humanity's powers, as a collectivity of individual subjects, take on an independent and hostile existence
and are experienced as if they are actually independently animate objects.[27]
In capitalism it has reached a fever pitch: it is 'a state of society, in which the
process of production has the mastery over [humanity]', an estranged social
power which is 'independent not only of isolated individuals but even all of
them together'.[28] Even though capital is not actually an autonomous power
independent of humanity, Marx claimed that 'the labourer looks at the social
nature of his labour, at its combination with the labour of others for a common

---

25   MECW 37, pp. 434–5.
26   MECW 34, p. 399.
27   See Chapter Six for further discussion of the concept of 'estrangement' and associated
      concepts.
28   MECW 35, p. 92; MECW 5, p. 245. Elsewhere he claimed that 'Capital comes more and more
      to the fore ... as an estranged, independent, social power, which stands opposed to society
      as an object, and as an object that is the capitalist's source of power' (MECW 37, p. 263).

purpose, as he would at an alien power', because 'the condition of realising this combination is alien property'.[29] Indeed, the 'estrangement' of the worker from the product they produce in the context of the capitalist mode of production is a core element of Marx's concept of 'estrangement'. These particular social relations of production are a manifestation of mind in our social existence – the social ethos or 'ethical order' which are an instance of 'the perceptibly existing human *psychology*'. Our 'estrangement' from *each other*, which is another central feature of Marx's 'materialist' conception of 'estrangement', is closely connected to this. It also provides further evidence of the fundamental importance of Marx's critical appropriation of Hegel's philosophy, which continues to be valuable for elucidating Marx's thinking about history. In particular, it resonates with the Hegelian idea that 'Reason' attains 'positive existence' through the 'desires' of individuals. This feature of 'the materialistic treatment of history' is present in a letter from Engels to Borgius:

> By economic relations, considered by us to be the determinant upon which the history of society is based, we understand the manner in which men of a certain society produce those products among themselves ...

> While men may make their own history, they have not hitherto done so with a concerted will in accordance with a concerted plan, not even in a given and clearly delimited society. Their aspirations arc at variance, which is why all such societies are governed by *necessity* of which the counterpart and manifestation is *chance*. The necessity which here invariably prevails over chance is again ultimately economic.[30]

The clash of interests that Engels referred to in connection to the social process of production is the aspect of 'estrangement' which manifests as historically dynamic social antagonisms that have progressive consequences for our development.

This kind of social antagonism plays a significant role in Kant's understanding of humanity's development as well. He called it 'unsociable sociability' and his treatment of it is informative for the purpose of interpreting Marx's view of human history. Kant was interested in making sense of 'the transition from the brutishness of a merely animal creature to humanity, from the leading reins of instinct to the direction of reason, in a word, from the guardianship of nature

---

29   MECW 37, p. 89.
30   MECW 50, pp. 264–6.

into the state of freedom'.[31] He also thought that our capacity for self-creation is a unique characteristic of our species, and yet he claimed that

> nature pursues a regular course ... and gradually leads our species from the low level of animal nature to the highest level of humanity by its own art (an art which nature compels humankind to invent) and develops, in this seemingly disorderly arrangement, those original predispositions [of our species] in a fully regular manner.[32]

In the end he did not think that we could 'reasonably hope' for our full development 'without presupposing a plan of nature'.[33] This 'plan of nature' unfolds through our 'tendency to enter into society' which is connected 'with a constant resistance that continually threatens to break up this society', and it is precisely 'this resistance that awakens all human powers'.[34] We are 'driven by lust for honor, power, or property, to establish a position' for ourselves among each other, and Kant thought that without this 'quarrelsomeness', 'jealously competitive vanity' and the 'insatiable appetite for property and even for power', all of 'the excellent natural human predispositions would lie in eternal slumber, undeveloped'.[35] According to him this is how 'the first true steps are taken from brutishness to culture' and 'a foundation is laid for a manner of thinking which is able, over time, to transform the primitive natural predisposition for moral discernment into definite practical principles and, in this way, to ultimately transform into an agreement a society that initially had been *pathologically* coerced into a *moral* whole'.[36] In his *Critique of Judgement*, Kant suggests that

---

31   Kant 2006, p. 29.

32   Kant 2006, p. 11.

33   Kant 2006, p. 16. According to Kant, 'if we consider the free exercise of the human will *broadly*, we can ultimately discern a regular progression in its appearances. History further lets us hope that, in this way, that which seems confused and irregular when considering particular individuals can nonetheless be recognised as a steadily progressing, albeit slow development of the original capacities of the species' (Kant 2006, p. 3).

34   Kant 2006, pp. 6–7.

35   Kant 2006, p. 7.

36   Ibid. He maintained that in the process we are 'thrust into work and hardship, only to find means, in turn, to cleverly escape the latter' (Kant 2006, p. 7). Cf. Hegel's claim that what 'is said about labour' in the biblical myth of the Fall is 'that it is both the result of the schism' – i.e., 'the abandonment of natural unity' which entails a 'marvellous inner schism of the spiritual' – 'and also its overcoming' (Hegel 1991b, pp. 61–2). Here Hegel is translating the language of religion into the language of philosophy. Consider also Kant's claim that 'if on the part of men war is a thoughtless undertaking, being stirred up by unbridled passions, it is nevertheless a deep-seated, maybe far-seeing, attempt on the part of supreme

a class relation between an oppressed labouring group and a group of expro-priators is a fundamental form that 'unsociable sociability' takes, but in this respect his thinking both converges and differs significantly with Marx's.[37]

Kant was ultimately unable to reconcile our bestial-corporeal element with our inherently rational character. From his perspective, on the one hand, the antagonism between the individual's self-interest and the moral demands of our social existence will never truly be overcome. On the other hand, a more profound problem is that our 'empirical-ego' is situated within what he under-stood as the mechanical determinism of the physical world which precludes the experience of freedom. We are forced to conclude that the 'goal always remains in the distance' as though it is our fate to perpetually strive toward an unattainable destiny.[38] Marx was aware of this problem in Kant's thought. He claimed that 'Kant makes' the 'republic' into 'the only rational form of state, a postulate of practical reason whose realisation is never attained, but whose attainment must always be striven for and mentally adhered to as the goal'.[39]

In his theory of the struggle between 'Lord' and 'Bondsman', Hegel incor-porated elements of Kant's 'unsocial sociability' but believed that the labourer is positioned for an advance in 'self-consciousness'. He focused his attention on the subjective aspect of this 'dialectical' socioproductive practice and Marx appropriated this idea in a sublated form; namely, that the historical 'self-creation' of humanity is a process of 'alienation' and 'transcendence of this alienation', and that labour 'is [humanity's] *coming-to-be for* [*itself*] within *alienation*'.[40] He agreed with Hegel that labour is a 'steeling school' for our self-transformation into a free being and that this development is 'only pos-sible in the form of estrangement', although in Marx's view 'the strict discipline of capital to which successive generations' of working-class individuals 'have

---

wisdom, if not to found, yet to prepare the way for a rule of law governing the freedom of states, and thus bring about their unity in a system established on a moral basis. And, in spite of the terrible calamities which it inflicts on the human race, and the hardships, perhaps even greater, imposed by the constant preparation for it in times of peace, yet – as the prospect of the dawn of an abiding reign of national happiness keeps ever retreat-ing farther into the distance – it is one further spur for developing to the highest pitch all talents that minister to culture' (Kant 2007, pp. 261–2).

37   He thought that 'the majority, in a mechanical kind of way that calls for no special art, provide the necessities of life for the ease and convenience of others who apply them-selves to ... science and art. These keep the masses in a state of oppression, with hard work and little enjoyment, though in the course of time much of the culture of the higher classes spreads to them also' (Kant 2007, p. 261).

38   Kant 2006, p. 167.

39   MECW 10, p. 114.

40   MECW 3, pp. 332–3.

been subjected' is the specific form that 'estrangement' has taken in the period immediately preceding its overcoming.[41] For instance, he claimed that the 'universally developed individuals' of communist society are a product of 'history' and that the

> degree and the universality of development of the capacities in which *this kind* of individuality becomes possible, presupposes precisely production on the basis of exchange value, which, along with the universality of the estrangement of individuals from themselves and from others, now also produces the universality and generality of all their relations and abilities.[42]

From this perspective human development entails the violent 'slaughterbench' of history.[43] This is inherent in Hegel's idea of the primeval 'life and death struggle' between the oppressed labourer and the oppressing exploiter – their 'fight for recognition' – which he thought 'constitutes a necessary moment in the development of the human spirit'.[44]

Hegel's influence on Marx's approach to the struggle between bourgeoisie and proletariat notwithstanding, there is a difference which has important implications for the problem of revolutionary subjectivity that will be explored in the next chapter. Hegel claimed that 'the fight for recognition pushed to the extreme ... can only occur in the natural state, where men exist only as ... separate individuals; but it is absent in civil society and the State because here

---

41   MECW 4, p. 37; MECW 3, p. 333; MECW 28, p. 250. Marx maintained that 'Hegel grasps man's self-estrangement, the alienation of man's essence, man's loss of objectivity and his loss of realness as self-discovery, manifestation of his nature, objectification and realisation. In short ... Hegel conceives labour as man's act of *self-genesis* – conceives man's relation to himself as an alien being and the manifestation of himself as an alien being to be the emergence of *species consciousness* and *species life*' (MECW 3, p. 342).

42   MECW 28, p. 99.

43   Hegel 1956, p. 21. Engels commented on the unavoidable necessity of development through 'estrangement': 'For it is a fact that man sprang from the beasts', he claimed, 'and had consequently to use barbaric and almost bestial means to extricate himself from barbarism' (MECW 25, p. 168). Cf. Löwith's claim that the 'outstanding element ... out of which an interpretation of history could arise at all' is 'the basic experience of evil and suffering, and of man's quest for happiness. The interpretation of history is, in the last analysis, an attempt to understand the meaning of history as the meaning of suffering by historical action' (Löwith 1949, p. 3).

44   Hegel 1971, pp. 172–3. Cf. Engels's claim that for Hegel 'the history of mankind no longer appeared as a chaotic jumble of senseless acts of violence' but 'as the process of the evolution of man himself' (MECW 25, p. 594).

the recognition for which the combatants fought already exists'.[45] He even claimed that though 'the State may originate in violence, it does not rest on it'.[46] For Marx, on the contrary, violence is perpetually present to a varying degree within the state and it takes many more or less overt forms within the conditions of bourgeois 'civil society'. This undercurrent of violence is still evident, for instance, in the social process of production. He wrote that the '*alienation* of the worker in [their] product means' that 'the life which [they have] conferred on the object confronts [them] as something hostile and alien', and 'if the product' of labour is 'an *alien, hostile*, powerful object independent of' the worker, it necessarily follows that 'someone else is master of this object, someone who is alien, hostile, powerful, and independent' of them.[47] Wage labour is thus 'an activity performed in the service, under the dominion, the coercion, and the yoke of another man'.[48] From the perspective of humanity as a whole this 'estrangement' in capitalism has the peculiar feature that the product of our labour – capital – becomes a power unto itself. According to Marx, it was shown in *Capital* how 'the social character' of human labour confronts the worker 'as not only alien, but hostile and antagonistic, and as objectified and personified in capital'.[49] The 'natural state' is thus still present, though in a canalised form, in the aggressive 'avarice' that drives the oppressive exploitation, competition and possessive individualism of capitalism.[50]

3   The 'Passions' of Capitalists and Their 'World-Historical' Activity

According to Hegel, the 'the material in which the Ideal of Reason is wrought out' is 'Personality itself – human desires – Subjectivity generally. In human knowledge and volition, as its material element, Reason attains positive exist-

---

45   Hegel 1971, p. 172.
46   Ibid. Cf. the following argument in Freud's response to a letter from Einstein in which he asked Freud whether there is 'any way of delivering mankind from the menace of war' (Einstein also claimed that 'law and might inevitably go hand in hand'): 'You begin with the relation between Right and Might. There can be no doubt that that is the correct starting-point for our investigation. But may I replace the word "might" by the balder and harsher word "violence"? Today right and violence appear to us as antitheses. It can easily be shown, however, that the one has developed out of the other; and, if we go back to the earliest beginnings and see how that first came about, the problem is easily solved' (Freud, n.d.).
47   MECW 3, pp. 272; 278.
48   MECW 3, pp. 278–9.
49   MECW 34, p. 429.
50   MECW 37, p. 92.

ence'.[51] The influence of this idea is palpable in Marx's writing about the historical role of capitalism, and capitalists in particular, in which he portrays 'estrangement' as a necessary phase in the process whereby 'reason' attains 'positive existence' through the 'desires' of individuals. In this connection, the 'passions' of the capitalist class – who are 'only capital personified', whose 'soul is the soul of capital' – play an analogous role to the Hegelian idea of 'passions' which are irrational motives that are unintentionally instrumental in the development of what Hegel termed 'self-conscious reason'.[52]

Marx argued that the capitalist is 'capital personified and endowed with consciousness and a will', whose 'subjective aim' and 'sole motive' is 'the appropriation of ever more wealth in the abstract' via 'the expansion of value', i.e. the 'unceasing movement of profitmaking', the 'boundless greed after riches' and 'passionate chase after exchange value'.[53] He depicts these 'passions' as a driving force behind the brutality and suffering that characterises the history of the capitalist mode of production.[54] But they are essential for the 'dialectical' movement of capitalism and there are various instances in Marx's writing in which the capitalist class is depicted as acting in ways that unintentionally accomplish 'deeds shared in by the community at large', as Hegel put it.[55] Marx identified the capitalists' avarice as the incessant urge which drives them to transform the production process. Capital wants to accumulate and the capitalist needs surplus value, and the consequences of their activity are world-historical because they create the foundation for a free society. As he wrote in *Capital*, for instance,

---

51   Hegel 1956, p. 38.

52   MECW 35, pp. 749; 241. A key difference is that Hegel theorised the 'passions' belonging to those who he described as 'world-historical individuals', such as Alexander of Macedon and Napoleon, whereas Marx emphasised the 'passions' of a particular social class.

53   MECW 35, pp. 163–4. He associates this with '*auri sacra fames*', i.e., the 'accursed hunger for gold' (MECW 35, p. 776). He elaborates the 'lust for enrichment' arising in the 'capitalist soul' as follows: 'In so far as he is a mere functionary of capital, that is, an agent of capitalist production, what matters to him is exchange-value, and the increase of exchange-value, not use-value and its increase. What he is concerned with is the increase of abstract wealth, the rising appropriation of the labour of others. He is dominated by the same absolute drive to enrich himself and the miser, except that he does not satisfy it in the illusory form of building up a treasure of gold and silver, but in the creation of capital, which is real production. ... [The capitalist] is always enjoying wealth with a guilty conscience, with frugality and thrift at the back of his mind. In spite of all his prodigality he remains, like the miser, essentially avaricious' (MECW 31, pp. 179–80).

54   For instance, in the third volume of *Capital* he claimed that 'the inordinate avarice of the mine owners' led to 'human sacrifices' (MECW 37, p. 92).

55   Hegel 1956, p. 24.

Except as personified capital, the capitalist has no historical value, and no right to that historical existence … And so far only is the necessity for his own transitory existence implied in the transitory necessity for the capitalist mode of production. But, so far as he is personified capital, it is not values in use and the enjoyment of them, but exchange value and its augmentation, that spur him into action. Fanatically bent on making value expand itself, he ruthlessly forces the human race to produce for production's sake; he thus forces the development of the productive powers of society, and creates those material conditions, which alone can form the real basis of a higher form of society, a society in which the full and free development of every individual forms the ruling principle.[56]

Thus his thoughts about history from the formative period in the mid-1840s, when he expressed ideas like 'the historical *necessity* of private property', find a renewed expression, in a more detailed form, in his mature writings on political economy.[57]

An encapsulated example of Marx's thoughts about the role of capitalist 'passions' in the 'dialectical' movement of history can be found in his writings on India:

England, it is true, in causing a social revolution in Hindustan was actuated only by the vilest interests, and was stupid in her manner of enforcing them. But that is not the question. The question is, can mankind fulfil its destiny without a fundamental revolution in the social state of Asia? If not, whatever may have been the crimes of England she was the unconscious tool of history in bringing about that revolution.[58]

He was clear about his view that the bourgeois 'passions' are an unavoidable phase in the historical process of humanity's maturation into a free being, and

---

56   MECW 35, pp. 587–8. Elsewhere in *Capital* he also claimed: 'Accumulation for accumulation's sake, production for production's sake: by this formula classical economy expressed the historical mission of the bourgeoisie, and did not for a single instant deceive itself over the birth-throes of wealth. But what avails lamentation in the face of historical necessity?' (MECW 35, p. 591).

57   MECW 3, p. 298.

58   MECW 12, p. 132. In the sense that Marx uses it, the term 'destiny' can be equated with 'inner driving force' or 'tendency' (MECW 34, p. 385). Cf. Avineri's claim that 'Marx's ultimate judgment on British rule in India is far removed from a purely moralistic and anti-imperialistic attitude. A strong Hegelian undercurrent of the "cunning of reason" can be traced in Marx's account' (Avineri 1968, p. 170).

yet he was never flippant about the suffering they brought about.[59] Thus Marx claimed that 'England has to fulfil a double mission in India: one destructive, the other regenerating'.[60] His description of the consequences of English imperialism and the colonial pursuit of the capitalist 'passions' in India also indicates that, in his view, the transformation of human subjectivity is a feature of the 'dialectic' of history:

> All the English bourgeoisie may be forced to do will neither emancipate nor materially mend the social condition of the mass of the people, depending not only on the development of the productive powers, but on their appropriation by the people. But what they will not fail to do is to lay down the material premises for both. Has the bourgeoisie ever done more? Has it ever effected progress without dragging individuals and peoples through blood and dirt, through misery and degradation?[61]

---

59 For instance: 'There cannot ... remain any doubt but that the misery inflicted by the British on Hindostan is of an essentially different and infinitely more intensive kind than all Hindostan had to suffer before' (MECW 12, p. 126). More generally, he thought that the 'profound hypocrisy and inherent barbarism of bourgeois civilisation lies unveiled before our eyes, turning from its home, where it assumes respectable forms, to the colonies, where it goes naked' (MECW 12, p. 221).

60 MECW 12, p. 217.

61 MECW 12, p. 221. Cf. the following passage from a *New York Times* article about women from rural communities becoming factory workers in cities in contemporary India:

> 'Much of what they learned in the village must be unlearned here. One evening when Baby begins preparing dinner, several of her roommates protest. She is menstruating, and caste tradition dictates that menstruating women must live in isolation, sleeping alone and taking care not to step into the kitchen, lest they contaminate the food and water. So two of the younger roommates cook, emerging an hour later with a glutinous, inedible glop. At this point, Baby is irritated. Menstruating women are allowed to work in the factory, aren't they? She walks into the kitchen, and the scent of spices and onions fills the room. After a brief discussion, they agree that the menstruation rules will be void for as long as they are living in Bangalore. Then they stuff themselves with food and fall into a deep sleep. When they are introduced to a factory supervisor and dive to touch her feet, a traditional gesture of respect toward elders, the supervisor jumps back as if she has been stuck with a hot poker. She then assumes a slight crouch, as if preparing to defend herself from further reverence. Back in their bedrooms, the girls laugh hysterically at this. From childhood, they have been told that it is disrespectful for a girl to laugh out loud in the presence of elders. In the event of irrepressible laughter, girls must cover their mouths with anything at hand: the corner of a dupatta, a hand, a washcloth. This lesson, too, flies out the window. In the hostel they laugh like tractors. They laugh so loud they spit their water out' (Barry 2016).

Marx's Hegelian conception of the capitalist 'passions' is evident in the many instances in which he depicts the 'bourgeois relations of production' as 'the last antagonistic form of the social process of production'.[62] According to him, 'the productive forces developing within bourgeois society create also the material conditions for a solution of this antagonism'.[63] As a consequence of the constant capitalist drive to increase surplus value extraction and perpetually accumulate profits, capitalism has exhibited the most marked tendency to revolutionise the productive process in order to increase efficiency. 'The directing motive, the end and aim of capitalist production', Marx claimed, 'is to extract the greatest possible amount of surplus value, and consequently to exploit labour power to the greatest possible extent'.[64] Engels claimed that political economy became a 'science' with the 'discovery' of surplus value – which in Hegelian terms is concerned with bringing the 'work which is accomplished by the reason of the thing itself' to consciousness. According to Marx, 'capital strives for an infinite enlargement of the productive forces of labour and calls them into being' because of 'an infinite drive for enrichment'.[65] Thus for him this so-called 'inner logic' of capitalism is animated by the inner drives of individuals which are in turn shaped through the activity of the sociohistorical process. In other words, this 'logic' has a fundamentally subjective component, hence his inclination to link money with human psychology and not only depict it solely as an element of socioproductive practice (in its function as a repository of exchange value, for instance). Statements about 'greed for money' or 'unbounded lust for enrichment', and terms like '*auri sacra fames*', 'thirst for profits', and so on, indicate that he thought of money simultaneously as an expression of the 'inner world' of 'the human mind', i.e., the 'perceptibly existing human *psychology*'.[66] Consider, for instance, his claim about the mercantilist monetary system characteristic of capitalism in its infancy: 'The prehistory of the development of modern industrial society opens with a general greed for money, on the part of both individuals and states. The actual development of the sources of wealth proceeds, as it were, behind its back, as a means to get possession of the representative of wealth'.[67] Marx's idea that money has a 'really magical significance' which occurs 'behind the backs of individuals' – whereby it 'becomes so potent an instrument in the real development of the

---

62   MECW 29, pp. 263–4.
63   MECW 29, p. 264.
64   MECW 35, p. 336.
65   MECW 28. p. 266.
66   MECW 28, pp. 155; 250; 365.
67   MECW 28, p. 157.

forces of social production' – also plays a role in his idea of the development of revolutionary subjectivity.[68] The productive capacities of the working class are an integral form of 'the forces of social production' that must develop to initiate the creation of 'communist society'. His claim that greed for money on the part of the working class is 'a driving force for the development of all productive forces, material and spiritual', will be returned to in the next chapter.[69]

Ultimately there is substantial textual evidence which indicates that Marx's 'materialist conception of history' has sublated the Hegelian idea that 'Reason' is 'at work' in human history, although it is clear that Marx chose to emphasise how it is at work through forms of subjective volition that are socially and historically determined in part by 'economic necessity'. In this connection Marx attributed the world-historical activity of capitalism to the 'concept' of capital. He claimed that capital is

> the condition for the development of the productive forces only so long as they require an external spur, a spur which at the same time appears as their bridle. It is a discipline over them, which at a certain level of their development becomes quite as superfluous and burdensome ... These inherent limits must coincide with the nature of capital, with the essential character of its very concept.[70]

This evokes Hegel's idea of the 'higher dialectic of the concept'. Recall that for Hegel it 'is only by' the 'Will, the activity of man in the widest sense', that the 'Idea as well as abstract characteristics generally' are 'realised, actualised; for of themselves they are powerless. The motive power that puts them in operation, and gives them determinate existence, is the need, instinct, inclination, and passion of man'.[71] Capital's 'concept' is 'actualised' by the capitalists possessed by their 'passions'.

4 The World Market of Global Capitalism and the Establishment of Worldwide Networks of Social Intercourse

A fundamental reason why Marx thought capitalism is *world-historical* is because it is a totalising system that spreads like wildfire across the globe 'through

---

68   MECW 28, p. 158.
69   MECW 28, p. 156.
70   MECW 28, p. 342.
71   Hegel 1956, p. 22.

the innate necessity of this mode of production, its need for an ever-expanding market'.[72] Indeed, he thought that the 'tendency to create the *world market* is inherent directly in the concept of capital itself'.[73] From his perspective the 'establishment of the world market' and 'the entanglement of all peoples in the net of the world market' is an integral part of 'the historical mission of the capitalist mode of production' which is an unavoidable phase in our development because it contributes to the creation of the 'material foundations of the new form of production' and the subjectivity required to initiate it.[74] He thought that the development of the world market establishes forms of globalised 'universal intercourse founded upon the mutual dependency of mankind, and the means of that intercourse'.[75] In particular, he thought that the activity of 'world-historical' capitalism creates conditions that facilitate the development of 'real connections' which enable individuals and entire societies to overcome forms of isolation that inhibit the development of 'intellectual wealth'.[76]

Marx analysed social conditions lacking such connections in French, German, Indian, and Russian communities, among others, and he drew a connection between the prevalence of prejudice rooted in isolated social units – 'home-bred conditions surrounded by superstition' – to the 'real intellectual wealth of the individual' which 'depends entirely on the wealth of [their] real connections'.[77] This was significant for Marx particularly because, on his assumptions, the growth of these connections are indispensable for the subjective development required for carrying out a successful revolutionary movement. This is one of the main reasons he considered proletarian conditions

---

72 MECW 5, p. 49; MECW 37, p. 236.

73 MECW 28, p. 335.

74 MECW 37, p. 439; MECW 35, p. 750. Cf. Marx's claim that the 'capitalist mode of production is, for this reason, a historical means of developing the material forces of production and creating an appropriate world market' (MECW 37, p. 249).

75 MECW 12, p. 222.

76 MECW 5, p. 51. Cf. Marx's claim that, as a result of the exploitation of the world market by the bourgeoisie, in 'place of the old local and national seclusion and self-sufficiency, we have intercourse in every direction, universal inter-dependence of nations. And as in material, so also in intellectual production. The intellectual creations of individual nations become common property. National one-sidedness and narrow-mindedness become more and more impossible, and from the numerous national and local literatures, there arises a world literature.

The bourgeoisie, by the rapid improvement of all instruments of production, by the immensely facilitated means of communication, draws all, even the most barbarian, nations into civilisation' (MECW 6, p. 488).

77 MECW 5, pp. 49; 51.

more favourable than peasant conditions for revolutionary development. As Engels claimed, 'the peasants ... everywhere are the embodiment of national and local narrow-mindedness'.[78] It is evident that Marx agreed with this assessment. 'What separates the peasant from the proletarian', he claimed, is not their 'real interest' but their 'delusive prejudice'.[79]

Marx also linked the lack of 'real connections' to populations that give rise to despotic state forms. 'Bonaparte', for example, represented 'a class', i.e., 'the *small-holding peasantry*', whose material conditions of life restrict the development of 'intellectual wealth'.[80] In such conditions, individuals develop a propensity to be led by others and become susceptible to manipulative control. 'Their representative', Marx wrote, 'must at the same time appear as their master, as an authority over them, as an unlimited governmental power that protects them against the other classes and sends them rain and sunshine from above'.[81] Marx's claim that it was 'the material conditions which made the feudal French peasant a small-holding peasant and Napoleon an emperor' is connected to the perspective that the conditions of the peasantry were not consistent with the development of 'intellectual wealth':

> Their mode of production isolates them from one another instead of bringing them into mutual intercourse. The isolation is increased by France's bad means of communication and by the poverty of the peasants. Their field of production, the smallholding, admits of no division of labour in its cultivation, no application of science and, therefore, no diversity of development, no variety of talent, no wealth of social relationships.[82]

He had a similar opinion of the Russian peasant commune. He claimed that

> There is one characteristic of the 'agricultural commune' in Russia which afflicts it with weakness, hostile in every sense. That is its isolation, the

---

78   MECW 8, p. 229.

79   MECW 22, p. 495.

80   MECW 11, pp. 186–7.

81   MECW 11, pp. 187–8.

82   MECW 11, pp. 189; 187. Cf. this similar point made by Engels: 'the agricultural population, in consequence of its dispersion over a great space, and of the difficulty of bringing about an agreement among any considerable portion of it, never can attempt a successful independent movement; they require the initiatory impulse of the more concentrated, more enlightened, more easily moved people of the towns' (MECW 11, p. 12).

lack of connexion between the life of one commune and that of the others, this *localised microcosm* which is not encountered everywhere as an immanent characteristic of this type but which, wherever it is found, has caused a more or less centralised despotism to arise on top of the communes.[83]

This way of thinking is also evident in Marx's writing on the 'idyllic village-communities' in India which, according to him, 'had always been the solid foundation of Oriental despotism' because 'they restrained the human mind within the smallest possible compass, making it the unresisting tool of superstition, enslaving it beneath traditional rules, depriving it of all grandeur and historical energies'.[84] Thus even if there are certain geographical conditions and forms of state which Marx associated with so-called 'Oriental despotism', it is evident that he thought despotism in the 'Orient' has essentially the same material and subjective basis as in the 'Occident'. Ultimately, the establishment of 'real connections' is a principal reason why Marx thought English imperialism would play a partly progressive role in India:

> The village isolation produced the absence of roads in India, and the absence of roads perpetuated the village isolation. On this plan a community existed with a given scale of low conveniences, almost without intercourse with other villages, without the desires and efforts indispensable for social advance. The British having broken up this self-sufficient *inertia* of the villages, railways will provide the new want of communication and intercourse.[85]

This, however, did not stop Marx from recognising that 'the history of the English management in India' was 'a string of futile and really absurd (in practice infamous) economic experiments'.[86]

In Marx's view, capitalism has a tendency to play a progressive role by transforming rural communities and agricultural production in a way that is necessary for 'the full development of the human race'.[87] As he claimed in manuscripts published posthumously as the *Grundrisse*, there is a

---

83   MECW 24, p. 353.
84   MECW 12, p. 132.
85   MECW 12, p. 220.
86   MECW 37, p. 332.
87   MECW 35, p. 507.

tendency which makes capital drive beyond national boundaries and prejudices and, equally, beyond nature worship, as well as beyond the traditional satisfaction of existing needs and the reproduction of old ways of
life confined within long-established and complacently accepted limits.
Capital is destructive towards, and constantly revolutionises, all this, tear-
ing down all barriers which impede the development of the productive
forces, the extension of the range of needs, the differentiation of production, and the exploitation and exchange of all natural and spiritual
powers.[88]

This way of thinking is displayed in *Capital* as well:

> In the sphere of agriculture, modern industry has a more revolutionary
> effect than elsewhere, for this reason, that it annihilates the peasant, that
> bulwark of the old society, and replaces him by the wage labourer ... The
> irrational, old-fashioned methods of agriculture are replaced by scientific
> ones.[89]

Ultimately, this indicates further that the 'dialectical' sociohistorical process
associated with the capitalist mode of production involves a developmental
transformation of 'the human mind' alongside changes in the 'material conditions' which provide 'real connections' and 'intellectual wealth'.

In Kant's elaboration of his idea of the *'sensus communis'* he articulated a
kind of mental capacity which is comparable to the one presupposed by Marx's
idea of 'real connections':

> [By] the name *sensus communis* is to be understood the idea of a *public*
> sense, i.e. a faculty of judging which in its reflective act takes account (*a
> priori*) of the mode of representation of everyone else, in order, *as it were*,
> to weigh is judgement with the collective reason of mankind, and thereby
> avoid the illusion arising from subjective and personal conditions which
> could readily be taken for objective, an illusion that would exert a prejudi-
> cial influence upon its judgement. This is accomplished by weighing the
> judgement, not so much with actual, as rather with the merely possible,
> judgements of others, and by putting ourselves in the position of every-
> one else, as the result of a mere abstraction from the limitations which
> contingently affect our own judging.[90]

---

88   MECW 28, p. 337.
89   MECW 35, p. 506.
90   Kant 2007, p. 123.

Kant associated it with three maxims: '(1) to think for oneself; (2) to think from the standpoint of everyone else; (3) always to think consistently. The first is the maxim of *unprejudiced* thought, the second that of *broadened* thought, the third that of *consistent* thought'.[91] His writing suggests that the 'reason' of subjects such as those that Marx understood as deeply superstitious is 'passive', and that to 'be given to such passivity, consequently to heteronomy of reason, is called *prejudice*'. In Kant's view, 'the greatest of all prejudices is that of fancying nature not to be subject to rules which the understanding by virtue of its own essential law lays at its basis, i.e., *superstition*'.[92]

Passages from Marx's work quoted above indicate that he also placed an emphasis on superstition in the context of social conditions which lack 'real connections'. Kant's claims here are also consistent with Marx's depiction of the subjectivity of individuals who provide a foundation in the population for – and who live under the yoke of – the despotic regimes which arise in conditions lacking 'real connections'. According to Kant, 'the condition of blindness into which superstition places us, and which it even demands from us as an obligation, makes the need of being led by others, and consequently the passive state of the reason, all too evident'.[93] This suggests that the contemporary rise of authoritarianism and, along with it, the prevalence of conspiracy theories (e.g., the QAnon movement) and pseudoscientific views (e.g., in relation to the COVID-19 pandemic and vaccines) is connected to a lack of 'intellectual wealth' and 'real connections'. The current 'post-Truth' era, in which public discourse is awash with 'alternative facts', indicates that Marx's thoughts about 'real connections' need re-evaluation. Indeed, as things have come to pass it appears that Marx was not entirely accurate with his claim about capitalism's ability to establish 'real connections' through the proliferation of markets and other networks of social intercourse worldwide. But 'real connections' have developed nonetheless insofar as we have created the technological means to connect to each other through networks of far-reaching, immediate mass communication, alongside advances in transportation. The innovations in the internet and social media, including all related technologies and infrastructure, in the last decades of the twentieth century have greatly expanded our horizons for 'intellectual wealth'. However, as things stand there is evidence which suggests that these technological advances and the global spread of communication networks do not necessarily provide people with mind expanding 'real con-

---

91   Kant 2007, p. 124.
92   Ibid.
93   Ibid.

nections'.[94] From the perspective of Marx's social philosophy, the efficacy of the 'real connections' that capitalism fosters presupposes the development of a subject that is sufficiently able to derive 'intellectual wealth' from them. A distinction can be made, for instance, between people who are susceptible to misinformation through social media, and those who consistently resist ideas which represent a lack of 'intellectual wealth'. From the standpoint of cognition, the ability to think reasonably for oneself is what qualifies the connections as 'real' in the sense that Marx uses the term.

Ultimately, Marx thought that only a 'communist' revolution 'will liberate separate individuals from the various national and local barriers, bring them into practical connection with the production (including intellectual production) of the whole world and make it possible for them to acquire the capacity to enjoy this all-sided production of the whole earth (the creations of man)'.[95] In his view, this revolution was steadily approaching. According to Marx, with the growth of the world market 'all contradictions are sent in motion', and these 'contradictions' (e.g., between the forces and relations of production in capitalism) lead to crises which he described as 'the urge to adopt a new historical form'.[96] But Marx's work suggests that the surfacing of crises in the world market alone are not enough to bring about the kind of revolution that he imagined; it ultimately depends on the development of revolutionary subjectivity. After all, crises can lead to the rise of both revolutionary and reactionary tendencies and their respective movements.

5   Marx's Teleological Theory of Humanity's Historical Development

Marx thought about human development in a teleological way. In his view our *telos* is the development of our implicit potential for 'universality' and, ultimately, freedom. His concept of *telos* is Aristotelian and it is connected to the idea that a thing's 'nature' is what it is when fully developed.[97] The idea that Marx's writing contains a teleological theory is controversial among read-

---

94   Consider, for instance, the article 'How WhatsApp Destroyed A Village' (Dixit and Mac 2018) which covers a spate of murders in India that are linked to the prevalence of WhatsApp, smartphones, and the spread of fake news among village residents in rural India.

95   MECW 5, p. 51.

96   MECW 28, p. 160.

97   As Scott Meikle put it, it is the 'form, state or condition toward which an entity develops by its nature', i.e., 'the final form attained in an entity's process of development' (Meikle 1985, p. 179).

ers and generally rejected.[98] For example, Ollman claimed that Marx's alleged propensity for reading history backward 'does not mean that Marx accepts a cause at the end of history, a "motor force" operating in reverse, a teleology'.[99] But Marx claimed that a 'final goal' is implicit in 'the forms *peculiar* to existing reality' from the perspective of an imminent critique of existing conditions and forms of consciousness, which does not entail reading history backward, but is teleological nonetheless.[100] As Meikle claimed,

> the form of teleology that [Marx] uses, in common with Aristotle, is not an occultism in which the future acts causally upon the present ... It is a theoretical correlate of recognising the fact that whole entities of their nature have potentials and lines of development, and in their development, in fully coming-to-be, those entities are simply realising the potentials constituted in their natures.[101]

In the interpretive literature on this aspect of Marx's thinking it is often the case that teleology is associated with ideas that do not reflect the kind of teleology found in Marx's thought, and the absence of those ideas in Marx's writings are taken to mean an absence of teleology. A common example of something that is correctly not attributed to Marx but incorrectly considered a necessary implication of a teleological theory of history is the assumption that teleological development is inevitable.[102] Some teleological ideas maintain that a *telos* is 'destined' to exist in the sense of developmental certainty,[103] but it is possible to conceive of a *telos* without maintaining that full develop-

---

98 Sayers, for instance, claimed that the idea of 'progress' in Marx's thought 'cannot be understood in teleological terms' because it 'is not a matter of approaching ever closer to some predetermined end point or ideal', and that 'the very notion of a final human end must be rejected' (Sayers 1998, p. 163).

99 Ollman 2003, p. 118. Cf. Bensaïd's claim that 'Present and future history is not the goal of past history ... Marx had no mania for posterity. He did not march to the beat of ultimate promises and last judgements' (Bensaïd 2002, p. 15).

100 MECW 3, p. 143.

101 Meikle 1985, p. 11. Ollman inadvertently recognises the idea of teleology in Marx's thinking because he believed that 'the unfolding of a potential has a privileged status in Marx's studies' (Ollman 2003, pp. 121–2).

102 For example, Mehmet Tabak claims that 'Marx does not assume an inevitable historical development on the basis of an eternal, extraneous, pre-given plan' (Tabak 2012, p. 39).

103 We see this notion of teleology in the writings of Kant, for example. He claimed that '*All of a creatures' natural predispositions are destined eventually to develop fully and in accordance with their purpose*' (Kant 2006, p. 4). Kant ended up maintaining contradictory positions on this matter.

ment is simply inevitable. For example, it is possible to maintain that the *telos* of an acorn is an oak tree without maintaining that a given acorn will become a tree (a squirrel could eat it before it does, for example). Marx's writing indicates that he did not think of humanity's freedom as our 'destiny' in the sense of an inevitable occurrence, or that 'full human development' and the society corresponding to it are inevitable, but this does not negate the existence of teleology.

This misinterpretation compliments the mistaken idea that a teleological conception of human history necessarily entails a kind of stagism. Ellen Wood, for instance, associated the idea of 'a mechanical sequence of modes of production' and 'some transhistorical drive which inevitably leads one social form to be succeeded by a more productive one' with teleology in a discussion of the 'essence of historical materialism and its general theory of history'.[104] In the literature on Marx's work there is a persistent tendency to make this association. While it is indeed arguable that Marx's work does not contain an idea of a simple linear process of inevitably successive developments, Ellen Wood mistakenly assumed that this therefore means there is no conception of teleology in his work. She argues that Marx

> has replaced teleology with history – not history as mere contingency, nor history as a mechanical succession of predetermined stages or a sequence of static structures, but history as a process with its own causalities, constituted by human agency in a context of social relations and social practices which impose their own demands on those engaged in them.[105]

What she says here does not undermine the notion of teleology in Marx's thought. The fact that Marx thought the specific determinations of each historical period circumscribe human agency and, in a sense, determine it – without dissolving human agency into an all-subsuming, mechanically fatalistic move-

---

104   Wood 2008, p. 88. Paresh Chattopadhyay, for example, claimed that 'As for the accusation that Marx viewed social development in a teleological way that is as serving a (predetermined) purpose or design, then Marx's conception of history is certainly not teleological' (Chattopadhyay 2006, p. 70). He argues that there was an 'anti-teleological rein' in the manner 'that communism is presented by Marx and Engels in their very first works on the materialist conception of history as a "movement," not a "doctrine"' (Chattopadhyay 2006, p. 71).

105   Wood 2008, p. 90. She claims further that by 'insisting on the specificity of capitalism, by refusing to read its principles of motion back into history, and by explaining how every mode of production is governed by its own specific rules for reproduction, Marx is offering precisely the antithesis of teleology' (Ibid.).

ment – is consistent with his notion of teleology. Marx's 'materialist conception of history' contains a philosophy of 'universal' or 'world' history in which there is a process tending toward an end with conditionally necessary phases of development, but he was not 'stagist' in a simple mechanical way that portrays history as an inevitable linear succession of modes of production.

From Marx's perspective there is not simply one human history even though there is essentially one humanity. There is history anywhere humans live; it depends on the relatedness of individuals as essentially 'rational' and 'social' beings and it is conditioned by the determinate circumstances in each instance, including the intersection of natural and sociocultural factors. Civilisations can rise and fall completely unknown to each other, and distinct histories of different peoples can entwine and fuse because of our 'universal' nature, whereby we become part of other histories and they become partly our own. Thus while Marx had an idea of 'world' history, he thought that 'World history did not exist always' and that 'history as world history' is itself 'a result' of a specific set of historical trajectories.[106] This kind of world history, which is bound by necessity rooted in our 'universal' development, underlies Marx's infamous claim that in 'broad outline, the Asiatic, ancient, feudal and modern bourgeois modes of production may be designated as epochs marking progress in the economic development of society'.[107] We must emphasise 'broad outline' because in Marx's view history does not proceed in a straight line of inevitably successive stages, but there is nevertheless necessity present in the historical movement of our development into free beings. After all, from Marx's perspective 'communist society' cannot emerge from merely any social form. The necessity in this instance is *conditional* necessity. Consider, for example, Marx's claim that

> The development of the industrial proletariat is, in general, conditioned by the development of the industrial bourgeoisie. Only under its rule does the proletariat gain that extensive national existence which can raise its revolution to a national one, and does it itself create the modern means of production, which become just so many means of its revolutionary emancipation. Only its rule tears up the material roots of feudal society and levels the ground on which alone a proletarian revolution is possible.[108]

---

106   MECW 28, p. 46.
107   MECW 29, p. 263.
108   MECW 10, p. 56.

To borrow a phrase from Daniel Bensaïd, there is no 'mechanical fatality' in Marx's theory of history.[109] However, Marx's writing indicates that there is necessity involved in the determination of its pattern nonetheless. The necessity he depicts corresponds to the degree of our 'universal' development as individuals and as a species, rooted in satisfying natural necessity and historically created needs. History is bound by necessity rooted in this development which proceeds in part like a natural process with phases of growth that are determined by 'universal' laws. From his perspective the development of our 'universality' as a species has taken place through the activity of individuals who are not determined by themselves entirely. Indeed, we were initially a result of *'natural history'* because we emerged from nature as creatures of the natural world, and for Marx 'History itself is a *real* part of *natural history* – of nature developing into [humanity]'.[110] Evidence suggests that we have originated in the womb of the cosmos, out of lower forms of animals, plants, simple cellular organisms and even apparently 'dead', inorganic matter. Thus a process has taken place from which our 'universal' capacities, the basis of our agency, began to emerge in the course of *'natural history'*.

Marx attempted to account for what he conceived as a discernable tendency upward not only in the evolutionary process of the natural world but human history as well – a trend which in the broad scheme of human activity has taken place unintentionally. The record of history shows groups and individuals motivated by particular interests and yet at certain moments our activity has had unintended results that changed the course of human history in ways which have proved necessary for the realisation of freedom. In Marx's view of history, the course of our species' 'universal' development has proceeded for the most part unknown to us. Insofar as this development results from activities of ours that are oriented toward some other end, it can be described as a process that we participate in unconsciously. For example, Marx thought the British bourgeoisie were the 'unconscious tool of history'.[111] Our activity as individuals taken collectively makes history, but as individuals we are also made by history, i.e., by the activity of those who came before us and those who exist contemporaneously with us. Marx claimed, for instance, that in 'the social production of their existence, men inevitably enter into definite relations, which are independent of their will, namely relations of production appropriate to a given stage in the development of their material forces of production'.[112]

---

109   Bensaïd 2002, p. 56.
110   MECW 3, pp. 303–4.
111   MECW 21, p. 132.
112   MECW 29, p. 263. The emphasis that Marx places on our corporeality, which is a key ele-

Readers may be inclined to criticise this interpretation because it appears to undermine Marx's conception of human agency in the historical process and portray Marx's idea of history as crudely deterministic.[113] But the teleological theory inherent in Marx's writing on human life and history contains these two theoretical positions sublated within it: 1) that there is a developmental process tending toward an implicit 'end' with conditionally necessary stages, and 2) that we can be agents of this process to the extent that human activity is a determining factor. While his pronouncements may seem paradoxical because of this, he was able to maintain a coherent view of the historical process of human development nonetheless. After all, Marx thought that human beings 'make their own history, but they do not make it just as they please; they do not make it under circumstances chosen by themselves, but under circumstances directly encountered, given and transmitted from the past'.[114]

In short, on Marx's premises our agency is dependent on our 'universal' development through the life movement of our species which is governed by 'universal' laws. Ultimately, our life process has 'transhistorical' characteristics, i.e., characteristics involved in all specific historical periods and modes of production, which reassert themselves in a different way in each particular form of society in sync with our 'universal' development and the corresponding circumstances. Thus each characteristic of ours which is common to all periods has the potential to transform during, and in accordance with, our species' developmental life-process. The labour process, for example, is a fundamental feature of human life activity which exists throughout all distinct modes of production and forms of society. On this matter it is worth quoting Marx at length:

> To the extent that the labour process is solely a process between man and Nature, its simple elements remain common to all social forms of development. But each specific historical form of this process further develops its material foundations and social forms. Whenever a certain stage of maturity has been reached, the specific historical form is discarded and

---

ment of the 'materialism' of his 'materialist conception of history', has profound implications for our conception of our agency. Consider, for example, Whitehead's claim that individuals 'are driven by their thoughts as well as by the molecules in their bodies, by intelligence and by senseless forces ... Our consciousness does not initiate our modes of functioning. We awake to find ourselves engaged in process, immersed in satisfactions and dissatisfactions, and actively modifying, either by intensification, or by attenuation, or by the introduction of novel purposes' (Whitehead 1967, p. 46).

113   Ellen Wood, for instance, associated teleology with a 'universal technological determinism' (Wood 2008, p. 91).

114   MECW 11, p. 103.

makes way for a higher one. The moment of arrival of such a crisis is disclosed by the depth and breadth attained by the contradictions and antagonisms between the distribution relations, and thus the specific historical form of their corresponding production relations, on the one hand, and the productive forces, the production powers and the development of their agencies, on the other hand. A conflict then ensues between the material development of production and its social form.[115]

In any given period we have developed our 'universal' capacities to some degree through activity which is partly self-determined and partly the result of broader interrelated processes inherent in the natural and sociohistorical elements of our mode of life. Thus, in his view, 'when a society has got upon the right track for the discovery of the natural laws of its movement' we 'can neither clear by bold leaps, nor remove by legal enactments, the obstacles offered by the successive phases of its normal development', although we can 'shorten and lessen the birth-pangs' by understanding it.[116] This way of thinking was prefigured in Hegel's philosophy. Engels claimed that the 'great merit' of 'the Hegelian system' was that with it, for the 'first time', the

> whole world, natural, historical, intellectual, is represented as a process, i.e., as in constant motion, change, transformation, development; and the attempt is made to trace out the internal connection that makes a continuous whole of all this movement and development. ... It was now the task of the intellect to follow the gradual march of this process through all its devious ways, and to trace out the inner law running through all its apparently accidental phenomena.[117]

Marx also possessed an idea of a *telos* which spans the natural world and human history, and he thought that human beings are the pinnacle of natural development. This is evident in his view of the origin and dissolution of 'the system of bourgeois economy' which he treated as a kind of natural life process, the 'ultimate result' of which is 'its negation'.[118] This 'system' of human life is a conditional necessity for another form of life: 'If, on the one hand, the pre-bourgeois phases appear as *merely historical*, i.e. transcended premisses, so

---

115   MECW 37, p. 870.
116   MECW 35, p. 10.
117   MECW 25, p. 24.
118   MECW 29, p. 98. He claimed to have recognised ways in which 'capital works to dissolve itself as the form which dominates production' (MECW 29, p. 86).

[on the other hand] the present conditions of production appear as conditions which *transcend themselves* and thus posit themselves as *historical premises* for a new state of society'.[119] After all, Marx claimed that capitalism's 'historical mission' is 'unconstrained development in geometrical progression of the productivity of human labour'.[120] However, its tendency to provide the foundation for the flowering of a 'higher' form of social life implies that while the life process of capitalism is akin to any other natural process, it is not simply a natural process because it involves the activity of human subjects. Nevertheless, according to Marx 'the material transformation of the economic conditions' of all social forms 'can be determined with the precision of natural science', and he thought that such transformations 'must be explained from the contradictions of material life, from the conflict existing between the social forces of production and the relations of production'.[121]

It has been well established (to a fault in some literature) that Marx thought 'the historical development of the antagonisms, immanent in a given form of production, is the only way in which that form of production can be dissolved and a new form established'.[122] He thought that such 'contradictions' within the capitalist mode of production 'lead to explosions, cataclysms', and 'crises' which are 'regularly recurring catastrophes' that 'lead to their repetition on a higher scale, and finally to' its 'violent overthrow'.[123] The 'economic laws' of distinct modes of production differ, however. Marx made it clear that 'a general historico-philosophical theory whose supreme virtue consists in being suprahistorical', is not sufficient for comprehending how 'events strikingly analogous, but occurring in different historical milieux', will lead 'to quite disparate results'.[124] But as McCarney pointed out, with a 'historical dialectic' of the sort involved in Marx's social philosophy,

---

119 MECW 28, p. 389. As Whitehead maintained, 'we have some knowledge of that counter-tendency which converts the decay of one order into the birth of its successor' (Whitehead 1929, p. 90).

120 MECW 37, p. 261. Capitalism 'goes back on its mission whenever ... it checks the development of productivity' (MECW 37, p. 261).

121 MECW 29, p. 263.

122 MECW 35, p. 491. As for the capitalist system, Marx was intent on demonstrating that there exists a 'contradiction between the general social power into which capital develops, on the one hand, and the private power of the individual capitalists over these social conditions of production, on the other', because this development 'becomes ever more irreconcilable, and yet contains the solution of the problem, because it implies at the same time the transformation of the conditions of production into general, common, social, conditions' (MECW 37, p. 263).

123 MECW 29, p. 134.

124 MECW 24, p. 201.

it is not enough that there should be contradictions continually coming into view and going under. There must be an imminent, progressive logic to the sequence of changes. What is required is, not simply an indefinite sequence of randomly revolving contradictions but, an essentially directed movement. In the language of the dialectical tradition, the question is how one can speak of reason in history.[125]

Presented in this way, however, the relationship between Marx's ontology and his teleological view of history is set up for misinterpretation which reanimates the debate about inevitability in the historical process. Even though Marx thought that 'the social antagonisms that result from the natural laws of capitalist production' are 'tendencies working with iron necessity towards inevitable results', it must be emphasised that he did not use his ontology, directly or indirectly, as a kind of philosophical guarantee for the emergence of freedom.[126] After all, Marx claimed that 'History does nothing' and 'is not, as it were, a person apart, using man as a means to achieve its own aims'; i.e., for him history is 'nothing but the activity of [humanity] pursuing [its] aims'.[127] It is thus imprecise to say that Marx thought there is a telos of history because history moves and changes in accordance with our activity and development. In other words, the telos of the historical process is more accurately described as the telos of human development. The 'historical dialectic' that he sublated from Hegel is not simply an external process of change in the cosmos which mechanically determines our behaviour in order to bring about freedom.

Thus the ontological idea that 'Reason directs the world' does not entail resignation to a kind of blind fate. Marx had no need for prophetic assertions about the 'impending revolution' because, of course, in his view it was impending. He did not proclaim that a successful revolution would inevitably happen apart from moments of revolutionary fervor, such as in the Manifesto during the revolutionary period of 1848,[128] or in Capital, which was intended to be a

---

125   McCarney 1987, p. 175.

126   MECW 35, p. 9. The view that proletarian revolution is inevitable is characteristic of the old school of 'historical dialectics' which developed in the Soviet Union. Moseley and Smith claim that 'the old Marxian dialectics (or Diamat)' was 'concerned primarily with the influence of Hegel on Marx's theory of history, and the eventual triumph of socialism' (Moseley and Smith 2014, p. 1). And according to McCarney it was the Marxism of the Second International which thought that the 'major achievement' of 'Marxist social theory' is 'the discovery of scientific laws of history and, specifically, of the mechanism that ensures the downfall of capitalism and its replacement by socialism' (McCarney 1990, p. 1).

127   MECW 4, p. 93.

128   In his book History, Labour and Freedom, Gerald Cohen incorrectly claims that 'Marx and

'scientific' exposition of the immanent manifestation of proletarian revolution from within capitalist society.[129] Ultimately, Marx only maintained that there are discernable tendencies toward a revolutionary transformation of society because from his perspective both the material conditions and the subjectivity that was going to bring it about were already in the process of formation. Thus from his perspective it is allegedly self-evident that *if* freedom is going to be achieved, we have to bring it about with consciousness and will. To suggest that freedom is inevitable on Marx's premises is to suggest, in effect, that it has *already* become realised. But unlike Hegel who thought that the 'infinite purpose' has already been accomplished, Marx's work puts forth the idea that the 'dialectic' which is evident in the record of history, and modern capitalism in particular, only entails that the experience of freedom is truly *possible*.[130]

This discussion overlaps with another objection to teleological notions of history; namely, that it is *theological* and that history thereby becomes a kind of theodicy. This, of course, would be an expression of alienation, a projection of our own purposeful activity onto some external, divine subject which resides above and beyond nature and humanity. Löwith, for instance, claimed that

---

Engels considered it inevitable that a socialist revolution would overturn capitalism', and he cites the statement in the *Manifesto* that the 'fall [of the bourgeoisie] and the victory of the proletariat are equally inevitable' as evidence of this (Cohen 1988, p. 51). Karl Löwith also claims that the Manifesto is 'eschatological in its framework, and prophetic in its attitude', and he went so far as to say that it 'is only in Marx's "ideological" consciousness that all history is a history of class struggles, while the real driving force behind this conception is a transparent messianism which has its unconscious root in Marx's own being, even in his race. He was a Jew of Old Testament stature ... It is the old Jewish messianism and prophetism ... and Jewish insistence on absolute righteousness which explain the idealistic basis of Marx's materialism' (Löwith 1949, pp. 38; 44).

129   He mentioned, for example, that the working class will 'inevitably' conquer political power (MECW 35, p. 491).

130   'The accomplishing of the infinite purpose', Hegel claimed, 'consists ... only in sublating the illusion that it has not yet been accomplished. The good, the absolute good, fulfills itself eternally in the world, and the result is that it is already fulfilled in and for itself, and does not need to wait upon us for this to happen. This is the illusion in which we live, and at the same time it is this illusion alone that is the activating element upon which our interest in the world rests. It is within its own process that the Idea produces that illusion for itself; it posits an other confronting itself, and its action consists in sublating that illusion. Only from this error does the truth come forth, and herein lies our reconciliation with error and with finitude. Otherness or error, as sublated, is itself a necessary moment of the truth, which can only be in that it makes itself into its own result' (Hegel 1991b, p. 286).

Historical materialism is essentially, though secretly, a history of fulfilment and salvation in terms of social economy. What seems to be a scientific discovery ... is, on the contrary, from the first to the last sentence
inspired by an eschatological faith ... It would have been quite impossible
to elaborate the vision of the proletariat's messianic vocation on a purely
scientific basis and to inspire millions of followers by a bare statement of
facts.[131]

Teleology in general is often associated with theological notions of a providential 'designer' god guiding the process as a conscious agent separate from
us. These ideas can be attributed to the medieval Scholastic tradition which
used Aristotelian teleology to bolster the Christian view, resulting in a 'divine
teleological cosmology'.[132] It is generally accepted that this idea of teleology is
absent from Marx's work. In fact, this is likely the sort of teleology that Marx
referred to in an 1861 letter to Ferdinand Lassalle, claiming that its presence in
the natural sciences was 'dealt a mortal blow' by Darwin.[133] The 'rational meaning' of teleology that Marx alludes to in this letter is the form of 'teleology'
in his own thinking. Nothing like Hegel's theological overtones and invoca-
tion of 'the superior design of providence', as Karel Kosík put it, will be found
in Marx's writings on history.[134] But Marx did not view the history of human
development merely as a Darwinian process of natural evolution, i.e., as a
series of random mutations and adaptations governed ultimately by a blind
process of natural selection. Even though it is evident that Darwin was influential for Marx's view of human life and development, Marx did not base his
'materialist conception of history' on the kind of materialist ontology found in
Darwin's theory of natural evolution.[135] The Darwinian view of natural life is

---

131   Löwith 1949, p. 45. He claims that 'the term "philosophy of history" is used to mean a
        systematic interpretation of universal history in accordance with a principle by which
        historical events and successions are unified and directed toward an ultimate meaning.
        Taken in this sense, philosophy of history is, however, entirely dependent on theology of
        history, in particular on the theological concept of history as a history of fulfilment and
        salvation but then philosophy of history cannot be a "science"; for how could one verify
        the belief in salvation on scientific grounds?' (Löwith 1949, p. 1).

132   Meikle 1985, p. 167.

133   MECW 41, p. 247. As Wood claimed, 'Marx and Engels respect for Darwin ... rests on the fact
        that he exhibited a progressive historical movement in the natural world, and provided a
        purely naturalistic account of biological organisation, undercutting explanations of nat-
        ural teleology in theological or supernaturalist terms' (Wood 2004, p. 109).

134   MECW 41, p. 247; Kosík 1969, p. 65.

135   Marx claimed that 'Darwin has interested us in the history of Nature's Technology, i.e.,

based on what Marx described as 'the abstract materialism' of 'natural science' which 'excludes history and its process', and on this basis we cannot adequately account for our development into a 'universal', 'free being'.[136] If the process of our evolutionary development into a sovereign being in nature is interpreted through the materialism of the natural sciences such as that of conventional Darwinian evolutionary theory, we cannot account for the 'upward trend' in the process whereby, as Whitehead put it, 'organic species of higher and higher types' tend to evolve.[137]

It is thus not accurate to claim that Marx understood history as a series of ultimately 'meaningless' transitions between cultural forms and social modes of life. For him, history was not merely a 'banal "succession of generations"' with 'no more meaning than the dreary genealogy of whales', as Daniel Bensaïd argued.[138] Bensaïd was referring to the idea that

> History is nothing but the succession of separate generations, each of which uses the materials ... the productive forces handed down to it by all preceding generations, and thus, on the one hand, continues the traditional activity in completely changed circumstances and, on the other, modifies the old circumstances with a completely changed activity.[139]

---

in the formation of the organs of plants and animals, which organs serve as instruments of production for sustaining life. Does not the history of the productive organs of man, of organs that are the material basis of all social organisation, deserve equal attention?' (MECW 35, p. 375).

136   MECW 35, pp. 376–7. Cf. Merleau-Ponty's claim that 'Marxism, as we know, recognises that nothing in history is absolutely contingent, that historical facts do not arise from a sum of mutually foreign circumstances but form an intelligible system and present a rational development. But the characteristic thing about Marxism – unlike theological philosophies or even Hegelian idealism – is its admission that humanity's return to order, the final synthesis, is not necessitated but depends upon a revolutionary act whose certainty is not guaranteed by any divine decree or by any metaphysical structure of the world' (Merleau-Ponty 1964, p. 120).

137   Whitehead 1929, p. 7. Whitehead claimed that the 'material universe has contained in itself, and perhaps still contains, some mysterious impulse for its energy to run upwards' (Whitehead 1929, p. 24).

138   Bensaïd 2002, p. 15.

139   MECW 5, p. 50. Marx's claim that this 'can be speculatively distorted so that later history is made the goal of earlier history', whereby 'history receives its own special aims', is not an accurate depiction of Hegel's philosophy or the 'speculative' character that Marx adopted, even if there were Hegelians who made the theoretical errors that Marx is describing (MECW 5, p. 50).

Misreading this is unavoidable if it is taken in abstraction from Marx's ontology and philosophical anthropology because the change of circumstances and
activity correspond to our 'universal' development which is bound by laws that
govern the life of our species, including the transitions in our development.[140]
Insofar as the realisation of 'human nature' (freedom) is our 'end', there are
necessary stages in our development; i.e., *if* there is progress in the process
of our development, certain necessary stages must be reached and surpassed,
and Marx thought that there was evidence of such progress. How are we to
make sense of Marx's claim, for instance, that the *'forming* of the five senses
is a labour of the entire history of the world' if we assume that he thought all
of our activity throughout history is simply 'meaningless'?[141] Substantial evidence indicates that, for Marx, our existence has an 'end' or 'purpose', and yet
interpretive positions akin to Bensaïd's are quite common. István Mészáros,
for example, claimed that for Marx 'history had to remain *radically open* to
qualify as history in order to make any sense at all of "self-activity" and "freedom" in terms of the objective potentialities of human self-realisation'.[142] This
notion of an open-ended movement is insufficient because Marx thought that
freedom is humanity's 'end', and it cannot adequately account for the fact that
certain kinds of society achieve freer relations and activities.[143] An example of
the inherent absurdity of such positions can be found explicitly in Bensaïd's
claim that in Marx's work we do not find 'a speculative philosophy of history'
but rather 'a deconstruction of universal History' which

> opens the way to a history that promises no salvation, offers no guarantee
> to redress injustice – not even the faintest possibility. A profane history
> emerges whose trajectory is unsettled, in that it is determined conjointly
> by struggle and necessity. Hence there is no question of founding a new
> philosophy of some unidirectional history.[144]

---

140   Cf. Marx's claim that at 'a certain stage of development' the mode of production founded
         on the small-scale industry of peasants and artisans 'brings forth the material agencies
         for its own dissolution. From that moment new forces and new passions spring up in the
         bosom of society; but the old social organisation fetters them and keeps them down. It
         must be annihilated; it is annihilated' (MECW 35, p. 749).

141   MECW 3, p. 302.

142   Mészáros 2011, p. 36.

143   It is arguable that Marx would agree with the essence of Kant's claim that 'if we aban-
         don' the 'teleological theory of nature' we 'can no longer understand nature as governed
         by laws, but rather only as playing aimlessly; and the dismal reign of chance thus replaces
         the guiding principle of reason' (Kant 2006, pp. 4–5).

144   Bensaïd 2002, pp. 2–3.

There is indeed no guarantee of freedom in Marx's writing – the only certainty is struggle, and the process of human emancipation can be disrupted at any point. But if Marx thought that there was 'not even the faintest possibility' of freedom, how are we to explain his life's work? If the possibility of progress exists there must be an 'end' toward which we can progress.[145]

While there is no idea of a providential force directing the course of history in Marx's writing, it is evident that attitudes toward revolutionary politics akin to religious faith exist nonetheless. And it is indeed possible that the ontological idea that 'Reason directs the world' could be mistakenly treated like some kind of omnipotent and inexorable providential will. It seems that even McCarney had a quasi-religious striving for salvation brought on by misgivings about the revolutionary potential of the proletariat and the development of 'communism'. He did not think capitalism was doing what Marx said it would and he was lamenting the absence of the revolutionary subject required to carry out a revolution. He went so far as to maintain that 'some version of the cunning of reason' is 'needed' to supplement Marx's revolutionary social theory by being 'placed explicitly at the center of the conceptual field', 'generalised in its application', and 'extended to the revolution of socialism'.[146] He did not recognise the extent to which Marx had critically reworked this idea into his writings – aside from 'isolated and opportunist, or at least not fully theorised, uses' – although, to his credit, he claims that *if* it were transferred into Marx's thought, it 'seems likely that a concept of Spirit as incorporating, and driven by, an impulse of reason, is indispensable'.[147] While this is true, Starosta's claim that an '*extrinsic* application of a *general* dialectic' of 'Spirit' is not sufficient for Marx's critique of political economy is also valid.[148] But is the 'dialectical'

---

145   Even Sayers – who maintains that Marx depicts historical events as 'not teleological in nature' – claims that Marx thought 'historical development' is 'leading in a progressive direction ... towards a situation in which human beings will be able to exercise increasing self-consciousness, control, and freedom' (Sayers 2019, pp. 56–7). Cf. McCarney's claim that 'At the most general level of all it is uncontroversially clear that' Marx 'shares' with Hegel 'the vision of history as the history of human emancipation. It is for him a record of progress leading to "that development of human energy which is an end in itself, the true realm of freedom"' (McCarney 1991, p. 22).

146   He claims that it is 'a device with which Marx was perfectly familiar', and he insightfully pointed out that this 'device has nothing mysterious or arbitrary about it in Hegel's scheme. On the contrary, it is directly grounded in, and required by, his basic ontological principles ... In the form that it is historically significant, reason is present in human beings as a "unconscious universal instinct"' (McCarney 2000, pp. 73; 72).

147   McCarney 2000, pp. 73–4.

148   Starosta 2015, p. 6.

development of 'Spirit' or 'mind' in history only capable of being *extrinsic-ally* applied? McCarney was on the right path to answering this question. He claimed that if 'Spirit is read immanently and anthropologically', it 'will not present a theoretical difficulty, but at most a shock[149] to conventional ways of thinking'.[150] Indeed, 'Spirit' must be read this way – Marx identified humanity with mind.[151]

Marx's work does not suggest that the revolution will be brought about by some kind of estranged cosmic νοῦς. We cannot rely on the ontological idea that 'Reason directs the world' as if it were a blind faith in an omniscient force tending the light at the end of the tunnel of human history; but it is evident that Marx thought he could see that light nonetheless. After all, he claimed that as 'the immanent laws of capitalistic production' proceed to unfold in the world – intelligible laws which are 'reason' implicit in the phenomena of capitalism – 'the mass of misery, oppression, slavery, degradation, exploitation [grows]; but with this too grows the revolt of the working class, a class always increasing in numbers, and disciplined, united, organised by the very mechanism of the process of capitalist production itself'.[152] Of course he may be wrong about this, but if it is determined that he is right then we will have to admit that there is indeed someone tending the light: you and I and everyone else who have 'become like one of us', as it were – i.e., 'universally developed individuals' living a free life.

---

149   In the words of Nietzsche's Zarathustra: 'Where is the lightning to lick you with its tongue?' (Nietzsche 1996, p. 14).

150   McCarney 2000, p. 74. 'The real problem', he continues, 'is whether ... Spirit can after all be detached from the Idea so as to form the basis of a viable, self-contained theory' (Ibid.).

151   Cf. Hegel's claim regarding the 'question of *perfectibility* and of the *education of the human race*': 'Those who have proclaimed this perfectibility have had some inkling of the nature of spirit, which is to have know thyself as the law of its *being*, and as it comprehends what *it is*, to assume a higher shape than that which its being originally consisted. But for those who reject this thought, spirit has remained an empty word, and history has remained a superficial play of *contingent* and allegedly "merely human" aspirations and passions' (Hegel 1991, pp. 372–3).

152   MECW 35, p. 750.

CHAPTER 5

Revolutionary Subjectivity

Have courage, for life is striding
To endless life along;
Stretched by inner fire,
Our sense becomes transfigured.
One day the stars above
Shall flow in golden wine,
We will enjoy it all,
And as stars we will shine.
The love is given freely,
And Separation is no more.
The whole life heaves and surges
Like a sea without a shore ...

NOVALIS[1]

∴

1   The Subjective Dimension of Revolutionary Transformation

Marx claimed that 'the communist proletarians who revolutionise society' put 'the relations of production and the forms of intercourse on a new basis – i.e., on themselves as new people'.[2] The subjectivity of the working class in capitalist society – like the subjectivity of all individuals in all societies – is internally related to the definite character of social relations and conditions of life activity that they live within. It is thus also a historical product like the revolution itself, which Marx depicts as the result of a broader historical process whereby we transform the socionatural world of life activity and our own 'inner world' simultaneously. In his view the specific form of 'estrangement' that we experience as wage labourers develops capacities that are required to engage in the 'revolutionary practice' through which revolutionary subjectivity develops fur-

---

1   Novalis 2000.
2   MECW 5, p. 214.

ther. Of course, revolutionary subjectivity is not the character of individuality that will populate a 'higher phase of communist society'. The 'present generation', Marx claimed, 'must go under in order to make room for the [individuals] who are able to cope with a new world'.[3] Revolutionary subjects are the individuals that will initiate the revolution by overthrowing the capitalist order and utilising the productive forces of social labour in the context of new, freer relations that take the place of the oppressive capitalist relations of dominance and servitude. They establish conditions through which, over time, we will remove any remaining barriers to the full and free development of everyone.

Marx's writing portrays the development of revolutionary subjectivity as a process that involves a kind of psychological – i.e., mental and emotional – transformation. This is expressed, for instance, in his depiction of 'greed' as an essential factor in the formation of the productive capacity that he called 'general industriousness'.[4] In short, this is an 'indifference' to the content of labour insofar as we are receiving wages, which is a kind of 'versatility' that is required for the revolutionary process and represents an embryonic form of the all-roundedness of 'universally developed individuals' sustained in 'a higher phase of communist society'. The development of the ethical character of revolutionary subjects also involves a kind of psychological process. In accordance with Marx's philosophical anthropology, this process entails the development of the 'mental' and 'practical senses' such as 'will' and 'love' to the extent required for the revolutionary appropriation of the productive forces beyond the character of capitalist relations of production. The development of revolutionary consciousness thus also involves a corresponding development of our 'emotional' and 'sensual' (i.e., 'moral') powers. This alteration of subjectivity underlies Marx's emphasis on the dissolution of the identity of revolutionary subjects themselves as a result of the revolution.[5] However, the kind of psychological transformation that Marx envisioned does not only begin after the revolution has reached a 'culminating point'. Instead, he thought that the

---

3   MECW 10, p. 117.

4   MECW 28, p. 156. See the next section below for further discussion of this idea.

5   Cf. Lukács's claim that the *proletariat only perfects itself by annihilating and transcending itself, by creating the classless society through the successful conclusion of its own class struggle. The struggle for this society, in which the dictatorship of the proletariat is merely a phase, is not just a battle waged against an external enemy, the bourgeoisie. It is equally the struggle of the proletariat against itself*: against the devastating and degrading effects of the capitalist system upon its class consciousness. The proletariat will only have won the real victory when it has overcome these effects within itself' (Lukács 1971, p. 80).

'proletariat goes through various stages of development' both during and leading up to revolutionary activity.[6]

Marx does not elaborate in detail about this process but we are able to
determine that he thought a primary impetus for the development of revolutionary subjectivity is the activity of 'estranged' wage labour in the capitalist
mode of production. In this connection it is evident that he critically appropriated Hegel's representation of the life and death struggle between oppressed
labourers and their exploiters, but the interpretative literature on this influence tends to overlook or underemphasise the extent to which Marx also treats
it as a kind of psychological process (alongside a process of material production and transformation of the social life world). Hegel claimed that within this
oppressive socioproductive relationship the labourer 'rids himself of attachment to natural existence' and their 'natural will'.[7] He thought the oppressed
labourers were driven to enter into a state of deferred desire by a fear of death
which completely consumes them.[8] In his view a consequence of this is that
'the slave', in 'the service of the master, works off his individualist self-will, overcomes the inner immediacy of appetite, and in this divestment of self and in
"the fear of his lord" makes "the beginning of wisdom"–the passage to universal
self-consciousness'.[9]

An analysis of Marx's critical appropriation of Hegel's idea of the intersubjective nature of class struggle makes the psychological aspect of it in Marx's
work more apparent. Consider, for instance, his idea of the 'life-and-death
struggle' between bourgeoisie and proletariat.[10] He claimed that as the 'poverty

6   MECW 6, p. 492.

7   Hegel 1977, p. 117.

8   Hegel claimed that 'this consciousness has been fearful, not of this or that particular thing
     or just at odd moments, but its whole being has been seized with dread; for it has exper-
     ienced the fear of death, the absolute Lord' (Ibid.). Cf. Aristotle's claim that 'the most
     frightening thing is death, for it is a limit' (Aristotle 2002, p. 48).

9   Hegel 1971, p. 175. In the process of elaborating this, Hegel also touched on its significance
     for the development of the human species overall: 'Since the slave works for the master
     and therefore not in the exclusive interest of his own individuality, his desire is expanded
     into being not only the desire of this particular individual but also the desire of another.
     Accordingly, the slave rises above the selfish individuality of his natural will ... This sub-
     jugation of the slave's egotism forms the *beginning* of true human freedom. This quaking
     of the single, isolated will, the feeling of the worthlessness of egotism, the habit of obedi-
     ence, is a necessary moment in the education of all men' (Ibid.).

10   Marx referred to 'the bourgeoisie's fear of the inevitable life-and-death struggle between
     itself and the proletariat' and also articulated class struggle in general as such a struggle
     (MECW 24, p. 265). He claimed, for instance, that there can be 'no peace' between feudal
     and aristocratic society and modern bourgeois society because their 'material interests

of the proletarian assumes an acute, sharp form' it 'drives him into a life-and-death struggle, makes him a revolutionary'.[11] It is important to note that Marx did not think of 'poverty' only in the 'material' sense; he also described a 'spiritual' form of 'poverty' which suggests that he thought of it from a psychological standpoint.[12] The life-and-death nature of the class struggle can be conceived from this perspective as well. In other words, the class struggle involves an 'inner' psychological struggle which is internally related to our struggles in the life world of material practice.

Class consciousness, of course, is unthinkable without at least implicitly presupposing the existence of psychological life. After all, Marx thought that the revolutionary working class is becoming conscious of their power as a class and the real potential for independence from economic bondage under the rule of the capitalists. This alone is unlikely to arouse controversy among scholars of Marx's work, although there is no consensus regarding how the development of revolutionary subjectivity and its relation to practice should be theorised within the bounds of Marx's social philosophy. He did not provide a substantial amount of elaborate detail about his view of the relationship between subjectivity and practice, nor the developmental process of revolutionary subjectivity in particular, but his writings contain some definite ideas about this nonetheless. Elements from the philosophies of Aristotle and Hegel that inspired Marx can be drawn on to enrich our understanding of his thinking on this matter as well. According to Hegel, a key moment in this process occurs as 'consciousness, *qua* worker, comes to see in the independent being [of the object] its *own* independence' from its exploitative oppressor.[13] Even though Marx maintained that there are significant – but not insurmountable – barriers

---

and needs bring them into mortal combat' in which one 'side must win, the other must lose'; and that the French bourgeoisie had attempted to 'indict the proletariat for not having risen in a bloody struggle, a life-and-death struggle on its behalf' (MECW 8, p. 336; MECW 11, p. 173).

11   MECW 5, p. 219.

12   MECW 3, p. 302.

13   Hegel 1977, p. 118. The worker 'posits *himself* as a negative in the permanent order of things, and thereby becomes *for himself*, someone existing on his own account ... [In] fashioning the thing, he becomes aware ... that he himself exists essentially and actually in his own right. The shape does not become something other than himself through being made external to him ... Through this rediscovery of himself by himself, the bondsman realizes that it is precisely in his work wherein he seemed to have only an alienated existence that he acquires a mind of his own. For this reflection, the two moments of fear and service as such, as also that of formative activity, are necessary, both being at the same time in a universal mode' (Hegel 1977, pp. 118–9).

hindering the wage worker's self-awareness and experience of their objectified power in the product they produce within capitalist relations of production, the influence of Hegel's representation of the maturation of revolutionary
independence is evident in Marx's writing:

> The recognition of the products as its own, and its awareness that its sep-
> aration from the conditions of its realisation is improper and imposed by
> force, is an enormous consciousness, and is itself the product of the mode
> of production based on capital, and just as much the knell to its doom as
> the consciousness of the slave that he cannot be the *property of another*,
> his consciousness of being a person, reduced slavery to an artificial linger-
> ing existence, and made it impossible for it to continue to provide the
> basis of production.[14]

There is a depth to Marx's idea of the wage worker's revolutionary independence that entails a psychological dimension of human life activity that he left
undertheorised. This is evident, for instance, in his writing about the role that
money plays in the development of revolutionary independence. In his view,
since it is 'the worker himself who turns the money into whatever use values
he wants', the wage worker 'acts as a free agent; he must pay his own way; he is
responsible to himself for the way he spends his wages' and thus *'learns to master himself, in contrast to the slave*, who needs a master'.[15] Marx also claimed that
'piece wages' in particular give a 'wider scope' to 'individuality' which 'tends to
develop ... that individuality, and with it the sense of liberty, independence, and
self-control of the labourers'.[16] The influence of Aristotle is perceptible in this
idea of self-transformative life activity because the development of independence through the habitual practice of using money is analogous to Aristotle's
idea of moral virtue ('excellence of character') which 'comes into being as a
consequence of habit'.[17] As Aristotle claimed, 'the things that one who has
learned them needs to do, we learn by doing'.[18] It follows that this also applies
to the development of what Marx described as 'that revolutionary audacity
which flings at the adversary the defiant words: *am nothing and I should be*

---

14   MECW 28, pp. 390–1.
15   MECW 34, pp. 100–1.
16   MECW 35, p. 554.
17   Aristotle 2002, p. 21. It should be noted that, for Aristotle, while 'habit' is required for the
      development of virtue, it is not equal to virtue.
18   Aristotle 2002, p. 22. We become courageous, for example, 'by doing things that are cour-
      ageous' (Ibid.).

everything.[19] His higher fusion of Aristotelian and Hegelian philosophy suggests that this revolutionary character requires the development of courage which is a moral virtue, and Marx's notes indicate that he thought of this as a kind of virtue.[20]

2　　Revolutionary Productive Capacities

Marx thought that the revolutionary appropriation of the productive forces of social labour by the working class involves the development of the abilities required to collectively control them in a manner consistent with the initiation of a 'communist organization of society'. In his view the process of appropriating the knowledge objectified in these forces, and attempting to exercise the technical capacities associated with their use, further develops the ability required for it. In particular, he claimed that

> private property can be abolished only on condition of an all-round development of individuals, precisely because the existing form of intercourse and the existing productive forces are all-embracing and only individuals that are developing in an all-round fashion can appropriate them, i.e., can turn them into free manifestations of their lives.[21]

As a feature of revolutionary subjectivity this 'all-round development of individuals' is more accurately described as the workers' 'indifference towards the

---

19　MECW 3, p. 185.
20　Aristotle defined courage as 'a mean condition concerned with fear and confidence' (Aristotle 2002, p. 48). A 'courageous person', he claimed, 'endures or fears what one ought, for the reason one ought, as one ought, when one ought, and is confident in similar ways', since they undergo things and act 'in accordance with what is worthy and in a way that is proportionate'. He states further that 'to a courageous person, courage is a beautiful thing, and so its end is something beautiful as well, since each thing is determined by its end. So it is for the sake of the beautiful that the courageous person endures and does the things that are in accord with courage' (Aristotle 2002, p. 49).
21　MECW 5, p. 439. 'This appropriation is first determined by the object to be appropriated, the productive forces, which have been developed to a totality and which only exist within a universal intercourse. Even from this aspect alone, therefore, this appropriation must have a universal character corresponding to the productive forces and the intercourse. The appropriation of these forces is itself nothing more than the development of the individual capacities corresponding to the material instruments of production. The appropriation of a totality of instruments of production is, for this very reason, the development of a totality of capacities in the individuals themselves' (MECW 5, p. 87).

particular content' of work.[22] However, his writing does not suggest that every individual must be able to operate all of the forces of production in order for the working class to overthrow the capitalist order. From the outset, the development of this 'indifference' is facilitated by the tendency to deskill the production process which increases the relative ease of transition from one occupation to another. He claimed that within the 'automatic workshop' of capitalist production, 'labour has ... completely lost its specialized character' and the 'need for universality, the tendency towards an integral development of the individual begins to be felt'.[23] He thought this was a positive consequence of the 'estrangement' experienced by wage labourers because the 'automatic workshop wipes out specialists and craft idiocy'.[24] Immature forms of the 'rational' indifference to the particularity of labour that Marx thought would be achieved in the 'communist organization of society' – i.e., 'the fully developed individual' – germinate through 'estrangement' in capitalism.[25]

In tandem with this process, the general mania for money encourages the movement which develops our *versatility*', i.e., the 'complete indifference to the specific content of work' and the 'ability to transfer from one branch [of

---

22   MECW 34, p. 421. In *Capital,* Marx included a statement on this matter by a French labourer who went to California for work: 'I never could have believed, that I was capable of working at the various occupations I was employed on in California ... In consequence of thus finding out that I am fit to any sort of work, I feel less of a mollusk and more of a man' (MECW 35, p. 490). Cf. the following claims by Marx: 'The fact that the particular kind of labour is irrelevant corresponds to a form of society in which individuals easily pass from one kind of labour to another, the particular kind of labour being accidental to them and therefore indifferent. Labour, not only as a category but in reality, has become here a means to create wealth in general, and has ceased as a determination to be tied with the individuals in any particularity' (MECW 28, p. 41); 'The higher the development of capitalist production in a country, the greater the demand for *versatility* in labour capacity, the more indifferent the worker is towards the *particular content* of his labour, and the greater the fluidity of capital's movement from one sphere of production to another. Classical political economy presupposes as axioms the *versatility* of labour capacity and the *fluidity* of capital, and justifiably so to the extent that this is the tendency of the capitalist mode of production, which asserts itself ruthlessly despite all obstacles, which are for the most part created by capitalist production itself' (MECW 34, p. 421).

23   MECW 6, p. 190.

24   Ibid. He claimed that the 'division of labour inside modern society ... engenders specialties, specialists', which is a kind of one-sided development (Ibid.).

25   MECW 35, p. 490. There are other similar tendencies that can be seen in capitalism, although it is not clear that they have anything positive to offer to the process of human development. For example, Bill Morneau, the former Finance Minister of Canada, claimed that Canadians 'should get used to so-called "job churn" – short-term employment and a number of career changes in a person's life' (*Canadian Press* 2016).

industry] to another'.[26] This aspect of the 'estrangement' experienced by wage labourers – which has positive transformative consequences – has a fundamental psychological dimension. The key significance that Marx ascribed to this psychological dimension for the development of revolutionary productive capacities makes it worthwhile to quote him at length:

> The quest for enrichment, being the driving force of everyone, since everyone wishes to produce money, produces general wealth. Only thus can the general quest for enrichment become the source of general wealth, wealth which continually reproduces itself anew. In that labour is wage labour and its immediate purpose is money, general wealth is *posited* as its purpose and object. ... Here, money as an end becomes the means to general industriousness. General wealth is produced in order to seize hold of its representative. In this way, the real sources of wealth are opened up.
>
> Since the aim of labour is not a particular product that bears a particular relation to the particular needs of the individual, but money, wealth in its general form, the industriousness of the individual firstly has no limits. It is indifferent to its particularity and assumes any form that serves the aim; it is inventive in the creation of new objects for social need, etc. It is clear, therefore, that with wage labour as its basis, the effect of money is not destructive but productive ... General industry is possible only where all labour produces general wealth, not a particular form of it; where, therefore, the wage of the individual is also money.[27]

Marx claimed that since 'the purpose of labour is for the wage labourer wages alone, money, a definite quantity of exchange value, in which any specific characteristics of use value have been extinguished', the wage labourer 'is completely indifferent to the *content* of his labour'.[28] This is a key ingredient in the developmental context of the proletariat as opposed to the slave. Marx claimed that wage labour is playing a vital role in the historical emergence of 'general industriousness ... as the universal asset of the new generation' and that slavery can 'never create *general industriousness*' because it fosters the perspective that freedom is 'loafing'.[29]

---

26   MECW 34, p. 101.
27   MECW 28, pp. 156–7.
28   MECW 34, pp. 437–8.
29   MECW 28, pp. 250–1.

In contemporary literature, Guido Starosta places a strong emphasis on Marx's idea of productive subjectivity.[30] Starosta recognises and attempts to explore the relationship between subjective powers and the socioproductive basis of society, but he fails to notice the depth of Marx's idea of subjectivity and the psychological dimension of the development of the productive capacities of revolutionary subjects.[31] To begin with, Starosta misinterprets Marx's idea that truly 'universal' productive subjects can only exist in a 'higher phase of communist society' and not as revolutionary subjects.[32] He does not place adequate emphasis on the 'universality' of humanity in the sense of our 'rational' and therefore 'free' nature, i.e., that which makes our productive activity unique among animals that 'also produce'. In effect, Starosta condenses Marx's idea of human 'universality' into the colloquial sense of the term (i.e., as all-rounded) and places excessive emphasis on productive capacities; e.g., he writes about 'a *universal worker*, that is, a productive subject capable of taking part in any form of the human labour-process'.[33] Marx's idea of 'general industriousness' incorporates the notion of 'all-sided development' in this sense. However, as demonstrated in previous chapters, his idea of our 'universality' involves all other aspects of human subjectivity and ultimately the fundamentally 'free' nature of human 'reason'.

---

30 He maintains that for Marx 'productive subjectivity' is a uniquely human trait, and that in Marx's writing from 1844 'the content of the history of the human species consists in the development of the specific material powers of the human being as a working subject, that is, of *human productive subjectivity*' (Starosta 2013, p. 233). Thus for Starosta the 'essence' of the 'capitalist transformation of the production-process of human life lies in the mutation of the productive attributes of the collective labourer according to a determinate tendency: the individual organs of the latter eventually becoming *universal productive subjects*' (Starosta 2013, p. 236).

31 He claimed, for example, that 'it is on the fully-expanded universal character of human productive subjectivity that the *material basis* for the new society rests' (Starosta 2013, p. 244).

32 Consider, for example, his claim that a 'passage from the *Grundrisse* mentions that the universality of "revolutionary" productive subjectivity must be the expression of a *scientific* consciousness, capable of organising work as "an activity regulating all the forces of nature"' (Starosta 2013, p. 247).

33 Starosta 2013, p. 239. He also claimed that 'Large-scale industry's tendency to produce an increasingly universal worker' is equal to 'the disappearance of the technical necessity for a particularistic development of the worker's productive subjectivity' (Starosta 2013, p. 240).

3   The Ethical Character of Revolutionary Subjectivity

Marx thought the transformation of working-class subjectivity in capitalism is more extensive than just the development of productive capacities. In particular, the development of our ethical character is an essential aspect of revolutionary subjectivity. Thus while the development of productive capacities is an integral subjective transformation for the revolutionary appropriation of the productive forces of social labour, the revolutionary character of this appropriation also requires a corresponding development of a more 'rational' ethical character among members of the working class so as to advance beyond the relations of current society and reorganise economic life in a manner consistent with the initiation of the 'communist' organisation of society. Marx's claim that capitalism 'creates the ... embryonic conditions' for 'a higher form of society' entails the development of the ethical capacities of the revolutionary proletariat, i.e., the 'mental' and 'practical senses'.[34] In keeping with Marx's primary philosophical influences, this can be articulated as a greater degree of 'moral virtuosity' *à la* Aristotle. Marx's writing indicates that he thought of it along the lines of a psychological transformation related to our 'sensuous will' and the development of rational desire.[35] As is the case with revolutionary productive capacities, Marx thought that the ethical character of revolutionary subjects is developing through their life practice in capitalism, including 'revolutionary practice'.

In the 'Provisional Rules' of the First International Marx described the emergent ethical character of revolutionary working-class movements. He claimed that the 'International Association and all societies and individuals adhering to it, ... acknowledge truth, justice, and morality, as the basis of their conduct towards each other, and towards all men, without regard to colour, creed, or nationality'.[36] He thought it was increasingly self-evident to working-class indi-

---

34   He claimed that the 'advance of industry, whose involuntary promoter is the bourgeoisie, replaces the isolation of the labourers, due to competition, by their revolutionary combination, due to association', and that it 'is one of the civilizing aspects of capital that it enforces ... surplus labour in a manner and under conditions which are more advantageous to the development of the productive forces, social relations, and the creation of the elements for a new and higher form' because 'it creates the material means and embryonic conditions, making it possible in a higher form of society to combine this surplus labour with a greater reduction of time devoted to material labour' (MECW 6, p. 496; MECW 37, p. 806).

35   In Hegelian terms this process requires 'an incalculable medial discipline of the intellectual and moral powers' (Hegel 1956, p. 41).

36   MECW 20, p. 15.

viduals that 'the cause of the producer is every[where] the same and its enemy everywhere the same, whatever its nationality (in whatever national garb)', and that their 'efforts, far from being narrow and selfish, aim at the emancipation of the downtrodden millions'.[37] It would be inaccurate to describe his view of revolutionary working people as though he thought they were acting 'altruistically', but they are not 'selfish' in the colloquial sense either insofar as he thought that workers were increasingly coming to experience each other's need for emancipation as their own self-interest.[38] Ultimately, on Marx's premises the reciprocal practice of 'justice' is the expression of a rational view of self-interest which is vital for a truly good existence. The picture of revolutionary individuals conveyed in Marx's writing indicates that they could not be perfectly 'just' because they are unable to practice 'complete virtue' in relations with others, and thus they would have to rectify the lack of development which still remains in order to 'complete' the revolutionary transition; but it also indicates that a key factor of the motivation of these individuals is the recognition of all human beings as inherently free.

Marx depicts this budding ethical character as partly expressed in the working class's 'need for society'. He thought this develops through our 'revolutionary activity' which is instrumental in the development of the desire for such relations as ends-in-themselves. Marx claimed that 'Association, society and conversation, which again has association as its end, are enough for them', and their association, which was initially approached as a means for resisting cap-

---

37   MECW 22, p. 501; MECW 20, p. 192.
38   Like many interpreters, Mihailo Marković would misinterpret this as 'abstract moralizing humanism' which he claimed is not 'Marx's standpoint' because he mistakenly thought that Marx 'does not expect emancipation to be the consequence of a higher moral consciousness' but rather 'the result of a social development which is unconscious and involuntary. The proletarians are not the agents of emancipation because they are morally superior and have noble and unselfish social aims' (Marković 1974, p. 173). Cf. Anthony Skillen's more accurate claim that the 'proletariat is the "revolutionary class" because of its capacity to seize power and its disposition to organise society on a different, nonoppressive basis. It is the "universal class," not because its members obediently perform a cluster of Kantian duties, but because its actual, historically formed "inclinations" correspond to the conditions for the realization of the human species' potential. It needs no moralistic form because its particular needs are, and are increasingly felt to be humanity's needs' (Skillen 1981, pp. 156–7). As Fromm claimed, the 'revolutionary character is humanist in the sense that he experiences in himself all of humanity, and that nothing human is alien to him', and they are 'the one who is identified with humanity and therefore transcends the narrow limits of his own society, and who is able, because of this, to criticize his or any other society from the standpoint of reason and humanity' (Fromm 1963, pp. 165; 158).

italism, 'becomes an end'.[39] Marx thought that he had recognised the embryo of 'communist' social relations developing within the already existing 'revolutionary activity' of the proletariat.[40] While he did not elaborate at length about this character we can still determine that even though 'the first phase of communist society' will be 'stamped with the birth-marks of the old society from whose womb it emerges', the 'first phase' of revolutionary transition must be brought about by a collectivity of revolutionary subjects that identify with all human beings and recognise that each individual is inherently free and an end-in-themselves. As Marx claimed, 'the emancipation of the producing class is that of all human beings without distinction of sex or race'.[41] This indicates that the subjectivity at the basis of the *'bourgeois right'* which characterises the social relations of the 'first phase' of revolutionary transition has the aim of universal human emancipation driving it to reorganise society. Marx did not venture to comprehensively explain this aspect of the revolutionary process but his work suggests that the development of the 'need for society' must be realised and transcended in order for the realisation of what he called the 'human' need for 'the *other* person as a person' to become widespread after

---

39   MECW 3, p. 313. Cf. Avineri's elaboration of this: 'Organization and association, even considered apart from their immediate aims, constitute a crucial phase in the liberation of the workers. They change the worker, his way of life, his consciousness of himself and his society. They force him into contact with his fellow-workers, suggest to him that his fate is not a subjective, particular and contingent affair but part of a universal scheme of reality. They make him see in his fellow-proletarians not competitors for work and bread but brothers in suffering and ultimately victory, not means but co-equal ends' (Avineri 1968, p. 143).

40   Avineri claimed that 'these proletarian associations are *in potentia* what future society will be in practice' and that they 'offer a glimpse into future society' because they 'create other-directedness and mutuality' (Avineri 1968, pp. 141–2). Cf. Skillen's claim that 'Marx tended to write as if it was solely in the struggle against the dominant class that the masses would gain the dispositions and capacities fitting them for self-emancipation. But ... [if] the new society is to develop in the womb of the old, its embryo must do more than kick against the walls of the old; it will have to be the case that it has exercised virtues and acquired habits (traditions) that will be required in the new age' (Skillen 1981, p. 170). This 'new age' has to be qualified as the initial phase of the revolutionary reorganisation of society because further development is required for the dawn of the age of 'true' freedom.

41   MECW 24, p. 340. He thought that the emancipation the workers contains 'universal human emancipation' because 'the whole of human servitude is involved in the relation of worker to production, and all relations of servitude are only modifications and consequences of the workers relation to production' (MECW 3, p. 280). Elsewhere he claimed that 'the economical subjection of the man of labour to the monopoliser of the means of labour, that is, the sources of life, lies at the bottom of servitude in all its forms, of all social misery, mental degradation, and political dependence' (MECW 20, p. 14).

a succession of post-revolutionary generations.[42] And while the full development of the need for 'the other' as a 'human being' (as well as its satisfaction) can only be achieved in the life activity of a 'higher phase of communist society' in which 'the human end-in-itself' is recognised and affirmed by all 'universally developed individuals', Marx depicted the revolutionary reorganisation of society (production, distribution, etc.) as motivated by the desire for the 'universal development' of everyone.[43] These revolutionary individuals are driven to act with the aim of remedying any situation in which human beings are subject to conditions that impede their full and free development.

Marx did not expound the psychological dimension of the process whereby we recognise everyone as potentially 'universally developed' – i.e., as inherently 'universal' and 'free' – but Hegel's philosophy provides a good starting point for attempting to elaborate this. He claimed that the 'servile obedience' arising in response to the worker's fear of the 'Lord' is the beginning of wisdom – but only the *beginning*,

> because that to which the natural individuality of self-consciousness subjects itself is not the truly universal, rational will which is in and for itself, but the single, contingent will of another person. Here, then, only one moment of freedom is manifested, that of the negativity of the egoistic individuality; whereas the positive side of freedom attains actuality only when, on the one hand, the servile self-consciousness, freeing itself both from the individuality of the master and from its own individuality, grasps the absolutely rational in its universality which is independent of the particularity of the subjects.[44]

Marx's work does not suggest that revolutionary subjects would be able to grasp 'the absolutely rational in its universality', but it does suggest that the *aufhebung* of the workers's 'egoistic individuality' through 'estrangement' facilitates the process of 'revolutionary practice' in which he glimpsed 'the brotherhood of man'.[45] He claimed, for instance, that the experience of 'poverty' in capitalism 'causes the human being to experience the need of the greatest wealth – the *other* human being'.[46] This phrase is somewhat cryptic but his dis-

---

42 MECW 3, p. 296.

43 MECW 28, p. 412.

44 Hegel 1971, pp. 175–6.

45 MECW 3, p. 313.

46 MECW 3, p. 304. Cf. Aristotle's claim that 'in both poverty and other misfortunes people believe that friends are the only refuge' (Aristotle 2002, p. 144).

tinction between 'material and spiritual wealth and poverty' is informative in this instance.[47] The 'spiritual' form of 'poverty' is connected to the experience of the need for 'the *other* human being' because it involves a 'passive bond', i.e., a kind of *relation*, with other individuals and society at large.[48] Does the condition of alienation for working people in a society determined by coldly indifferent and hostile market forces contribute to a 'spiritual' malaise and ensuing psychological struggle which primes them to collectively transcend their atomised 'egoistic individuality'? 'All that is solid melts into air', as it were, and on Marx's premises we must assume a metamorphosis of subjectivity that facilitates the workers' consciousness of their class identity which is 'independent of the particularity of the subjects' – a liberatory consciousness 'which has a universal character by its universal suffering'.[49]

Comprehending the development of the working class as the 'universal class' and the ethical character that corresponds to it on Marx's premises requires a theorisation of the psychological dimension of this process, but this element of his social philosophy remained undertheorised. The result is that a gap exists in his work which ultimately undermines the coherence of his revolutionary theory. After all, 'material poverty' is also connected to the psychological dimension of human life. Consider, for example, the significance of his claim that the 'material privation' of the working classes 'dwarfs their moral as well as their physical stature'. In general, the 'estranged' condition of working-class life, including both their 'spiritual' and 'material' poverty, detrimentally effects the development of the ethical character required for revolution.

4   The Problem

Our encounters with considerable counter-revolutionary tendencies[50] during the course of history since Marx was active compels us to entertain – to borrow a phrase from McCarney – 'the question of what could justify a rational confidence in the proletariat as the historical subject which brings to an end the era of capitalism'.[51] McCarney responded to this question by claiming that

---

47   MECW 3, p. 302.

48   MECW 3, p. 304.

49   MECW 6, p. 487; MECW 3, p. 186.

50   Consider, for instance, the rise of fascism in the twentieth century and the contemporary intensification of right-wing politics worldwide in the years scarred by the fallout of the global economic crisis – the 'Great Recession' – of 2008.

51   McCarney 1990, p. 143.

'no greater theoretical contribution to the dialectic of human freedom could be conceived' than a 'systematic study of "the world market and crisis" which [Marx] projected'.[52] But it must be reiterated that a crisis of capitalism alone is not sufficient to compel the working class to participate in revolutionary struggle, even though Marx thought the crises of capitalism could act as potential galvanising moments. He also proposed the theory of the 'falling rate of profit' and predicted ever-expanding and volatile capitalist crises, but in his view the most decisive factor was the development of a group of revolutionary subjects who act as agents of this process. Consider, for instance, the emphasis he placed on this in a discussion about the Civil War in France, in which he claimed that the 'Paris proletariat was still incapable of going beyond the bourgeois republic otherwise than in its *fancy*, in *imagination*; how everywhere it acted in its service when it really came to action'.[53] Indeed, history since Marx's time indicates that various kinds of revolutionary forces arise in periods of social and economic crisis, but so do reactionary ones which are at times very extreme.

Aside from consideration of whether revolutionary subjectivity is actually developing in the world, Marx's idea of the development of revolutionary subjectivity is inconsistent. Even if it is just undertheorised, he indicated consequences of the 'estrangement' in capitalism that undermine his own ideas of this process. This is a profound problem inherent in Marx's social philosophy. According to him, capital 'usurps the time for growth, development, and healthy maintenance of the body', 'mortifies [our] body and ruins [our] mind', squandering 'not only blood and flesh, but also nerve and brain'.[54] It thus ruins our mind, resulting in 'ignorance', 'mental degradation', 'stupidity', and 'cretinism'.[55] A conspicuous impediment to 'revolutionary practice' is the fact that capitalism profoundly exhausts the physical and mental energies of the working class. Marx described this as the 'physical and mental degradation' brought on by 'the torture of overwork'.[56] Hence his support for reforms that limit the duration of the working day, which he considered a 'preliminary condition, without which all further attempts at improvement and emancipation must

---

52   McCarney 2000, p. 75.

53   MECW 10, p. 66.

54   MECW 35, p. 271; MECW 3, p. 274; MECW 37, p. 92. Capitalist manufacturing in particular 'converts the labourer into a crippled monstrosity' (MECW 35, p. 365).

55   MECW 35, p. 640; MECW 3, p. 273.

56   MECW 35, pp. 275–6. In capitalism 'the highest development of productive power together with the greatest expansion of existing wealth will coincide' with 'degradation of the labourer, and a most straitened exhaustion of his vital powers' (MECW 29, p. 134).

prove abortive', because it 'is needed to restore the health and physical energies of the working class ... as well as to secure them the possibility of intellectual development, sociable intercourse, social and political action'.[57]

The debilitating effects of working-class life in capitalist society are laid bare throughout Marx's work. In *Capital*, for example, he claimed that

> within the capitalist system all methods for raising the social productive-ness of labour are brought about at the cost of the individual labourer; all means for the development of production transform themselves into means of domination over, and exploitation of, the producers; they mutil-ate the labourer into a fragment of a man, degrade him to the level of an appendage of a machine, destroy every remnant of charm in his work and turn it into a hated toil; they estrange from him the intellectual potenti-alities of the labour process in the same proportion as science is incor-porated in it as an independent power; they distort the conditions under which he works, subject him during the labour process to a despotism the more hateful for its meanness; they transform his lifetime into working time, and drag his wife and child beneath the wheels of the Juggernaut of capital.[58]

Of course, in Marx's view, continued struggle can lead to gradual development over a span of generations as the brutality of capitalism is resisted and con-ditions improve so that individuals are able to experience development even within 'estrangement'. But he also suggested that development can be stunted, such as in the 'many cases' when a working person is 'too ignorant to under-stand the true interest of [their] child, or the normal conditions of human development'.[59] This is particularly significant because of the intergenerational nature of class struggle. And while Marx undoubtedly witnessed progress in the development of working-class resistance to capitalism, such as the 'workers'

---

57   MECW 20, p. 187. Marx claimed that 'After a thirty years' struggle, fought with most admir-able perseverance, the English working classes, improving a momentaneous split between the landlords and money-lords, succeeded in carrying in the Ten Hours Bill' which led to 'immense physical, moral, and intellectual benefits' for the 'factory operatives' (MECW 20, p. 10). In *Capital* he sarcastically remarked: 'Time for education, for intellectual develop-ment, the fulfilling of social functions and for social intercourse, for the free-play of [our] bodily and mental activity ... – moonshine!' (MECW 35, p. 270).

58   MECW 35, p. 639.

59   MECW 20, p. 189. He claimed further that 'the more enlightened part of the working class fully understands that the future of its class, and, therefore, of mankind, altogether depends upon the formation of the rising working generation' (MECW 20, p. 189).

desire to establish the conditions for co-operative production on a social scale', he was also aware of detrimental elements of working-class life that impede the development of revolutionary subjectivity.[60]

Thinking of resistance to capitalism from the perspective of a theory of subjectivity is consonant with Mark Fisher's work which is notable for the way that he focused on human subjectivity as a site of social and political struggle. Alongside his concept of 'capitalist realism', which is 'an attitude of resignation, defeatism and depression', he argued that capitalism has taken a form with profoundly negative implications for the psychology of resistance.[61] He wrote about 'the deleterious psychic effects of neoliberalism' which 'instills a perpetual anxiety – there is no security'.[62] Marx was aware of this general tendency and he claimed that 'all fixity and security in the situation of the labourer' is undermined in capitalist society.[63] This has been intensified with the situation of the contemporary 'precariat' whose life, according to Fisher, is characterised by 'constant conditions of instability and insecurity, short-term employment, [and] casualization', which are demonstrably debilitating for mental health.[64] In such conditions, individuals are increasingly habituated into 'the deflationary perspective of a depressive who believes that any positive state, any hope, is a dangerous illusion'.[65] In this state our oppressive conditions appear fixed as a permanent feature of our reality while all positive expectations dissolve in hopelessness, undermining the development of a politics of resistance. In relation to this frontier of the struggle, Marx's work provides a positive perspective that resists the deleterious effects of 'estrangement'. He claimed, for instance, that capitalism, 'along with the universality of the estrangement of individuals from themselves and from others, ... also produces the universality and generality of all their relations and abilities'.[66] But not enough attention was given to circumstances that exacerbate the inherently hostile relations at the heart of our social life activity in capitalism. After all, in capitalist society we are habituated into an individualistic and possessive hostility as individuals who are united through relations of exchange on the foundation of private property. Marx described this ethos of our 'estrangement', which is fundamental for life activity in capitalism, as 'mutual plundering':

---

60   MECW 24, p. 93.
61   Fisher 2018, p. 521.
62   Fisher 2018, p. 631.
63   MECW 35, p. 490.
64   Fisher 2018, p. 638.
65   Fisher 2009, p. 5.
66   MECW 28, p. 99.

The intention of *plundering*, of *deception*, is necessarily present in the background, for since our exchange is a selfish one, on your side as on mine, and since the selfishness of each seeks to get the better of that of the other, we necessarily seek to deceive each other ... For me, you are rather the means and instrument for producing this object that is my aim ... Our *mutual* value is for us the *value* of our mutual objects. Hence for us [humanity itself] is mutually of *no value*.[67]

In such conditions where others are habitually treated as a 'means and instrument' rather than ends-in-themselves, the stage is set for particularly adverse circumstances to significantly stunt the development of our ethical character and impair the initiation of the revolutionary reorganisation of society on a radically democratic basis within which we will have the opportunity for 'universal' development. Anthony Skillen describes this as 'situationally generated tendencies to possess, to submit, to escape, to "scab"' which act as 'internal enemies' of the 'universal human values' that the proletariat is supposed to be the bearer of.[68] But aside from the possibility for the anti-social tendencies endemic to the ethos of capitalism to intensify in certain circumstances, Marx's revolutionary theory presents us with a problem that demands attention insofar as 'the emancipation of the working classes requires their fraternal concurrence'.[69]

While it might be premature to simply maintain that the inconsistency inherent in Marx's theory of revolutionary subjectivity indicates that 'estrangement' cannot be overcome, there are relentless counter-revolutionary tendencies that need to be taken into account. Indeed, historical evidence indicates that the working class is not immune to waves of extreme reaction, and Marx's writing indicates that he had experience with reactionary tendencies of working people. Consider, for instance, this statement of his on the situation in English industrial and commercial centres in 1870:

---

67   MECW 3, pp. 226–7.
68   Skillen 1981, p. 166. Skillen insightfully articulated the development of revolutionary character but underemphasised the significance of the 'internal enemies' to 'universal human values': 'it is the case that direct and habitual experience, not only of reciprocities, of taken-for-granted "mutual aid," but also of *common* suffering and *common* joy where community enters into the nature of the passions, fosters a capacity directly to appreciate and respond to situations "disinterestedly," as "one of many." In this sense, "the universal class" received its epithet from Marx in part because he thought that "the brotherhood of man" could be "a fact of life" to its members; because the proletariat ... is the bearer in a qualitative, though not *unqualified* way, of universal human values' (Skillen 1981, p. 166).
69   MECW 20, p. 12.

All industrial and commercial centres in England now have a working class *divided* into two *hostile* camps, English proletarians and Irish proletarians. The ordinary English worker hates the Irish worker as a competitor who forces down the standard of life. In relation to the Irish worker, he feels himself to be a member of the *ruling nation* and, therefore, makes himself a tool of his aristocrats and capitalists *against Ireland*, thus strengthening their domination *over himself*. He harbours religious, social and national prejudices against him. His attitude towards him is roughly that of the poor whites to the n****** in the former slave states of the American Union. The Irishman pays him back with interest in his own money. He sees in the English worker both the accomplice and the stupid tool of *English rule in Ireland*.

This antagonism is kept artificially alive and intensified by the press, the pulpit, the comic papers, in short by all the means at the disposal of the ruling class. *This antagonism* is the *secret of the English working class's impotence*, despite its organisation. It is the secret of the maintenance of power by the capitalist class. And the latter is fully aware of this.[70]

Even though he maintains that the antagonism within the ranks of the working class is 'kept artificially alive and intensified', his writing suggests that such politics are not merely molded by external manipulation but rather rely on organic tendencies within the life of the population and their sociomaterial conditions of existence.

5   Marx's Idea of 'Revolutionary Practice' and the Limitations of Vanguardism

The intensification of neoliberal capitalism and fractured state of the working-class movement encourages the growth of a terminal vanguardism – the perpetual call to rebuild the radical left – which serves to obfuscate the fact that the absence of a robust revolutionary working class in an era when capitalism is in crisis cannot be ameliorated by the organisational efforts of Marxists.[71] For those who find inspiration in Marx's revolutionary theory, this problem

---

70   MECW 43, pp. 474–5.
71   Consider, for example, the claim made by Kostas Lapavitsas and Stathis Kouvelakis, in the context of the defeat of the Left in Greece, that 'today's singular imperative' is 'the process of re-founding the radical Left' (Lapavitsas and Kouvelakis p. 2019).

demands a reemphasis of the philosophy underlying his claims that the 'proletarian movement is the self-conscious, independent movement of the immense majority' and that 'the emancipation of the working classes must be conquered by the working classes themselves'.[72] On Marx's premises, revolutionary subjectivity implies *revolutionary practice* which he defined as the 'coincidence of the changing of circumstances' and 'self-change'.[73] The developmental consequences of this 'revolutionary activity' is necessary for the working class to 'become fitted to found society anew'.[74] Marx claimed that for

> the production on a mass scale of ... communist consciousness, and for the success of the cause itself, the alteration of men on a mass scale is necessary, an alteration which can only take place in a practical movement, a *revolution*; the revolution is necessary, therefore ... because the class *overthrowing* it can only in a revolution succeed in ridding itself of all the muck of ages.[75]

His writing indicates that he thought 'revolutionary practice' precedes any kind of culminating moment of a revolution when the class struggle comes to a head and the rule of private property and the bourgeois state are overthrown. In general, the development of revolutionary subjectivity is not limited to activity which begins when working people are consciously resisting capitalist rule.

An issue arises, however, insofar as Marx's idea of the 'coincidence of the changing of circumstances' and 'self-change' poses an incomprehensible paradox for the kind of abstract thinking that Hegel called 'the Understanding'. Such thinking is unable to comprehend the dialectical 'coincidence' at the centre of Marx's idea of subjects who are 'engaged in revolutionising themselves and things, in creating something that has never yet existed'.[76] Marx's claim that 'revolutionary practice' can only be 'rationally understood' indicates that it is only comprehensible for 'speculative' thinking.[77]

---

72 MECW 6, p. 495; MECW 20, p. 14.

73 MECW 5, p. 4. As David McNally claims, 'the self-transforming powers of mass struggle' is 'central to Marx's view of revolution' (McNally 2006, p. 375).

74 MECW 5, p. 53.

75 MECW 5, pp. 52–3. He also claimed that 'through a revolution ... there develops the universal character and the energy of the proletariat, which are required to accomplish the appropriation, and the proletariat moreover rids itself of everything that still clings to it from its previous position in society' (MECW 5, p. 88).

76 MECW 11, p. 103.

77 MECW 5, p. 4.

We encounter an abstract rendering of the paradoxical 'coincidence' at the basis of Marx's idea of 'revolutionary practice' in Michael Löwy's *The Theory of Revolution in the Young Marx*. Löwy posits the notion of a culminating 'moment of the revolution, during which the broad masses "change" and become conscious of their role by changing circumstances through their action', but this is just the process of revolutionary activity itself.[78] Marx had an idea of a so-called decisive hour in the process of the class struggle, but Löwy's formulation becomes problematic because it implies that the 'moment of the revolution' is necessary for the process of 'revolutionary practice'. On this basis we would have to posit it *ad infinitum*, in which case it would never begin – unless a Marxist vanguard would come along and guide the masses to this 'moment'.

Lenin's work serves as a classical example of Marxist-vanguard theory. He stressed the 'need for a strong revolutionary organization' composed of '*professional revolutionaries*' whose 'attention must be devoted *principally* to the task of *raising* the workers to the level of revolutionaries'.[79] The 'vanguard' is thus required 'to bring political knowledge to the workers' and for 'training the masses in revolutionary activity'.[80] Vanguardism has become presupposed as a legitimate tendency among countless groups and independent thinkers – although the extent to which they practice it and emphasise it varies – that consider themselves to be within the tradition of Marx's thought, even though his idea of 'revolutionary practice' is inconsistent with it. His third thesis on Feuerbach suggests that anyone who maintains a vanguardist position 'forgets' that 'the educator must ... be educated'.[81] An analogous problem arises in Kant's writing on the development of the human species. Kant put it thus: 'The human being must ... be *educated* to be good. The one who educates [us] is, however, also a human being, one who also therefore is subject to the same brutish nature and is supposed to bring about that of which [they are] in need'.[82]

---

78   Löwy 2005, p. 106.
79   Lenin 1943, pp. 157; 147; 153.
80   Lenin 1943, pp. 112; 109. He claimed that 'our very first and most imperative duty is to help train working class revolutionaries who will be on the same level in *regard to Party activity* as intellectual revolutionaries (we emphasize the words "in regard to Party activity", because although it is necessary, it is not so easy and not so imperative to bring the workers up to the level of intellectuals in other respects)' (Lenin 1943, p. 153).
81   MECW 5, p. 4. Cf. Lenin's claim that 'We can and must *educate* workers (and university and high-school students) so as to enable them to understand us when we speak to them' (Lenin 1943, p. 154).
82   Kant 2006, p. 168. Kant also articulated this problem another way. He claimed that 'the human being is an *animal* which, when he lives among others of his own species, *needs a*

Compare this to the following statement by Marx about a 'speaker from the knightly estate' who was opposed to freedom of the press:

> In his view, true education consists in keeping a person wrapped up in a cradle throughout his life, for as soon as he learns to walk, he learns also to fall, and only by falling does he learn to walk. But if we all remain in swaddling-clothes, who is to wrap us in them? If we all remain in the cradle, who is to rock us? If we are all prisoners, who is the prison warder?[83]

While textual evidence suggests that Marx would agree, in a qualified way, with Kant's claim that the 'human being is capable of and requires education in the form of both instruction and discipline', Marx's idea of the 'estrangement' that shapes our development from nature into human beings (e.g., 'the strict discipline of capital to which successive generations have been subjected') avoids the problem of needing an 'educator' in the Kantian or Leninist sense of the term.[84]

With this in mind, Löwy's *Theory of Revolution* contains awkward and inconsistent formulations about the self-emancipation of the proletariat and the role of a vanguard for consolidating this self-activity into a successful revolutionary 'moment'. One of the many examples of this is his claim that the 'communist's' goal consists in 'helping the proletariat to find, through its own historical prac-

---

master ... But where does he find such a master? In no place other than in the human species. But such a master is just as much an animal in need of a master ... This task is thus the most difficult of all. Indeed, its perfect solution is impossible: nothing entirely straight can be fashioned from the crooked wood of which humankind is made' (Kant 2006, p. 9). Cf. Schiller's reflection on an analogous paradox of human development: 'Theoretical culture should engender practical culture, while practical culture is still the condition of theoretical culture? All improvement in the domain of politics should derive from the refinement of character – but how can character be refined under the influence of a barbaric state order?' (Schiller 2016, p. 29).

83   MECW 4, p. 153.
84   Kant 2006, pp. 166–7; MECW 28, p. 250. Draper describes the problem thus: 'It was Owen's type of materialism which *one-sidedly* emphasized that men are the products of their environmental circumstances and upbringing, and which concluded that to change men for the better, one had to change the environmental circumstances and upbringing. Marx's thesis cuts straight to the heart of the difficulty in this reasoning: *who* are the men who are going to operate this change? These men apparently stand exempt from the very law they enunciate; for they, who are also the product of their environmental conditioning, are going to act to change the world which conditioned them' (Draper 1971, p. 95).

tice, the path of communist revolution', but the Party 'cannot set itself above the masses and "make the revolution" in their place'.[85] This inconsistency is even present in a single sentence in which Löwy claims that Marx's activity during the 1846–48 period 'had a definite aim: to form a communist vanguard freed from utopian socialism and the "true," conspiratorial, or "sentimental" varieties, and to create, on the international scale, but first of all in Germany, a revolutionary and "scientific" Communist Party which must be theoretically coherent, yet not become a sect cut off from the proletarian masses'.[86] Even though Löwy claimed that Marx's writing contains the idea of the 'self-liberation of the working class through communist revolution' and 'self-education of the proletariat through its own revolutionary practice' – i.e., that 'in the course of its struggle against the existing state of affairs, the proletariat transforms itself, develops its consciousness, and becomes capable of building a new society' – he overemphasised the significance of Marx's vanguardist tendencies and presented him as a vanguardist of the Leninist variety.[87] And it makes no difference if we point out, as Löwy did, that Marx may have had some vanguardist tendencies in a relatively early period, because his theory of 'Scientific socialism' is anti-vanguardist in principle.[88] What he chose to emphasise about his experience of revolutionary social movements is of greater importance for our understanding of his idea of the role of revolutionary theorists like himself and the possible role of any kind of vanguard group. His account of the role of the International in the affairs of the Paris Commune is informative in this instance:

> The insurrection in Paris was made by the workmen of Paris. The ablest of the workmen must necessarily have been its leaders and administrators; but the ablest of the workmen happen also to be members of the International Association. Yet the Association as such may be in no way responsible for their action.[89]

---

85   Lowy 2005, pp. 136–7.
86   Lowy 2005, p. 120.
87   Lowy 2005, p. 106.
88   It is possible that Marx had some vanguardist tendencies later on as well. In 1870 he claimed that the 'The English have all the *material* necessary for the social revolution. What they lack is the *spirit of generalisation and revolutionary ardour*. It is only the General Council that can provide them with this, that can thus accelerate the truly revolutionary movement in this country, and consequently *everywhere*' (MECW 21, p. 87).
89   MECW 22, p. 601. 'The Association does not dictate the form of political movements', he claimed, 'it only requires a pledge as to their end' (MECW 22, p. 602).

No iteration of vanguardist politics, including any idea of a vanguard that is somehow connected to the working class, can escape inconsistency with Marx's 'Scientific socialism'. According to him this term was 'used only in contrast to Utopian socialism which wishes to foist new illusions onto the people instead of confining its scientific investigations to the social movement created by the people itself'.[90] This also applies to vanguardists because as an 'advanced layer' they bring in knowledge about the 'social movement' that is not 'created by the people itself'. As Engels claimed,

> Marx ... entirely trusted to the intellectual development of the working class, which was sure to result from combined action and mutual discussion. The very events and vicissitudes of the struggle against capital, the defeats even more than the victories, could not help bringing home to men's minds the insufficiency of their various favourite nostrums, and preparing the way for a more complete insight into the true conditions of working-class emancipation. And Marx was right.[91]

Whether he was right or wrong, Marx was clear about his belief that members of the working class

> know that in order to work out their own emancipation, and along with it that higher form to which present society is irresistibly tending by its own economical agencies, they will have to pass through long struggles, through a series of historic processes, transforming circumstances and men. They have no ideals to realize, but to set free the elements of the new society with which old collapsing bourgeois society itself is pregnant. In the full consciousness of their historic mission, and with the heroic resolve to act up to it ...[92]

Of course, Marx was not opposed to the organisation of a revolutionary political party.[93] However, in his view such activity presupposes that 'a class in

---

90   MECW 24, p. 520.

91   MECW 26, p. 515. Cf. Marx's claim that 'the material and intellectual elements' for the 'collective form' of control of the means of production 'are shaped by the very development of capitalist society' (MECW 24, p. 340).

92   MECW 22, pp. 335–6. As Draper put it, 'against all varieties of socialism and reform which looked on the working masses in the accusative case ("we will emancipate *them*"), Marx developed the principle of the self-emancipation of the working class' (Draper 1977, p. 216).

93   He claimed that 'even under the most favourable political conditions all serious success

which the revolutionary interests of society are concentrated' has developed and 'finds the content and the material for its revolutionary activity directly in its own situation: foes to be laid low; measures dictated by the needs of the struggle to be taken', and he thought that 'the consequences of its own deeds drive it on'.[94]

Marx maintained that the presence of vanguard sects is unavoidable in the early, immature phases of revolutionary struggle when 'the working class is not yet ripe for an independent historical movement'.[95] He claimed that when the working class 'has not yet developed sufficiently to act as a class', independent theoreticians 'criticise social antagonisms and suggest fantastic solutions thereof, which the mass of workers is left to accept, preach and put into practice'.[96] For the sake of clarity it is worth quoting Marx at length:

> All the socialist founders of sects belong to a period in which the working classes themselves were neither sufficiently trained and organized by the march of capitalist society itself to enter as historical agents upon the world's stage, nor were the material conditions of their emancipation sufficiently matured in the old world itself ... The utopian founders of sects ... found neither in society itself the material conditions of its transformation, nor in the working class the organized power and the conscience of the movement. They tried to compensate for the historical conditions of the movement by phantastic pictures and plans of a new society in whose propaganda they saw the true means of salvation.[97] From the moment the

---

of the proletariat depends upon an organization that unites and concentrates its forces' (MECW 21, p. 17).

94   MECW 10, p. 56. He claimed that 'Our party can come to power only when the conditions allow it to put *its own* views into practice' (MECW 10, p. 628). This is consistent with Avineri's claim that 'Even during 1857–8, when he envisaged a possible radicalization that might lead to revolution, Marx did not try to prepare for it by forming or joining a revolutionary group. Quite the contrary: when he saw the gathering storm, he immersed himself with additional intensity in his economic studies, so that his Political Economy would be ready once the revolution broke out' (Avineri 1968, p. 257).

95   MECW 44, p. 252. He maintained that 'sects are justified (historically)' in such instances and that the 'development of socialist sectarianism and that of the real labour movement always stand in indirect proportion to each other' (MECW 44, p. 252).

96   MECW 23, p. 106.

97   Engels claimed that the 'the means of getting rid of the incongruities [of the capitalist system] that have been brought to light must also be present, in a more or less developed condition, within the changed modes of production themselves. These means are not to be *invented*, spun out of the head, but *discovered* with the aid of the head in the existing material facts of production' (MECW 25, p. 255). This idea was already essentially present

workingmen class movement became real, the phantastic utopias evanesced, not because the working class had given up the end aimed at by these utopians, but because they had found the real means to realize them, and in their place came a real insight into the historic conditions of the movement and a more and more gathering force of the military organization of the working class.[98]

If there is a single statement that best sums up Marx's idea of the role of who he called 'the theoreticians of the proletarian class', it is his claim that as 'history moves forward' and 'the struggle of the proletariat assumes clearer outlines', these theoreticians 'have only to take note of what is happening before their eyes and to become its mouthpiece'.[99] Thus in his view the theoretician's voice has been 'called forth' by the situation 'from which emanates the consciousness of the necessity of a fundamental revolution, the communist consciousness'.[100] This outlook is yet another indication of the significance of Hegel's influence on Marx's revolutionary theory and orientation. In the midst of a discussion on 'the subject of *issuing instructions* on how the world ought to be', Hegel notoriously claimed that 'philosophy, at any rate, always comes too late to perform this function. As the *thought* of the world, it appears only at a time when actuality has gone through its formative process and attained its completed state'.[101] Marx not only carried out this approach in his theoretical work, he also affirmed it in his political practice. While he was involved with the First International Workingmen's Association he put forward a program which was limited to presenting 'a general outline of the proletarian movement', and which left 'its theoretical elaboration to be guided by the needs of the practical struggle and the exchange of ideas in the sections'.[102] Thus while Marx was indeed a revolutionary intellectual who sought to engage with the working-class movement,

---

in the *Manifesto*: 'When people speak of ideas that revolutionize society, they do but express the fact, that within the old society, the elements of a new one have been created' (MECW 6, p. 503).

98   MECW 22, pp. 499–500.

99   MECW 6, p. 177. Cf. McCarney's claim that for 'Hegel and Marx ... what is required of the dialectical thinker is not to moralise the immanent movement of reason and of reality but to surrender to it and seek to articulate it, to "become its mouthpiece"' (McCarney 2000, p. 68).

100   MECW 5, p. 52. In his 1843 'Introduction' to his critique of Hegel's *Philosophy of Right* he claimed that 'Theory can be realised in a people only insofar as it is the realisation of the needs of that people' (MECW 3, p. 183).

101   Hegel 1991, p. 23.

102   MECW 22, p. 107.

his activity also serves as an example of the limits to interventions in social movements by revolutionary theorists. After all, his interventions in the First International Workingmen's Association (which he was invited to participate in) could not keep it from disintegrating.

Ultimately it is inconsistent to maintain that 'the masses' of working people will liberate themselves but that they also need direction – on how to think and act, and therefore how to feel, will, etc. – from the superior intellects of a vanguard in order to do so. Löwy, for example, claimed that Marx thought that 'the proletariat tends towards the totality through its practice of the class struggle, thanks to the role of *mediation*, which is played by its communist vanguard', whereby the vanguard 'is the *instrument* of the masses for coming to consciousness and taking revolutionary action. Its role is not to act in place or "above" the working class but to *guide* the latter towards the path of its self-liberation, towards the communist "mass" revolution'.[103] A similar inconsistency is found in Guido Starosta's book *Marx's Capital, Method and Revolutionary Subjectivity* which presents an opportunity to look closer at this significant interpretive problem and refocus the analysis of Marx's idea of revolutionary subjectivity.

Starosta claims that without 'a detailed positive account of the laws of motion of alienated labour and the determinations of the political action of the workers as personifications of the former, no significant guide to action can be drawn from revolutionary theory' because the 'scientific critique of capital' would be 'bound to remain external and thus impotent to fully unite with practice'.[104] This diverges considerably from Marx's position. First of all, Marx's work indicates that he was not concerned with uniting 'theory' and 'practice' but instead presupposed that they were already in unity. Indeed, his work suggests that a theory of 'the political action of the workers' entails that they are already engaged in the process of transcending capitalism and thus corresponds to the development of revolutionary subjectivity to the extent required for participating in the intersubjective experience that the theory reflects. Starosta even argues that 'dialectical cognition must provide the necessity of the transformative action of the workers in the *totality* of its determinations', i.e., 'all the determinations involved in the different forms of political action of the workers necessary for its production as fully conscious revolutionary action'.[105] Any

---

103 Löwy 2005, p. 137.
104 Starosta 2016, p. 45. Starosta's position on this question is inconsistent because he also claims that 'science as practical criticism does not need to be applied to or guide an externally conceived practice' (Starosta 2016, p. 54).
105 Starosta 2016, pp. 106–7. He wrote about 'the need to grasp the specific qualitative determ-

such 'necessity' is what Marx sought to comprehend in a clear and comprehensive way within the phenomena of the workers' already existing 'revolutionary practice'.

To his credit, Starosta recognised the compulsion to 'associate' in capitalism
as well as the fact that Marx saw 'associations as a necessary "training ground"
for the revolutionary struggle', but he did not take into account that it leads to
the development of 'needs' (e.g. the 'need for society') and a state of character
that cannot be imparted by the guidance of another, as well as the fact that 'the
necessity of a fundamental revolution' is connected to this 'inner necessity'.[106]
In accordance with Marx's Aristotelianism, the transformation of the 'mental'
and 'practical senses' associated with our 'inner world' can be conceived of as
coinciding with the development of a degree of both moral virtue and 'practical
judgement'. Aristotle defined the latter as 'concerned with things that are just
and beautiful and good for a human being' and claimed that 'we are no more
able to perform these actions by knowing about them, if indeed the virtues
are active conditions of the soul', because 'active states come into being from
being at work in similar ways'.[107] On the premises of this Aristotelianism, even
if a vanguard asked us to imagine 'the capitalist form of society to be abolished
and society organised as a conscious and planned association', their prompt is
not enough to get us to understand it, desire its existence, and act to bring it
about, even if we were also given directions for how to achieve it.[108]

In the *Manifesto*, Marx and Engels attempted to make it clear that the 'theoretical conclusions of the Communists are in no way based on ideas or principles that have been invented, or discovered, by this or that would-be universal
reformer. They merely express, in general terms, actual relations springing from
an existing class struggle, from a historical movement going on under our very
eyes'.[109] Starosta, on the contrary, claimed that 'what was at stake in [Marx's]
investigation was the conscious organization, i.e., the discovery of the social
necessity, of the political action of the working class', and that Marx attempted
to provide 'scientific grounds for his political position concerning the content
and form of proletarian action antagonistic to capital'.[110] With the *Manifesto*

---

ination immanent in each of the forms of the class struggle in order to discover their
necessity' (Starosta 2016, p. 114).

106   Starosta 2016, p. 111.
107   Aristotle 2002, pp. 115; 23.
108   MECW 37, p. 654.
109   MECW 6, p. 498.
110   Starosta 2016, pp. 100–1. Cf. Lenin: 'We must take upon ourselves the task of organizing a
      universal political struggle under the leadership of *our Party* in such a manner as to obtain
      all the support possible ... for the struggle and for our Party' (Lenin 1943, p. 117).

Marx intended to articulately vocalise the 'necessity' of the 'real' needs of the revolutionary working-class movement, i.e., of the workers that were 'already *conscious*' of their 'historic task' and were 'constantly working to develop that consciousness into complete clarity'.[111] Marx was contributing to the 'clarity' of the worker's consciousness of their 'historic task' on the premises that the working class had been 'sufficiently trained and organized by the march of capitalist society itself to enter as historical agents upon the world's stage'. On these premises it makes sense to give a speech or write a pamphlet about what he considered 'real insight into the historic conditions of the movement' because the working class itself is 'the organized power and the conscience of the movement'. From the perspective presented in Starosta's work it is as if Marx was writing *Capital* so that those of us who cannot engage in 'dialectical research' can come 'to know what concrete form our action should take in order to achieve the willed transformation of the world'.[112] Evidence suggests, however, that in Marx's view it is only in the wake of the development of requisite 'subjective and objective conditions' engendered through our 'estranged' activity and 'revolutionary practice' that we discover for ourselves the necessity of our revolutionary action.[113]

At the end of Starosta's book we are told that it is the task of 'communist intellectual labourers' to provide the 'form of political action that could mediate the immediate needs of the workers with the "historical interests of the proletariat as a whole."'[114] In the vanguardist view, revolutionary subjects are in need of a perspective beyond theirs 'in order to account for the necessity of the practical abolition of alienated life' – instead of being able to think, feel,

---

111 MECW 4, p. 37. It is evident that Marx thought sections of the workers of the world were 'already conscious'. Consider, for instance, his view of the revolt of the Silesian textile workers in 1844. He claimed that the 'The Silesian uprising *begins* precisely with what the French and English workers' uprisings *end*, with consciousness of the nature of the proletariat. The action itself bears the stamp of this *superior* character. Not only machines, these rivals of the workers, are destroyed, but also *ledgers*, the titles to property. And while all other movements were aimed primarily only against the *owner of the industrial enterprise*, the visible enemy, this movement is at the same time directed against the banker, the hidden enemy. Finally, not a single English workers' uprising was carried out with such courage, thought and endurance' (MECW 3, p. 201).

112 Starosta 2016, pp. 189–9. According to Starosta, 'Dialectical research must ... analytically apprehend all relevant social forms and synthetically reproduce the "inner connections" leading to the constitution of the political action of wage labourers as the form taken by the revolutionary transformation of the historical mode of existence of the human life-process' (Starosta 2013, p. 234).

113 MECW 28, p. 530.

114 Starosta 2016, pp. 315–6.

will and act in a way that is necessary for self-emancipation.[115] Textual evidence suggests that Marx had come across this kind of perspective. He wrote that

> the sole task of one who thinks and loves the truth consisted not in playing the role of *schoolmaster* in relation to this event, but instead in studying its *specific* character. This, of course, requires some scientific insight and some love of mankind, whereas for the other operation a glib phraseology, impregnated with empty love of oneself, is quite enough.[116]

Rather than attempting to 'unleash a revolutionary thunderbolt', Marx was occupied with an 'objective analysis of the situation and the movement' for those who are able to recognise them as such.[117] In this way he acted as a mouthpiece for a clarified and unified voice of the revolutionary working class. He played the role of an 'educator' only as part of a broader social process of development through which individuals are fitted for revolutionary practice.[118] Formal education alone, such as attempting to teach revolutionary theory or 'Scientific Socialism', is not edifying to the extent required for the kind of transformation that a revolution entails.

---

115   Starosta 2016, p. 196.

116   MECW 3, p. 202. Fisher's analysis of depression as 'a pathology of the left' suggests that some particularly fanatic vanguardist attitudes might be tied, paradoxically, to a depressiveness arising in conditions in which the working-class movement is contracting and the left is largely defeated, whereby revolutionary fanaticism is a kind of manic defense which exaggerates positive prospects for revolution (Fisher 2018, p. 522). The association of Left vanguardism with this kind of underlying depressiveness is also consistent with Fisher's claim that it is 'a pathology of responsibility: you feel intensely responsible for the state you're in' (Fisher 2018, p. 667).

117   MECW 42, p. 485. Compare this approach to the one espoused by Lenin: 'Why is it that the Russian workers as yet display so little revolutionary activity in connection with the brutal way in which the police maltreat the people, in connection with the persecution of the most innocent cultural enterprises, etc.? ... We must blame ourselves, our remoteness from the mass movement; we must blame ourselves for being unable as yet to organize a sufficiently wide, striking and rapid exposure of these despicable outrages. When we do that (and we must and can do it), the most backward worker will understand, *or will feel*, that the students and religious sects, the muzhiks and the authors are being abused and outraged by the very same dark forces that are oppressing and crushing him at every step of his life, and, feeling that, he himself will be filled with an irresistible desire to respond to these things ... As yet we have done very little, almost nothing, to *hurl* universal and fresh exposures among the masses of the workers' (Lenin 1943, pp. 105–6).

118   Cf. Marx's claim that society 'has in truth first to create for itself the revolutionary point of departure, the situation, the relations, the conditions under which alone modern revolution becomes serious' (MECW 11, p. 106).

Instead of offering mere dictates for action, Marx attempted to contribute his theoretical work to our 'combined action and mutual discussion' through which we attain a kind of 'reconciliation' with the world. It is a form of 'reconciliation' in the sense that our initial, reflexive discontent born of struggle and alienation is transformed from the negative experience of suffering into a positive affirmation of emancipatory thought and will. This idea of 'reconciliation' is akin to the idea in Hegel's philosophy. According to Michael Hardimon, Hegel sought 'to enable his contemporaries to overcome their alienation from this world by providing them with a philosophical theory that will reveal its true nature'.[119] He claims that Marx also offered a vision of 'reconciliation', and that 'if we generalize the idea of the project of reconciliation, we can think of Hegel and Marx as being engaged in different forms of the same basic enterprise'.[120] As he put it,

> Marx is engaged in the 'political' project of reconciliation and Hegel is engaged in the 'philosophical' project of reconciliation. The political project gets its start from the proposition that the modern social world is not a home. It seeks to secure the objective conditions of reconciliation by transforming the central social institutions so as to make them worthy of reconciliation. Instead of seeking to reconcile people to the social world directly, it seeks to change the social world so as to make it worthy of reconciliation. It is 'political' in that it seeks to make reconciliation possible through political change.[121]

On Marx's premises, finding resonance with the theoretical expression of a blossoming mass movement motivated by the aim of 'universal human emancipation' requires a corresponding degree of our ethical 'powers'. But he did not elaborate a consistent and realistic vision of how these capacities will develop amid the 'estranged' social relations of capitalist society – and vanguardism is not the answer to the problem of revolutionary subjectivity. In a letter to Arnold Ruge in 1843, Marx adamantly maintained that

> we do not confront the world in a doctrinaire way with a new principle: Here is the truth, kneel down before it! We develop new principles for the world out of the world's own principles. We do not say to the world: Cease

---

119   Hardimon 1992, p. 165.
120   Hardimon 1992, p. 171.
121   Ibid.

> your struggles, they are foolish; we will give you the true slogan of struggle.
> We merely show the world what it is really fighting for.[122]

This statement is an indication of his confidence that the subjectivity of the working class was positioned to undergo a process of revolutionary maturation. And yet in the same piece he also claimed that 'consciousness is something that [the world] *has to* acquire, even if it does not want to'.[123] This could be misread as suggesting that revolutionary theorists are responsible for reforming the consciousnesses of others, in which case it would not be consistent with the previous statement. He meant, rather, that such awareness is required to be free, and the context in which it was uttered implies that he thought there is a tendency to resist what he considered a 'reform of consciousness'. But Marx's position does not lead to fatalistic resignation in the absence of a robust revolutionary movement. The aim of a revolutionary theorist of this sort would remain the attainment of insight into the peculiar character of their age and its struggles for the sake of human emancipation. On Marx's premises this would involve insight into human subjectivity alongside analysis of socioproductive life, but he neglected to put it into adequate relief. For those who seek to practice social philosophy on similar premises, a foray into the subjective dimension of human life activity – a frontier not beyond the bounds of Marx's social philosophy but one which he did not sufficiently explore in his writing – is integral for comprehending the vicissitudes of the class struggle and the resistance to a 'reform of consciousness'.

---

122   MECW 3, p. 144.
123   Ibid.

CHAPTER 6

'Show the World What It Is Really Fighting for': Prospect for a Psychosocial Theory of 'Estranged' Political Struggle

Death and love are the myth of negative dialectic, for dialectic is the inner, simple light, the piercing eye of love, the inner soul which is not crushed by the body of material division, the inner abode of the spirit. Thus the myth of it is love, but dialectic is also the torrent which smashes the many and their bounds, which tears down the independent forms, sinking everything in the one sea of eternity. The myth of it is therefore death.

Thus dialectic is death, but at the same time the vehicle of vitality, the efflorescence in the gardens of the spirit, the foaming in the bubbling goblet of the tiny seeds out of which the flower of the single flame of the spirit bursts forth.

MARX[1]

∴

1 'Estrangement' and the Human 'Soul'

Marx's work suggests that comprehending the world of human activity for the sake of 'universal human emancipation' requires an exploration of subjectivity as a fundamental determinant of social and political phenomena. His desire to 'show the world what it is really fighting for' brings this problem into focus. However, Marx left his thoughts about human subjectivity and the psychological dimension of life undeveloped, and he ultimately lacked 'a satisfactory psychology' from which to understand these ideas in a more elaborate or systematic form.[2] But this is not the result of an 'antipathy to psychology'.[3] According to Reich,

---

1 MECW 1, p. 498.
2 Fromm 1970, p. 155. Fromm maintained that Marx's work contained 'a *dynamic psychology*' nonetheless (Fromm 1970, p. 64).

for Marx it is the living, productive man, with his psychic and physical disposition, who is the first presupposition of history and of politics. The character structure of active man, the so-called "subjective factor of history" in Marx's sense, remained uninvestigated because Marx was a sociologist and not a psychologist, and because at that time scientific psychology did not exist.[4]

However, Marx's thoughts about the human 'soul', i.e., his nascent reflections on mental and emotional life and the nature of our mind in general, are substantial enough to warrant serious attention.

His concept of 'estrangement' is a fitting starting point for unravelling central elements of his incipient psychology and theory of mind. He depicts 'estrangement' as rooted in us, our 'inner world', but inexorably related to 'objective' social life nonetheless. Although it is a complex concept with various features, 'estrangement' can be described as a process whereby humanity's powers, as a collectivity of individual subjects, take on a controlling and even hostile existence, and are experienced as if they are 'independent not only of isolated individuals but even all of them together'.[5] Marx's idea of 'the Fetishism which attaches itself to the products of labour, so soon as they are produced as commodities' is a pertinent example.[6] At the root of this is the 'estranged' social power of humanity. In *Capital* he summarises our 'estrangement' in the capitalist mode of production by claiming that our 'own social action' has for us 'the form of the action of objects, which rule the producers instead of being ruled by them'.[7] This involves an 'inverted consciousness' because of our actually 'inverted' social life activity. The inversion is summed up in his claim that a 'commodity is ... a mysterious thing, simply because in it the social character of [human] labour appears to [us] as an objective character stamped upon the product of labour'.[8]

Insofar as Marx thought that we live in conditions which 'require illusions', he was implicating a decisive subjective component in the determination of this social life even though he did not extensively elaborate it. A key instance in which Marx depicted the 'mystical consciousness' of 'estrangement' is his claim that the 'social relation between' human beings takes the 'fantastic form

---

3   Wolfenstein 1993, p. 390.
4   Reich 1980, p. 25.
5   MECW 5, p. 245.
6   MECW 35, p. 83.
7   MECW 35, p. 85.
8   MECW 35, pp. 82–3.

of a relation between things'.[9] Even though it is clearly linked to a definite form of sociomaterial life practice, his description of it as 'fantastic' distinguishes it as fundamentally psychological in nature despite the fact that it is connected to 'material' practice. Consider also, for instance, his claim that the 'transposition of the social productive powers of labour into material attributes of capital is so strongly rooted in people's minds that the advantages of machinery, the application of science, inventions, etc., in this *alienated* form are conceived of as the *necessary* form, and therefore all these things are regarded as *attributes of capital*'.[10] Indeed, he thought that a fundamental aspect of 'the basis' for this is 'the form in which the matter appears on the basis of capitalist production, and therefore also in the consciousness of those whose ideas are confined within that mode of production'.[11]

The psychological aspect of the concept 'estrangement' is implicated in a paradox that arises at this point in Marx's theory; namely, that throughout the process of 'estrangement' our consciousness can be characterised as 'illusory' (or 'mystical') even though it arises from the 'actual life process'. As he claimed, 'the labourer looks at the social nature of his labour, at its combination with the labour of others for a common purpose, as he would at an alien power' because 'the condition of realising this combination is alien property'.[12] In his view, when the 'material conditions necessary for the realisation of labour are therefore themselves *alienated* from the worker' they 'appear' as '*fetishes* endowed with a will and a soul of their own'.[13] He did not attempt to rectify the inversion by saying that the apparently ensouled commodity cannot be ensouled because there is no 'soul' whatsoever. He thought, rather, that psychological processes are a fundamental basis for this inversion. It is the human 'soul' that gives life to the activity of capital. After all, the capitalist's 'soul is the soul of capital', and the workers find themselves confronted by the capital 'which lives in the person of the capitalist'.[14] The capitalist is 'capital personified' because their 'soul' is such that this definite form of life activity satisfies an 'inner necessity' of theirs, such as greed.[15] Insofar as it is our 'soul' that is alienated and projected onto capital in this way, 'estrangement' is a kind of psychosocial phenomenon.

---

9   MECW 35, p. 83.
10   MECW 34, p. 461.
11   Ibid.
12   MECW 37, p. 89.
13   MECW 34, p. 411.
14   MECW 35, p. 241; MECW 34, p. 458. Hence Marx speaks of 'capital' itself as having a '*compulsion to perform surplus-labour*' and an 'innate urge to shorten the necessary labour-time' (MECW 32, p. 41).
15   MECW 3, p. 304. Marx claimed that every person under the rule of capitalist private prop-

His writing about this also touches other aspects of the mental dimension of this process. He claimed that when the product of labour that we experience with our senses becomes a commodity it 'is changed into something transcendent'.[16] In doing so he equated a feature of our social activity with that which is 'imperceptible by the senses', which is a manifestation of the human mind.[17] Thus he could emphasise that consciousness is 'practical' but also focus on it as an *experience*. It is within consciousness that the world appears to us, whether real or illusory, such as this 'fantastic form' of life. Marx's approach to the experience of the 'mystical consciousness' of 'estrangement' is akin to the phenomenological method displayed in Husserl's work. In the process of analysis, Marx explored an embryonic form of what Husserl elaborated as 'intentionality'. Husserl claimed that

> when we are fully engaged in conscious activity, we focus exclusively on the specific thing, thoughts, values, goals, or means involved but not on the psychical experience as such, in which these things are known *as* such. Only reflection reveals this to us. Through reflection, instead of grasping simply the matter straight out – the values, goals, and instrumentalities – we grasp the corresponding subjective experiences in which we become "conscious" of them, in which (in the broadest sense) they "appear." For this reason, they are called "phenomena," and their most general essential character is to exist as the "consciousness-of" or "appearance-of" the specific things, thoughts (judged states of affairs, grounds, conclusions), plans, decisions, hopes, and so forth.[18]

It was this kind of 'reflection' that Marx intimated to Ruge when he said he was starting out 'from any form of theoretical and practical consciousness' – i.e., taking 'the forms *peculiar* to existing reality' as his 'point of departure' – and he followed through with this in a more developed form in *Capital*. This indicates that the incipient psychology in Marx's social philosophy has an affinity to Husserl's 'phenomenological psychology'.[19] For Husserl, however, this psy-

---

erty 'tries to establish over the other an *alien power*, so as thereby to find satisfaction of his own selfish need' (MECW 3, p. 306).

16   MECW 35, p. 82.

17   MECW 35, p. 83.

18   Husserl 1999, p. 323.

19   Husserl wrote that if the 'realm of what we call "phenomena" proves to be the possible field for a pure psychological discipline related exclusively to phenomena, we can understand the designation of it as *phenomenological psychology*' (Ibid.).

chology 'simply knows nothing other than the subjective',[20] whereas Marx's concentration on social life activity is what foremost shaped the various nebulous expressions of his incipient psychology and theory of mind. The consciousness being reflected on is fundamentally co-determined by the 'material life-process'. As Marx wrote, the 'phantoms formed in the brains of men ... necessarily, sublimates of their material life-process, which is empirically verifiable and bound to material premises ... It is not consciousness that determines life, but life that determines consciousness'.[21] If consciousness 'can never be anything else except conscious being, and the being of men is their actual life-process', the experience of 'estrangement' is a kind of 'irrational' activity.[22] As Marx claimed, the

> irrational forms in which certain economic relationships appear and assert themselves in practice does not concern the active agents of these relations in their everyday life. And since they are accustomed to move about in such relations, they find nothing strange therein. A complete contradiction offers not the least mystery to them. They feel as much at home as a fish in water among manifestations which are separated from their internal connections and absurd when isolated by themselves.[23]

On Marx's premises, a focus on 'material' practice is essential for comprehending such 'irrational' activity and the 'irrational' forms of consciousness connected to it. In the context of his 'materialist conception of history', the satisfaction of 'natural necessity' is a fundamental feature of humanity's 'material' life practice.

2   The Confluence and Divergence of Freud's Psychoanalytic Theory and Marx's 'Materialist Conception of History' on Human Development

Marx's 'materialist conception of history' is premised on the fact that human beings are part of a natural 'life process'. After all, he thought that 'the sphere

---

20   Cf. his idea of a 'scientifically rigorous form of a psychology purely of inner experience' in his article 'Phenomenological Psychology and Transcendental Phenomenology' (Husserl 1999, p. 328).
21   MECW 5, pp. 36–7.
22   MECW 5, p. 36.
23   MECW 37, pp. 765–6.

of material production' is 'the real social life process'.[24] 'Life' is an onto-cosmological principle for Marx and as such it is ultimately affirmed in everything that exists. He claimed, for instance, that 'in history, as in nature, putrefaction is the laboratory of life'.[25] This entails that even so-called inorganic matter is an active moment in the pulsing process of effervescent life, the creative force animating the interconnected totality of all being. 'Reason' may 'govern the world', but the force of 'Eros' also has a hand in the cosmos.[26]

The urge to life, to survive, drives us to modify our environment and ourselves in the process. Marx's writing suggests that 'estrangement' arises through our struggles around the social satisfaction of bio-physical needs determined by a process of natural evolution and further modified throughout history. By tying 'estrangement' to the 'dialectic of negativity' in the labour process, he depicts it as a necessary phase in the movement whereby we raise ourselves 'above the rank of animals'.[27] But he also maintained that

> [*Humanity*] is directly a *natural being*. As a natural being and as a living natural being [we are] on the one hand endowed with *natural powers, vital powers* – [we are] an *active* natural being. These forces exist in [us] as tendencies and abilities – as *instincts*.[28]

Thus even though we have developed to a level of mentality beyond our initial animal nature and have lived in civilisations for millennia, the state of nature is not simply a thing of the past because we are still partly animals with bodies that are driven in part by bio-physical, instinctual forces. Marx's depiction of this aspect of the complex 'inner world' of the human being indicates that he understood it as an element of the 'soul' which, together with our higher mental faculties, is the subjective basis of the 'perceptibly existing human *psychology*' in our life activity.[29]

Freud's psychoanalytic theory complements Marx's perspective on the historical transformation of our 'natural' needs and desires through life activity

---

24   MECW 35, p. 398.

25   Marx 1965, p. 995.

26   'We have to ask', Whitehead mused, 'whether nature does not contain within itself a tendency to be in tune, an Eros urging towards perfection' (Whitehead 1967, p. 251).

27   MECW 35, p. 513.

28   MECW 3, p. 336.

29   MECW 3, p. 302. Cf. Fromm's claim that the 'realm of human drives is a natural force which, like other natural forces ... is an immediate part of the substructure of the social process. Knowledge of this force, then, is necessary for a complete understanding of the social process' (Fromm 1970, p. 157).

which unavoidably involves the socioproductive satisfaction of 'natural necessity'. Even though their thinking diverges in key ways, a comparative analysis of
their writing helps to illuminate Marx's incipient psychology. Freud thought
that 'civilisation is to a large extent being constantly created anew' because
'each individual who makes a fresh entry into human society repeats' the 'sac-
rifice of instinctual satisfaction for the benefit of the whole community'.[30] He
described this process as 'frustration by reality' under 'the pressure of vital
needs – Necessity', and the role it plays in his theory of the human psyche is
a major point of intersection with the foundational premises of Marx's historical materialism.[31] According to Marx the 'first premise of all human existence'
and 'all history' is the 'production of the means to satisfy' the 'needs' of 'material life' (for example, 'eating and drinking, housing, clothing', and so on).[32] He
claims that this is 'a fundamental condition of all history, which today, as thou-
sands of years ago, must daily and hourly be fulfilled merely in order to sustain
human life'.[33] The satisfaction of these 'material' needs leads to the development of new needs. Another premise is that human beings must 'propagate
their kind' which puts focus on 'the relation between man and women, parents
and children, the family'.[34] These are universal features of human existence

---

30   Freud 1966, p. 27. According to Hegel, 'constraint put upon impulse, desire' and the 'mere
      brute emotions and rude instincts', as well as the 'limitation' of 'premeditated self-will of
      caprice and passion', is 'the indispensable proviso of emancipation' because the 'state of
      Nature' is 'predominantly that of injustice and violence, of untamed natural impulses, of
      inhuman deeds and feelings' (Hegel 1956, p. 41). Cf. Freud's claim that for 'incalculable
      ages mankind has been passing through a process of evolution of culture. (Some people, I
      know, prefer to use the term "civilisation.") We owe to that process the best of what we have
      become, as well as a good part of what we suffer from ... The process is perhaps compar-
      able to the domestication of certain species of animals and it is undoubtedly accompanied
      by physical alterations; but we are still unfamiliar with the notion that the evolution of
      civilisation is an organic process of this kind. The psychical modifications that go along
      with the process of civilisation are striking and unambiguous. They consist in a progress-
      ive displacement of instinctual aims and a restriction of instinctual impulses. Sensations
      which were pleasurable to our ancestors have become indifferent or even intolerable to
      ourselves; there are organic grounds for the changes in our ethical and aesthetic ideals.
      Of the psychological characteristics of civilisation two appear to be the most important: a
      strengthening of the intellect, which is beginning to govern instinctual life, and an intern-
      alisation of the aggressive impulses, with all its consequent advantages and perils' (Freud
      n.d.).
31   Freud 1966, p. 441. According to Freud 'it is a characteristic feature of the libido that it
      struggles against submitting to the reality of the universe – to Ananke' (Freud 1966, p. 534).
32   MECW 5, pp. 41–2.
33   MECW 5, p. 42.
34   MECW, 5, pp. 42–3.

which have existed 'since the dawn of history' and 'still assert themselves' today even though they undergo historical transformation.[35] In other words, they are determined by natural processes and modified further through social and historical ones.

In an analogous way, Freud thought that the 'motive of human society is in the last resort an economic one', and 'since [society] does not possess enough provisions to keep its members alive unless they work, it must restrict the number of its members and divert their energies from sexual activity to work. It is faced, in short, by the eternal, primaeval exigencies of life, which are with us to this day'.[36] From the perspective of psychoanalytic theory, the sociohistorical alteration of our natural 'drives' entails that our instincts have become sublimated or repressed but still operative in our unconscious and redirected.[37] To put Freud's view briefly, if the struggle to satisfy the portion of 'natural necessity' connected to the bestial-instinctual part of our psyche becomes overwhelming, it leads to psychical repression with the consequence that our behaviour becomes unconsciously influenced by these reoriented drives (the source of which is obscured by the fundamental structure and functioning of the psyche itself). Freud maintained that what psychoanalysis 'aims at and achieves is nothing other than the uncovering of what is unconscious in mental life', and thus freedom requires that we become conscious of the mysterious, alien power of our 'unconscious'.[38] Marx did not conceive of an idea like Freud's 'unconscious' but the record of his thought about our *'instincts'* – which are a kind of 'natural necessity' – are amenable to linking with Freud's psychoanalytic theory.[39] The role of the 'unconscious' in Freud's conception of psychical life is comparable with Marx's idea of 'estrangement' specifically in relation to the notion that our own activity is 'alienated' and driven from an unintelligible

---

35   MECW 5, p. 43.

36   Freud 1966, p. 386.

37   'We believe', Freud wrote, that 'civilisation has been created under pressure of the exigencies of life at the cost of satisfaction of the instincts', e.g., 'the sexual impulses' which 'are diverted from their sexual aims and directed to others that are socially higher and no longer sexual' (Freud 1966b, pp. 26–7). Compare Hegel's claim that as 'the passions of men are gratified' they 'develop themselves and their aims in accordance with their natural tendencies, and build up the edifice of human society; thus fortifying a position for Right and Order *against themselves*' (Hegel 1956, p. 27). For Freud, however, this ultimately leads to 'discontent' which is inconsistent with the actualisation of what Hegel understood as freedom.

38   Freud 1966b, pp. 482–3.

39   Cf. Plato's classic treatment of 'inner natural necessity' in his *Republic* (Plato 1997, p. 137).

source which is, at least in part, within us, and which in some circumstances is an unavoidable and necessary phase in our species' development.[40]

Despite this affinity, Freud's theory diverges fundamentally from the philosophical anthropology and corresponding theory of mind in Marx's work. From Freud's perspective, the socioeconomic frustration of instinctual desire entails a psychological process whereby the 'ego-instincts' work 'towards obtaining pleasure' and, 'under the influence of the instructress Necessity', the 'ego discovers that it is inevitable for it to renounce immediate satisfaction' whereby the ego is 'educated' and 'has become "reasonable."'[41] However, Freud's idea of 'reason' is inconsistent with Marx's. For Freud, the operation of the inexorable 'pleasure principle' within our psyche will perpetually come into conflict with the demands of reality, including other people that inhabit the world with us, insofar as our 'id', the primordial and inextinguishable seat of the instincts, perpetually strives for immediate instinctual gratification.[42] Thus he maintained that human beings 'have always found it hard to renounce pleasure' and 'have contrived to alternate between remaining an animal of pleasure and being once more a creature of reason'.[43]

In this respect Freud's work parallels the writings of Kant, for whom a truly just society remains ultimately unattainable. In Kant's view, freedom cannot be achieved because the crudity of our instinctual-bestial nature clings so strongly that we need a master to discipline us and educate us for the demands of a peaceful and free social order, but this master can only come from among humanity itself.[44] As we have seen, the problem of needing an educator to educate the educator is an insoluble one. It is evident that the same kind of problem arises in psychoanalytic theory if it is maintained that we need an analyst to overcome the discontent of civilised life. Psychoanalysis is thus bound

---

40   This comparison illustrates a connection between instinctual activity and the exercise and development of human powers which was left unexplored by Marx.

41   Freud 1966, p. 444. This idea of 'pleasure postponed' is comparable with Hegel's depiction of the psychological process of deferred desire in the section on the 'Independence and dependence of self-consciousness' in the *Phenomenology*.

42   Hence Freud's claim that 'Ethics ... means restriction of instinctual gratification' (Freud 1939, p. 152). As Norman Brown put it, for Freud the 'pleasure-principle is in conflict with the reality principle, and this conflict is the cause of repression. Under the conditions of repression the essence of our being lies in the unconscious, and only in the unconscious does the pleasure-principle reign supreme' (Brown 1959, p. 8).

43   Freud 1966, p. 463.

44   This kind of problem is reflected, for instance, by the case of the judge from Oklahoma who was found to be masturbating with a penis-pump under the bench in court while presiding over trials. He was sentenced to four years in prison (Associated Press 2006).

by a contradiction like the vanguardist fallacy which is common to Marxism. This is particularly evident in the thought of the psychoanalytic-Marxist Wilhelm Reich whose work is bound by both of these fallacies. If psychoanalysis is the solution to the neurotic discontent rooted in the crudity of our instinctual nature which acts as a barrier to 'integral development' and expresses itself as a constant check on the progress of human civilisation, it follows that the analyst must also be analysed, but we would still have to account for how the first analyst was capable of spontaneous self-analysis. After all, Sigmund Freud analysed himself, and yet given the barriers to such insight that he himself pointed out it seems that self-analysis is inadequate in principle. Ultimately, from this perspective our history is, and can only be, a record of perpetual striving for unattainable freedom, characterised predominantly by suffering and unhappiness.

Herbert Marcuse's work serves as a classic example of an attempt to resolve this problem on its own foundations. In *Eros and Civilisation* he railed against the 'the tyranny of reason' and tried to 'extrapolate the hypothesis of a non-repressive civilisation from Freud's theory of the instincts', which on the premises of Freud's psychoanalytic theory is ultimately impossible.[45] As a result of his search for 'mental forces' which 'remain essentially free from the reality principle', he ended up positing the imaginative power of 'phantasy' as the path to liberation because he thought that it 'has a truth value of its own', and only with it lies the possible 'surmounting of the antagonistic human reality' and 'the liberation of sensuousness from the repressive domain of reason'.[46] In Marcuse's *Essay on Liberation* he attempted to describe a 'new sensibility' in which the 'sensuous power of the imagination' would 'fashion [our] reason', and he thought that 'the freedom of the imagination is restrained not only by the sensibility, but also, at the other pole of the organic structure, by the rational faculty of man, his reason'.[47] He left it up to the 'imagination' to mediate 'between the rational faculties and the sensuous needs'.[48]

This limitation of Freudian psychology from the standpoint of Marx's social philosophy can be illustrated further in conjunction with what Erich Fromm considers the key conception of psychoanalysis: the adaptation of the instinctual structure to 'social reality' and 'real needs in life'.[49] Fromm maintained that the 'phenomena studied in social (or mass) psychology ... should

---

45   Marcuse 1962, pp. 164; 122.
46   Marcuse 1962, pp. 130; 126; 164.
47   Marcuse 1969, pp. 30; 21; 29.
48   Marcuse 1969, p. 30.
49   Fromm 1970, p. 139.

be understood as the result of the adaptation of the instinctual apparatus to the social reality'.[50] Any such social psychology could not adequately incorporate an idea of the manifestation of 'mind' as depicted in Marx's writing because where Freudian anthropology puts forth instinctual adaptation and sublimation, Marx posits a fundamental transformation through the development of 'species powers' which enable 'free activity'. From Marx's perspective, the character of social relations in 'communist society' is not derived from the sublimation of the desire 'to bring one's own genitals into contact with those of someone' else.[51] Its full actualisation is found in 'universally developed individuals' who are able to experience and actualise 'universal existences', a truly 'beautiful' kind of 'love', through 'rational' thought and feeling.

Alongside this divergence from Marx's thought is the deeper inconsistency of ontological principles associated with the 'materialism' of the natural sciences on which Freud's work is based. In Freud's early essay titled 'Project for a Scientific Psychology' he claimed that his 'intention' was 'to represent psychical processes as quantitatively determinate states of specifiable material particles, thus making those processes perspicuous and free from contradiction'.[52] Views like this are typical of the natural sciences founded on the 'materialism' of Newtonian physics. As Whitehead put it, this kind of 'materialism' conceives of 'nature as composed of permanent things, namely bits of matter, moving about in space which is otherwise empty', in which the 'connections between such bits of matter consists purely of spatial relations'.[53] 'We assume', Freud wrote, 'that mental life is the function of an apparatus to which we ascribe the characteristics of being extended in space and of being made up of several portions'.[54] Whitehead maintained that it is impossible to interweave the concepts of 'Life' and 'Mind' within this 'general concept of nature' because the locomotion 'of matter involves change in spatial relationship' and 'nothing more than that'.[55] Freud left his 'Project' unfinished but he did not fully cast aside the 'materialist' foundations of natural science.[56] Thus he ultimately remained

---

50   Fromm 1970, p. 147.

51   Freud 1969, p. 22.

52   Freud 1966, p. 295.

53   Whitehead 1968, p. 128.

54   Freud 1966, p. 13.

55   Whitehead 1968, pp. 129; 132. 'Matter involves nothing more than spatiality, and the passive support of qualifications. It can be qualified, and it must be qualified. But qualification is a bare fact, which is just itself. This is the grand doctrine of nature as a self-sufficient, meaningless complex of facts. It is the doctrine of the autonomy of physical science' (Whitehead 1968, p. 132).

56   As his work progressed he attempted to take account of 'the subtleties which were being

unable to consistently maintain that we can potentially direct ourselves intel-
ligently and live freely because his 'metapsychology' rests on the ontological
premises of a mechanistic 'materialism' which precludes a coherent conception of self-determination and the life of 'mind'. Near the end of his life he
described psychoanalytic psychology as 'a natural science like any other', and
according to him the 'processes with which it is concerned' are akin to 'those
dealt with by other sciences' such as 'chemistry or physics'.[57] His work indicates
that even until that point his 'metapsychology' was still part of the same kind of
'materialism' in which nature is ultimately composed of 'dead' matter in strictly
determined motion. Consider, for example, his view that our innate 'instincts'
(i.e., the 'somatic demands upon the mind', including the physical-chemical
processes associated with such bodily impulses) 'are the ultimate cause of all
activity'.[58]

Reich's work is an example of an attempt to synthesise the work of Marx and
Freud which failed to sufficiently overcome this inconsistency, even though he
recognised the problem with 'a certain "materialist" conception of psychology
widespread in Marxist circles', i.e., 'the concept of mechanistic materialism',
which he did 'not accept'.[59] But Reich never completely overcame this 'materialism' in his appropriation of Freud's psychoanalytic theory and his thinking
on the matter remained beset with problematic contradictions. In the first edition of *Dialectical Materialism and Psychoanalysis* (1929) he claimed that if a
psychology 'is to deserve the right to be called a materialistic psychology', it
'has to be clear about whether psychological activity can be viewed as a metaphysical fact – i.e., a fact outside the organic world – or as a secondary function
bound up with the organic world'.[60] And in the second edition (1934), he wrote:

---

brought to light by "psychological analysis" and which could only be accounted for in
the language of mental processes' (Freud 1991, p. 163). At that point he thought that the
'physical characteristics' of 'latent states of mental life' are 'totally inaccessible to us: no
physiological concept or chemical process can give us any notion of their nature' (Freud
1991, p. 169).

57   Freud 1969, p. 30.
58   Freud 1969, p. 17. Cf. Rousseau's claim that 'Nature commands all animals, and the beast
obeys. Man receives the same impulsion, but he recognises himself as being free to acqui-
esce or resist; and it is above all in this consciousness of his freedom that the spirituality
of his soul reveals itself, for physics explains in a certain way the mechanism of the senses
and the formation of ideas, but in the power to will, or rather to choose, and in the feeling
of that power, we see pure spiritual activity, of which the laws of mechanics can explain
nothing' (Rousseau 1984, p. 88).
59   Reich 2012, p. 11.
60   Reich 2012, p. 13.

Sexual economy, if it wants to become a proper scientific discipline, must study the sexual process in all its functions, psychical as well as physiological, biological as well as social, and must equally investigate all the functions of the basic law of sexuality; thus it is faced with the difficult task of deducing sexual-psychical functions from sexual-biological functions. In this task it is assisted by the dialectical method which it consciously employs. We may put forward the following principle: it is certainly true that the psychical is the product of the organic and must consequently follow the same laws as the organic; but at the same time, it is the opposite of the organic, and in that function, it develops a set of laws which are its own and peculiar to itself. Only the study of these latter laws has been the task of psychoanalysis; and in the main, this task has been completed. Sexual economy may be expected to solve the problem of this relationship between physical and psychological functions; whether it does so depends on conditions outside our control.[61]

3   Husserl's Phenomenological Psychology and Marx's Incipient Psychology

In contrast to Freudian psychology, the vision of the 'soul' that Husserl put forth with his 'phenomenological pure psychology' involves a conceptual framework which is more consistent with the philosophical premises of Marx's incipient psychology.[62] 'In no way', Husserl maintained, 'can a science of soul be modeled on natural science or seek methodical counsel from it'.[63] He spoke directly to the issues arising from a psychological theory which shares the same ontological materialism as the natural sciences, as with psychoanalysis. 'Psychology failed', Husserl claimed, because 'it let its task and method be set according to the model of natural science or according to the guiding idea of modern philosophy as objective and thus concrete universal science'.[64] Freudian psychoanalysis would fit in this general description. Husserl claimed that

psychology began with a concept of soul which was not at all formulated in an original way but which stemmed from Cartesian dualism, a concept furnished by a prior constructive idea of a corporeal nature and of a math-

---

61   Ibid.
62   Husserl 1999, p. 326.
63   Husserl 1970, p. 223.
64   Husserl 1970, p. 203.

ematical natural science. Thus psychology was burdened in advance with the task of being a science parallel [to physics] and with the conception that the soul – its subject matter – was something real in a sense similar to corporeal nature, the subject matter of natural science.[65]

In his view, for 'the realm of souls there is in principle no ... ontology, no science corresponding to the physicalistic mathematical ideal' characteristic of the natural sciences.[66] This stands in contrast to the essentially physicalistic idea of the 'soul' in Freud's psychoanalytic psychology. According to Husserl,

> Phenomenology frees us from the old objectivistic ideal of the scientific system, the theoretical form of mathematical science, and frees us accordingly from the idea of an ontology of the soul which could be analogous to physics. Only blindness to the transcendental, as it is experienceable and knowable only through phenomenological reduction, makes the revival of physicalism in our time possible.[67]

He maintained that 'the psychic, considered purely in terms of its own essence, has no [physical] nature, has no conceivable in-itself in the natural sense, no spatiotemporally causal, no idealizable and mathematizable in-itself, no laws after the fashion of natural laws'.[68] But he also claimed that psychology is like 'natural science' insofar as it 'can only draw its "rigor" ("exactness") from the rationality of the essence'.[69] In this case it is 'the mind's [*Geist*] own essence' which 'refers not to a mystical "metaphysical" essence but to one's own being-in-oneself and for-oneself which ... is accessible to the inquiring, reflecting ego through so-called "inner" or "self-perception."'[70] This is related to the distinc-

---

65   Husserl 1970, p. 212. The 'psychology of Locke', which developed with 'the natural science of a Newton before it as a model', is a classic example (Husserl 1970, p. 117).

66   Husserl 1970, p. 265.

67   Husserl 1970, p. 265.

68   Husserl 1970, p. 222.

69   Husserl 1999, p. 326.

70   Husserl 1970, p. 213. In his view, the 'soul "is," of course, "in" the world. But does this mean that it is in the world in the way that the physical body is and that, when men with living bodies and souls are experienced in the world as real, their reality, as well as that of their living bodies and souls, could have the same or even a similar sense to that of the mere physical bodies? Even though the human living body is counted among the physical bodies, it is still "living" – "my physical body," which I "move," in and through which I "hold sway," which I "animate." If one fails to consider these matters – which soon become quite extensive – thoroughly, and actually without prejudice, one has not grasped at all what is of a soul's *own essence* as such' (Husserl 1970, p. 212).

tion that Husserl made between 'the psychological ego (the human ego, that is, made worldly in the spatiotemporal world) and the transcendental ego'.[71] Husserl described this 'duality' in our being by explaining that we are 'psychological, as human objectivities in the world, the subjects of psychic life, and at the same time transcendental, as the subjects of a transcendental, world-constituting life-process'.[72]

There are strong parallels between Husserl's idea of 'transcendental subjectivity' and the thinking expressed in Marx's fragmentary writings on human subjectivity.[73] Consider, for example, the following passage form Marx's writing:

> My *general* consciousness is only the *theoretical* shape of that of which the *living* shape is the *real* community, the social fabric ... The *activity* of my general consciousness, as an activity, is therefore also my *theoretical* existence as a social being. Above all we must avoid postulating 'society' again as an abstraction vis-à-vis the individual. The individual *is the social being* ... In his *consciousness of species* man confirms his real *social life* and simply repeats his real existence in thought, just as conversely the being of the species confirms itself in species consciousness and exists for itself in its generality as a thinking being. Man, much as he may therefore be a *particular* individual ... is just as much the *totality* – the ideal totality – the subjective existence of imagined and experienced society for itself; just as he exists also in the real world both as awareness and real enjoyment of social existence, and as a totality of human manifestations of life. Thinking and being are thus certainly *distinct*, but at the same time they are in *unity* with each other.[74]

---

71   Husserl 1970, p. 205.

72   Husserl 1999, pp. 330–1. He thought that we have 'direct access' to 'this transcendental subjectivity' through 'a transcendental experience' (Ibid.).

73   'Transcendental subjectivity ... is none other than again "I myself" and "we ourselves"; not, however, as found in the natural attitude of everyday or of positive science; i.e., apperceived as components of the objectively present world before us, but rather as subjects of conscious life, *in* which this world and all that is present – for "us" – "makes" itself through certain apperceptions. As [human beings], mentally as well as bodily present in the world, we are for "ourselves"; we are appearances standing within an extremely variegated intentional life-process, "our" life, *in which* this being on hand constitutes itself "for us" apperceptively, with its entire sense-content. The (apperceived) I and we on hand presuppose an (apperceiving) I and we, *for* which they are on hand, which, however, is not itself present again in the same sense' (Husserl 1999, pp. 329–30).

74   MECW 3, pp. 298–9.

According to Husserl, 'each soul' stands 'in community with others which are intentionally interrelated, that is, in a purely intentional, internally and essentially closed nexus, that of intersubjectivity'.[75] On his premises this entails 'a transcendental intersubjectivity constituting the world as "world for all."'[76] This phenomenological theory aligns more than psychoanalytic psychology with the philosophy underlying the depiction of 'mind' in Marx's social philosophy and his idea of 'universal' experience in particular. As Husserl claimed,

> phenomenology recognises ... the absolute norms which are to be picked out intuitively from [the life of humanity], and also its ... directedness towards disclosure of these norms and their conscious practical operation ... Or, in different words, it is a striving in the direction of the idea (lying in infinity) of a humanness which in action and throughout would live and move [be, exist] in truth and genuineness.[77]

This entails the existence of 'universal' values which are precluded by the 'materialist' foundations of Freud's psychoanalytic psychology. At the same time, its physicalistic conception of the psyche also precludes the possibility for the self-determination of these values by 'free' individuals in the sense that Marx meant by 'free'. This is particularly significant for Marx's social philosophy because 'universal' ethical values are also essential for his conception of human freedom.

4   Kleinian Psychoanalysis and the Development of 'Human Need'

Freud's theory ultimately stands opposed to Marx's idea that it is possible for us to develop the ability to desire in accordance with 'universal' ethical values – i.e., in a conscious, ratiocinative way – that would permeate the ethos of

---

75   Husserl 1970, p. 238. In other words, 'there is a sole universal nature as a self-enclosed framework of all souls, which are united not externally but internally, namely, through the intentional interpenetration which is the communalisation of their lives' (i.e., in 'a pure, intentional, mutual internality') (Husserl 1970, pp. 255–6).

76   Husserl 1970, p. 184. Cf. what Hegel described as 'the experience of what Spirit is', i.e., the 'absolute substance which is the unity of the different independent self-consciousnesses which, in their opposition, enjoy perfect freedom and independence: "I" that is "We" and "We" that is "I"' (Hegel 1977, p. 110).

77   Husserl 1999, pp. 334–5. Cf. Marx's claim that 'the senses and enjoyment of other [individuals can] become my *own* appropriation' (MECW 3, p. 300).

a 'rational' social order. His view of ethical life is inconsistent with the idea of being able to know such values and actualise them in our relationships, even though he was concerned with the development of an individual whose desires are 'reasonable' because they seek 'to attain pleasure' which 'is assured through taking account of reality'.[78] This is because the only basis for determining ethical behaviour from his perspective is the character of our 'superego' morality. This denotes the sense of conscience inherited from one's elders and broader sociocultural environment. Evaluative claims about the way we behave in our relations with others are inconsistent with this relativism. Ultimately, the 'superego' is not a substantial basis for self-determined ethical behaviour because it is a predominantly unconscious internal authority that influences behaviour through fear roused by a sense of guilt.

This renders Freud's psychoanalysis inconsistent with the politics of 'universal human emancipation' in Marx's work. For Marx this entails a 'universal' ethic that is such not simply because a specific group (such as one's parents or culture) give it credence or a social majority experience it, but rather because it is true in-and-for-itself (and yet only takes on an actual existence through intersubjective activity). Marx's idea of 'universally developed individuals' suggests that it is possible for us to develop beyond the need for a 'superego' to govern ethical behaviour. For him, such individuals would be determined by their own 'reason' which affirms the freedom and infinite worth of the human person and consequently treats the flourishing of all individuals as an end-in-itself. This philosophical foundation is particularly necessary for orienting our understanding of the psychosocial nature of the extreme politics of the far-right which displays the tendency to divide the human community, promote supremacism, devalue some of us based on various kinds of prejudice, and affirm oppressive relations of dominance and servitude between groups and individuals.

Melanie Klein's revision of Freud's psychoanalytic theory is more compatible with the philosophical premises underlying Marx's idea of ethical life practice and experience. Her elaboration of the human psyche and its development also overlaps with significant elements of Marx's depiction of human subjectivity and helps to further illuminate his incipient psychology. Her theoretical orientation is also more amenable to the kind of social and political theory that Marx developed. Klein attempted to take account of an 'ethical pattern' which she claimed is 'universal'.[79] A key idea in this connection is the 'integration'

---

78   Freud 1966b, p. 444.
79   In her view, 'When the imperatives: "Thou shalt not kill" (primarily the loved object), and

of the 'ego'. For Klein, 'elements of an integrated personality' are 'emotional
maturity, strength of character, [the] capacity to deal with conflicting emotions, a balance between internal life and adaptation to reality, and a successful
welding into a whole of the different parts of the personality'.[80] It 'expresses
itself in the capacity for love' and more specifically corresponds to 'Understanding of other people, compassion, sympathy and tolerance'.[81] The process
of 'integration' is essentially the coming together of initially discordant parts of
the ego and 'internalised objects'.[82] According to her, as the process of 'integration' proceeds, 'the adaptation to external reality' improves and there is 'a
fuller synthesis of unconscious processes' whereby 'the demarcation between
conscious and unconscious is more distinct'.[83] The 'growing sense of reality'
associated with 'integration and synthesis' is a step away from Freud's ethical
relativism toward the kind of 'rational' self-determination presented in Marx's
work insofar as 'integration' entails the gradual 'assimilation' of the 'superego'
by the ego.[84] Thus from the perspective of Klein's psychoanalytic psychology
it is possible to conceive of a subject capable of engaging in relations that are
good from a 'universal' standpoint.[85]

From a Kleinian perspective, the experience of the ethical relationship that
Marx conceived as 'human' – namely, relations in which we would experience
each other 'as a completion of [our] own essential nature and as a necessary
part of [ourselves]', and would be 'confirmed both in [our] thought and [our]

"Thou shalt save from destruction" (again the loved objects, and in the first place from the
infant's own aggression) have taken root in the mind, an ethical pattern is set up which is
universal and the rudiment of all ethical systems' (Klein 1997, p. 322).

80   Klein 1997, p. 268.
81   Klein 1997, pp. 191; 269. She maintained that in 'the depths of the mind, the urge to make
people happy is linked up with a strong feeling of responsibility and concern for them,
which manifests itself in genuine sympathy with other people and in the ability to understand them, as they are and as they feel' (Klein 1998, p. 311).
82   The 'integration of the ego is accomplished by the different parts of the ego ... being able
to come together in spite of their conflicting tendencies' (Klein 1997, p. 289). Cf. her claim
that the 'ego's growing capacity for integration and synthesis leads more and more ... to
states in which love and hatred, and correspondingly the good and bad aspects of objects,
are being synthesized' (Klein 1997, p. 50).
83   Klein 1997, p. 86.
84   Klein 1997, pp. 304.
85   In relation to Marx's social philosophy it is noteworthy that her definition of successful
individual development is articulated as a kind of mean akin to Aristotelian virtue ethics;
e.g., with the development of 'tolerance'. Cf. Klein's claim that 'tolerance does not mean
being blind to the faults of others. It means recognizing those faults and nevertheless not
losing one's ability to co-operate with people or even to experience love towards some of
them' (Klein 1997, p. 260).

love' – involves developmental processes in infancy that 'make possible the feeling of unity with another person', whereby 'such unity means being fully understood'.[86] Her understanding of the psychology of 'love' also overlaps with Marx's idea of the 'human' need for 'the *other* person as a person' rather than as a mere object to be used instrumentally, as in the relationship between wage labour and capital.[87] In the context of Klein's work this kind of relationship is prefigured in the development of the infant's ability to experience their mother as independent and a 'person'. Klein claimed that our mother is first experienced as an object (the breast) and gradually becomes recognised as an independent subject with the infant's further development.[88] Her theory corresponds with Marx's claim that 'love' is what 'first really teaches man to believe in the objective world outside himself, which not only makes man into an object, but even the object into a man'.[89]

Another key concept related to this is her idea of 'reparation' which is the desire to repair loved objects (including people) that a child (in a delusional way) believes they have harmed with their destructive impulses. She associates this with the capacity to love and feel concern for others. In particular, she thought that the 'drive to make reparation' is 'a consequence of greater insight into psychic reality and of growing synthesis, for it shows a more realistic response to the feelings of grief, guilt and fear of loss resulting from the aggression against the loved object'.[90] C. Fred Alford claimed that 'reparative reason' is a 'Kleinian alternative' to 'what the Frankfurt School calls instrumental reason' and that 'Klein's psychoanalytic studies reveal a potential for morality that flies higher than Freud's'.[91] According to Alford, with Klein's ver-

---

86   MECW 3, p. 228; Klein 1997, p. 188. She claimed that this experience is 'essential for every happy love relation or friendship' and, in the context of infant development, that 'such an understanding needs no words to express it' (Ibid.).

87   Here it is worth highlighting that Marx's concept of 'estrangement' fundamentally entails 'estrangement' from each other. In Marx's depiction it does not just involve the projection of subjective powers onto objects, but also the habitual objectification of other subjects. As Marx wrote, 'When man confronts himself, he confronts the *other* man ... In fact, the proposition that man's species-nature is estranged from him means that one man is estranged from the other, as each of them is from man's essential nature. The estrangement of man, and in fact every relationship in which man stands to himself, is first realised and expressed only in the relationship in which a man stands to other men. Hence within the relationship of estranged labor each man views the other in accordance with the standard and the relationship in which he finds himself as a worker' (MECW 3, pp. 277–8).

88   Klein 1997, p. 71.

89   MECW 4, pp. 21–2.

90   Klein 1997, p. 14.

91   Alford 1989, pp. 22; 38–9.

sion of psychoanalysis we encounter the idea of 'a morality based not merely upon the desire to make sacrifices, in order to make reparation for phantasised acts of aggression; it is also based upon an ability to deeply identify with others, to feel connected with their fates. Their pain becomes our pain'.[92] But this also indicates that Klein did not completely overcome the inadequacy of Freudian psychoanalytic theory in the realm of ethical life from the perspective of Marx's social philosophy. Insofar as she thought the 'reparative' tendency requires an element of depressive guilt tied to 'phantasy', a degree of delusion remains at the basis of Kleinian ethics. This is a major shortcoming of her psychological theory from the standpoint of Marx's social philosophy because she essentially precludes the possibility of the development of individuality akin to 'universally developed individuals'.[93] Indeed, Marx's work suggests that such individuals would require what Klein termed 'Complete and permanent integration' which she maintained is 'never possible' even though she thought that a tendency toward 'integration' is inherent in the ego.[94]

Despite the fact that this issue with Klein's theory is incongruent with the premises of Marx's social philosophy, it provides an opportunity from within psychoanalysis for theorising beyond 'estranged' interpersonal relations on the basis of ethical universalism. Coming from a 'socialist' perspective, Michael Rustin claimed that Klein's psychological theory is consistent with the idea of 'a universal ethic' of 'essential human equality' at the basis of 'a social order providing a fulfilling life for all'.[95] At the same time, her view of the psychological processes underlying human development complements Marx's perspective on 'estranged' sociohistorical practices through which humanity

---

92   Alford 1989, p. 41.

93   She thought that 'the young child's perception of external reality and external objects is perpetually influenced and coloured by his phantasies, and ... this in some measure continues throughout life' (Klein 1997, p. 40).

94   Klein 1997, p. 233. Cf. David McIvor's claim that 'integration's fragile and incomplete nature is not only a lamentable shortcoming to be transcended; it is an unavoidable ongoing obstacle to social and psychic peace. The self is never fully integrated, but it can achieve moments of coherence where incompletion and ambivalence are faced down in ways that make gratitude and reparation towards self and other possible. Practically speaking, this implies the search for spaces and modes of interaction that tilt us towards a countenancing of the damage we do to ourselves and to others through acts of violent misrecognition. The sociopolitical challenge is to identify spaces and practices that provide non-manic forms of reassurance – what Bion called "containment" – which can mitigate (but not eliminate) some of the meanness that we find and continually create in the world' (McIvor 2016, p. 245).

95   Rustin 1982, p. 95.

transforms into 'the new generation'.[96] In particular, the psychosocial practices through which our collective powers and relations become transferred onto objects that then dominate us as alien and hostile entities resembles Klein's concept of 'projective identification' which denotes the unconscious process whereby parts of the self (such as an infant's own impulses like greed and aggressiveness) are projected onto other objects and people and experienced as though they actually belong to them.[97] For Klein, some unconscious 'projection' is necessary for the development of a healthy, 'integrated' mind, and Marx had an analogous view of the role that 'estrangement' in capitalist society plays in the process of human development. In his view, 'estranged' labour in capitalism 'is exactly *the same* relation ... as is represented by *religion*' – namely, 'the inversion of subject into the object and *vice versa*' – in 'the real social life process', and he claimed that it 'is necessary to pass through this antagonistic form, just as [humanity] had first to shape [our] spiritual forces in a religious form, as powers independent of [us]'.[98]

5   A Psychology of Political Struggle in the 'Bourgeois Epoch'

Notwithstanding its limitations, Klein's version of psychoanalysis presents a possible starting point for reconceptualising the psychological determinations of the social and political struggles which parallel Marx's analysis of the struggle for human emancipation in the 'bourgeois epoch'.[99] Her writings offer a complementary approach to a theory of the 'soul' of individuals who have revolutionary or reactionary attitudes and participate in their respective social

---

96   MECW 28, p. 251. After all, Marx thought that a 'communist' revolution concludes human-
     ity's 'prehistory'. Cf. Engels's claim that 'the common management of production by the
     whole of society and the resulting new development of production require and also pro-
     duce quite different people. The common management of production cannot be effected
     by people as they are today, each one being assigned to a single branch of production,
     shackled to it, exploited by it, each having developed only *one* of his abilities at the cost
     of all the others and knowing only *one* branch, or only a branch of a branch of the total
     production. Even present-day industry finds less and less use for such people. Industry car-
     ried on in common and according to plan by the whole of society presupposes moreover
     people of all-round development, capable of surveying the entire system of production'
     (MECW 6, p. 353).
97   Klein 1997, p. 12. See R.D. Hinshelwood's 'Projective Identification and Marx's Concept of
     Man' in which he argues that 'Marx described an unmistakable and very concrete form of
     projective identification' (Hinshelwood 1983, p. 221).
98   MECW 34, pp. 398–9.
99   MECW 6, p. 487.

movements in a way that is amenable to Marx's social philosophy because the 'universal' ethic in her work provides a basis for coherently articulating the polarised strife of extreme far-right politics. The psychological framework she put forth enables a conceptualisation of political orientations as more or less reasonable in a way that is more consistent with the philosophical premises of Marx's social theory than Freud's original work is. It also furnishes these orientations with corresponding traits that can be observed in political attitudes and behaviours.

Klein's idea of the series of psychological 'positions' that individuals pass through in the early phases of psychological development is particularly suitable for theorising attitudes and behaviours associated with extreme politics. These developmental phases are the 'paranoid-schizoid' and 'depressive', and they function in accordance with the particular forms of anxiety ('persecutory' and 'depressive', respectively) and corresponding defenses that pertain to each of them. Initially, in the 'paranoid-schizoid' position, the undeveloped ego and its objects (primarily the mother's breast) are unintegrated and experienced in an idealised form as either wholly 'good' or 'bad', satisfying or frustrating. As the infant develops and its world becomes more realistic, its objects are increasingly recognised as composites of both 'good' and 'bad', leading to a more realistic picture of the world. But it also presents a psychological conflict for the developing psyche and leads to 'depressive' feelings because the conflicting impulses (e.g., love and hostility) are now directed toward the same object rather than the idealised object that was split into separate and diametrically opposed identities. For example, an infant that has destructive urges toward its mother's breast when it is frustrating and perceived as wholly 'bad' will come to realise that its aggressiveness was directed to the 'good' object that it loves. If the 'depressive' anxiety evoked by this realisation is too much for the infant to manage, their psyche will revert to the more primitive defense mechanisms of the 'paranoid-schizoid' position. Chief among these is 'splitting'. In short, 'splitting' is the process whereby the object becomes idealised as either 'good' or 'bad' and the other aspect is split off from it. The infant self is also split in the process and the paranoid element arises because one's own 'badness' (e.g., harmful aggression) is disavowed and projected onto 'bad' objects.

Parallels to this regressive psychological orientation are observable in political phenomena. When this kind of psychological mechanism is operative in the behaviour of adults in society as political actors, it undermines the perception of people/groups as composite wholes and is associated with devaluation and hostility insofar as political others are perceived as simply 'bad', dangerous and even sinister to varying degrees in a way that is unrealistic. This can be observed, for example, in the discourse of the migrant crises in Europe and the United States. During his presidency, Donald Trump was a very public example of someone who displays a marked tendency to invoke this splitting mechanism and encourage it among his supporters. Splitting facilitates the process of devaluing others which makes any mistreatment of them seem justified.

Disruptions of the developmental process of the psyche (e.g., when the 'depressive' phase is not fully completed) will lead to lasting effects on the personality of individuals.[100] It is relatively straightforward to recognise that a toddler who has not developed properly cannot be held accountable for it. But in the case of adults who have regressive tendencies or characteristics that correspond to a malformed psyche or an unintegrated ego it is more difficult to recognise the limitations of their agency over their maladaptive traits and behaviours. Aristotle's *Nicomachean Ethics* opens with the claim that everyone acts with a view toward some perceived good. This applies to all human beings, even to the most extreme, such as an individual with a fascistic orientation, which on Klein's premises is someone whose mind has been vitiated and whose perspective is warped as a result of disturbances of development, with detrimental consequences for their political behaviour. She claimed that the 'universal ethical pattern' is 'capable of manifold variations and distortions, and even of complete reversal', and she mentioned 'the Nazi attitude' as an example of a 'reversal' of this 'primary pattern'.[101] This idea was formed within the context of her reconceptualisation of the subject's 'inner world' on the basis of her 'object relations' theory. She explained that

> the processes of introjection and projection from the beginning of life lead to the institution inside ourselves of loved and hated objects, who are felt to be 'good' and 'bad,' and who are interrelated with each other and with the self: that is to say, they constitute an inner world. This assembly of internalised objects becomes organised, together with the organisation of the ego, and in the higher strata of the mind it becomes discernible as the super-ego. Thus, the phenomenon which was recognised by Freud ... as the voices and the influence of the actual parents established in the ego is, according to my findings, a complex object-world, which is felt by

---

100   As Aristotle claimed, 'It makes no small difference ... to be habituated in this way or that straight from childhood, but an enormous difference, or rather all the difference' (Aristotle 2002, p. 23).

101   Klein 1997, p. 322.

the individual, in deep layers of the unconscious, to be concretely inside himself, and for which I and some of my colleagues therefore use the term 'internalised objects' and an 'inner world.'[102]

In her explanation for the distortion of the 'universal ethical pattern' that corresponds to the 'Nazi attitude', she referred to 'the early unconscious relation towards the first persons attacked or injured in phantasy'.[103] She wrote:

> Here the aggressor and aggression have become loved and admired objects, and the attacked objects have turned into evil and must therefore be exterminated ... The object then turns into a potential persecutor, because retaliation by the same means by which it had been harmed is feared. The injured person is, however, also identical with the loved person, who should be protected and restored. Excessive early fears tend to increase the conception of the injured object as an enemy, and if this is the outcome, hatred will prevail in the struggle against love.[104]

At the basis of this is her 'conceptual distinction between depressive anxiety, guilt and reparation on the one hand, and persecutory anxiety and the defenses against it on the other'.[105] She cited Roger Money-Kyrle's application of this 'to attitudes towards ethics in general and towards political beliefs in particular'.[106]

Money-Kyrle approached 'the conflict of different social ideologies within one nation' – namely, 'the old conflict between socialism and individualism, radicalism and conservatism' – from a Kleinian perspective.[107] In his work he reanimates the connection between psychological development and politics and illuminates the Kleinian view of mental and emotional development at the basis of our ethical capacities with an aim of understanding the political personality underpinning extreme authoritarian politics. From this psychoanalytic perspective, if an individual emerges from the formative period in early childhood development with a relatively 'unintegrated ego' and an inability to manage psychological stress and anxiety without reverting to regressive defense mechanisms, they are more likely to develop traits that predis-

---

102   Klein 1998, p. 362.
103   Klein 1997, p. 322.
104   Ibid.
105   Klein 1997, p. 37.
106   Klein 1997, p. 38.
107   Money-Kyrle 1944, p. 114.

pose them to extreme politics. True to his psychoanalytic roots, Money-Kyrle emphasises the role of the 'unconscious'. He maintained that 'our political beliefs' about 'political affairs' are 'often very greatly influenced by unconscious phantasies surviving from early childhood which distort our conscious inferences and deductions'.[108] Thus in his view, some 'ideological attitudes' are 'ultimately conditioned by unconscious distortions of reality and must therefore be classed as pathological'.[109] Similar to when a 'patient's emotional behaviour is irrational', pathological ideological attitudes and beliefs are 'not justified by the situation' that an individual 'is really in'; these individuals behave as if they are 'in different situations' because they are 'in unconscious phantasy' and 'unconsciously deluded'.[110]

In the context of political environments, effective propaganda plays on these unconscious forces. Money-Kyrle pointed out how the propaganda of the Nazi's 'raised the sleeping bogeys of the unconscious and identified them with Jews and Democrats and Communists', and that 'propaganda often seems to be a method of inducing a series of temporary psychoses'.[111] Such propaganda relies on the existence of a paranoid propensity in the individuals who are susceptible to it. According to Money-Kyrle, paranoid

> symptoms are not confined to certifiable lunatics. Indeed, under conditions of sufficient stress, most people seem capable of producing them ... Even in peace time, there are many otherwise sane people who attribute all the ills of the world to some one evil and mysterious source, which they identify, according to their religious or political prejudices.[112]

After all, following Ernest Jones, Money-Kyrle claimed that our 'political egos' can 'remain as it were the seat of an encapsulated illness in otherwise sane and normal personalities'.[113] In a similar vein, Richard Hofstadter believed that it is 'the use of paranoid modes of expression by more or less normal people that makes the phenomenon significant'.[114]

From a Kleinian perspective, 'the Nazi attitude' is connected to a predominance of 'unconscious phantasy' associated with the 'paranoid-schizoid posi-

---

108   Money-Kyrle 1952, p. 233.
109   Money-Kyrle 1944b, p. 168.
110   Money-Kyrle 1952, pp. 228–9.
111   Money-Kyrle 2015, pp. 170; 168.
112   Money-Kyrle 2015, p. 164.
113   Money-Kyrle 1951, p. 99.
114   Hofstadter 1964.

tion'. According to Klein, 'if early schizoid mechanisms and anxieties have not been sufficiently overcome, the result may be that instead of a fluid boundary between the conscious and unconscious, a rigid barrier between them arises', indicating that 'development is disturbed'.[115] Prominent during this phase of psychological development is the drive to destroy and kill – i.e., *death*, a primary force in the onto-cosmology of Freudian psychoanalysis. Klein maintained that when 'there is a very rigid barrier' between the conscious and unconscious 'produced by splitting' of the 'ego' and 'internalised objects' as a defense from persecutory anxiety, the 'conclusion would be that the death instinct is dominant'.[116] Furthermore, when 'the persecution-anxiety for the ego is in the ascendant, a full and stable identification with another object, in the sense of looking at it and understanding it as it really is, and a full capacity for love, are not possible'.[117] A connection can therefore be drawn between these psychological processes and the ethno-supremacy, conspiratorial paranoia, and other related traits of far-right extremism.[118]

In Money-Kyrle's work our 'political egos' are also conceived as connected to the 'super-ego' which is 'a being in the world of unconscious phantasy'.[119] From the psychoanalytic perspective, the 'super-ego' is a significant component of the ethical capacities involved in political life. Aside from the theoretical differences discussed above, the concept of the 'super-ego' happens to correspond with Marx's assertion that through a 'reform of consciousness' it will become evident that 'it is not a question of drawing a great mental dividing line between past and future'.[120] As Freud claimed, the 'super-ego' 'unites in itself the influences of the present and the past'.[121] In other words, 'we have before us, as it were, an example of the way in which the present is changed into the past'.[122] Inspired by Freud, Klein maintained that the 'super-ego derives'

---

115 Klein 1997, p. 87.
116 Klein 1997, p. 244. Some of the strongest imagery from the history of fascist movements are depictions of mass death, which also expresses itself in the symbolism associated with these movements, such as the skull and bones that adorned Nazi ss uniforms and have since been reappropriated by the contemporary far-right fringe group Atom Waffen (which dreams of nuclear holocaust).
117 Klein 1998, p. 271.
118 Cf. McIvor's claim that 'Critical theory rooted in the work of Klein would be more attuned to the ways that paranoid-schizoid fantasies mediate social groups and mitigate a politics of solidarity across lines of division' (McIvor 2016, p. 255).
119 Money-Kyrle 1951, p. 67.
120 MECW 3, p. 144.
121 Freud 1969, p. 97.
122 Ibid.

from 'the people whom we first loved and hated', and she thought that these 'phantasy-relationships' form 'part of our continuous, active life of feeling and of imagination'.[123] She claimed that

> However far we feel removed from our original dependencies, however much satisfaction we derive from the fulfilment of our adult ethical de-mands, in the depths of our minds our first longings to preserve and save our loved parents, and to reconcile ourselves with them, persist. There are many ways of gaining ethical satisfaction; but whether this be through social and co-operative feelings and pursuits, or even through interests which are further removed from the external world – whenever we have the feeling of moral goodness, in our unconscious minds the primary longing for reconciliation with the original objects of our love and hatred is fulfilled.[124]

While her idea of the 'super-ego' remains essentially Freudian, her revision of Freud's theory brings it closer to the philosophical premises of Marx's social theory because the 'growing assimilation of the super-ego by the ego' entails a tendency toward growing awareness of the 'universal' *present* of 'rational', 'inter-subjective' life activity and experience.

Money-Kyrle gave a Kleinian account of the 'super-ego' in his attempt to explain the forms of 'moral character' that are observable in ideological atti-tudes. He arranged these forms of 'conscience' on a spectrum in which the 'humanist' type is closest to the 'integrated' and 'rational' individual who has essentially passed through the 'depressive' phase, and at the other end is the 'authoritarian' which is subdivided further into more irrational forms of 'dis-turbed morality' (namely the 'hypo-manic' and 'hypo-paranoid').[125] From this perspective, these different forms of 'moral character' correspond to an uncon-scious sense of 'guilt' that is composed of some combination of 'persecutory' and 'depressive' anxiety, and they are expressed in different political ideolo-gies and the activities associated with them. Thus while this conceptualisation is appropriate for theorising the ontogenesis of fascism (and other particular expressions of the authoritarian moral character), Money-Kyrle's work indic-ates that Klein's theory is also suitable for articulating the psychological dimen-sion of the opposite tendency characterised by what Marx described as the

---

123   Klein 1997, pp. 322–3; Klein 1998, p. 340.
124   Klein 1997, p. 323.
125   Money-Kyrle 1951, pp. 71–2.

desire for the emancipation of 'all human beings without distinctions of sex or race'. The experience of a sense of unity and love for all humanity is consistent with the radical solidarity and humanism of socialist politics expressed in Marx's revolutionary social theory.[126]

In the work of both Marx and Klein the development of the capacity to 'love' is portrayed as a condition of freedom and associated with increasing 'universal' awareness of the world, including other individuals and our relationships with them. Marx proposed that revolutionary subjects strive to organise society on the basis of a common plan which ensures that everyone can be properly nurtured. Such individuals identify with all human beings and recognise that each individual is inherently free and an end-in-themselves.[127] They thus stand in stark contrast to far-right ethno-nationalist supremacists, but also those who create 'crude communism', with their 'greed', 'envy', and proclivity for 'possession', as well as individuals drawn to violent and authoritarian power structures.[128] From a Kleinian perspective the form of individuality expressed in Marx's idea of the revolutionary subject is characteristic of the 'depressive' type for whom the 'division between unconscious and conscious is less pronounced', whereby they are 'much more capable of insight'.[129] This association between 'moral character' and perception resembles the relationship between moral virtue and perception in Aristotle's philosophy which had a marked influence on Marx's thought. Consider his claim that 'in each sort of active condition there are special things that are beautiful and pleasant, and the person of serious moral stature is distinguished most of all, perhaps, for seeing what is truly so

---

126 Because of this fundamental consistency with a core feature of Marx's social theory, the Kleinian approach allows for a more concrete perspective of the psychological character of social and political phenomena in comparison to the abstract and formulaic application of psychoanalytic theory to the study of the revolutionary character presented in the work of E. Victor Wolfenstein. He claimed that the 'basic attribute' of the revolutionary 'personality is that it is based on opposition to governmental authority' (Wolfenstein 1967, p. 308). He focused on men, such as Lenin and Ghandi, 'who shared a commitment to ending an existing political order and replacing it with a new one' (Wolfenstein 1967, p. vii). Wolfenstein roots this phenomenon abstractly in the Oedipus complex: 'the root psychological condition appears to be a particular kind of relationship with parental authority, specifically with the father. That relationship is a highly ambivalent one, an intense focusing of love and hate on the same person' (Wolfenstein 1967, p. 167).

127 Cf. Fromm's description of the individual 'who has emancipated himself from the ties of blood and soil, from his mother and his father, from special loyalties to state, class, race, party, or religion. The revolutionary character is humanist in the sense that he experiences in himself all of humanity, and that nothing human is alien to him' (Fromm 1963, p. 165).

128 MECW 3, pp. 294–5.

129 Klein 1997, p. 67.

in each kind, since such a person is like a rule and measure of what is beautiful and pleasant'.[130]

Klein believed that the 'experience of depressive feelings' – that is, the specific kind of 'suffering' associated with them – 'has the effect of further integrating the ego, because it makes for an increased understanding of psychic reality and better perception of the external world, as well as for a greater synthesis between inner and external situations'.[131] This is consistent with the findings presented in *The Authoritarian Personality* by Adorno et al., which focused on a study of the 'potential fascist'. The authors developed a scoring system of personality traits to measure individual authoritarianism. The subjects who scored low on the test are comparable with this Kleinian reading of Marx's depiction of the revolutionary subject. The capacity to bear depressive feelings and mental stresses without regressing to primitive defence mechanisms and a flight into phantasy is consistent with the kind of revolutionary individuals that Marx's theory entails. This is typical of people who would score low on the 'F scale' (as presented in *The Authoritarian Personality*) which was an instrument developed to measure 'antidemocratic potential' and 'implicit prefascist tendencies'.[132] As the authors wrote, such individuals tend to 'manifest open anxieties and feelings of depression, due perhaps at least in part to their greater capacity of facing insecurity and conflict'.[133] These individuals are less likely to develop forms of 'morality based on irrational anxiety', which has positive implications for their political attitudes and behaviour.[134]

---

130 Aristotle 2002, p. 44. Cf. Fromm's claim that the 'revolutionary character is the one who is identified with humanity and therefore transcends the narrow limits of his own society, and who is able, because of this, to criticise his or any other society from the standpoint of reason and humanity. He is not caught in the parochial worship of that culture which he happens to be born in, which is nothing but an accident of time and geography. He is a man who is awake and who finds his criteria of judging the norms which exist in and for the human race' (Fromm 1963, p. 158).

131 Klein 1997, pp. 14; 44.

132 Adorno et al. 1950, p. 224.

133 Adorno et al. 1950, p. 441.

134 Money-Kyrle 1952, p. 230.

Conclusion

If to be human is to suffer we are not human to suffer only
this is why I think so often, these days, of the great river
of this meaning that goes forward between banks of herbs and weeds
and animals that graze and slake their thirst and people that sow and
   reap
and even of great tombs and small dwellings of the dead.
This flowing that follows its course and is not so different from human
   blood
or from human eyes when they gaze fixedly and without fear into their
   own hearts ...[1]

Marx's idea of revolutionary subjectivity is not limited to a sterile conception of class *consciousness*. To conceive it as such would be to treat it abstractly, one-sidedly, because it would be depicted in separation from emotional life and broader somatic experiencing which together constitute the totality of human experience. Satisfying the needs of our bodies – including the emotional needs associated with the psyche, the nexus of the human mind and body – is a perennial feature of the human experience. Marx's notion of revolutionary subjectivity is more thoroughly psychological, in which mentality is conceived as a component of the ensouled human organism along with emotional and somatic life.

The problem of revolutionary subjectivity as it exists in Marx's thought is located within the domain of his incipient psychological ideas. Ultimately, it is a psychosocial issue which cannot be remedied by vanguardism. Marx's writings convey a sensitivity to the depth of human suffering that has a greater value than worn out platitudes about raising the consciousness of the masses. His social philosophy is oriented toward developing a 'scientific' comprehension of social life that assists with the clarity of perspective required for social transformation. This is not a philosophical practice that leads to the kind of comprehension that Marx derided in his infamous eleventh thesis on Feuerbach. Instead, true to his Hegelian heritage, on the premises of Marx's social philosophy such comprehension takes place as human beings engaged in revolutionary practice change the sociomaterial world they inhabit and themselves simultaneously. The implication is that the revolutionary social theorist must undergo a corresponding transformation of their own subjectivity.

---

1 Seferis 2016, p. 113.

Social philosophy on Marx's premises works toward revolutionary awakening not as a vanguard who guides workers with 'false consciousness' through the motions of revolution. Instead, it acts as a comrade in the struggle who has had the opportunity to clearly comprehend and articulate the situation. But its ability to 'show the world what it is really fighting for' is determined in part by the receptivity of the working class – a receptivity which rests on their independent development of revolutionary subjectivity, which Marx claimed was happening.[2] And he also knew that certain social conditions undermine the labour of this kind of philosopher, such as when societies are 'deep in the mire' of a *patriotism*' that buttresses a despotic state, as he described Germany in 1843.[3] At the time he claimed that a 'real anarchy of the mind, the reign of stupidity itself, prevails'.[4] Similar difficulties confront the social philosopher today.

Without an adequate theory of the subjectivity at the basis of our life practice, social philosophy unavoidably falls short of explaining to the world 'the meaning of its own actions' and giving 'religious and philosophical questions the form corresponding to man who has become conscious of himself'.[5] At a formative period in Marx's life he expressed the desire to contribute to the 'self-clarification ... to be gained by the present time of its struggles and desires'.[6] He described the possibility of a 'reform of consciousness' as the awakening of the world 'out of its dream about itself' which involves '*realising* the thoughts of the past' and 'consciously carrying into effect' the 'old work' of humanity.[7] This goal corresponds to the essential aim of psychoanalytic theory which, in its own way, is concerned with what Marx called an analysis of the 'mystical consciousness that is unintelligible to itself'.[8] From the psychoanalytic perspective, the past bears on the present insofar as the formative period in early life determines the development of our adult character. More specifically, it is present mentally through wishes, instinctual impulses, emotional ties, and so on, that were repressed in the process of psychological development and have returned to influence us from our 'unconscious'. This perspective was reanimated in the Kleinian school's idea of 'unconscious phantasy'. As Money-Kyrle put it, when 'phantasy' is at work there is 'an undercurrent of patterns' in an individual's behaviour that belong 'to other situations than the present one. Something is

---

2   MECW 3, p. 144.
3   MECW 3, p. 133.
4   MECW 3, p. 142.
5   MECW 3, p. 144.
6   MECW 3, p. 145.
7   MECW 3, p. 144.
8   Ibid.

being repeated from the past ... The perceptual world ... is being distorted –
perhaps only to a slight and barely perceptible degree – by unconscious phantasy, and it is the distorted picture to which' we 'emotionally' react.[9] He claimed
that when 'the phantasy world' is gradually recognised as unreal,

> the belief systems expressed by it are to this extent corrected. The process
> is analogous to the awakening from a dream. No one is entirely awake even
> when he is out of bed, for everyone has moods of irrational depression,
> anxiety or irritation which reflect the unconscious influence of phantasy.
> The neurotic or psychotic is someone who lives more in an unconscious
> dream world than other people, the unrecognised influence of which
> accounts for the irrationality of his emotional behaviour. As he gradually
> wakes under the influence of analysis, he may have to face some sorrows
> which he previously evaded; but he will also discard some nightmare-like
> anxieties.[10]

To put it in the allegorical words of Heraclitus, 'The waking have one world in
common. Sleepers meanwhile turn aside, each into a darkness of his own'.[11]

The experience of 'phantasy' as represented in Klein's version of psychoanalysis parallels Marx's idea of the 'mystical consciousness' of 'estrangement'
because it involves illusions that are unavoidable and at times instrumental for
development. Marx's depiction of this consciousness – e.g., as expressed in religious life or the fetishism which attaches itself to commodities – is analogous
to the Freudian sense of 'illusion' which he maintained is 'not the same thing
as an error'.[12] In Freud's view, such 'illusions' are

> derived from human wishes. In this respect they come near to psychiat-
> ric delusions. But they differ from them, too, apart from the more com-
> plicated structure of delusions. In the case of delusions, we emphasise
> as essential their being in contradiction with reality. Illusions need not
> necessarily be false – that is to say, unrealisable or in contradiction with

---

9   Money-Kyrle 1951, p. 85.
10   Money-Kyrle 1951, pp. 85–6. As Norman Brown put it, in 'the case of the neurotic indi-
      vidual, the goal of psychoanalytical therapy is to free him from the burden of his past ...
      And the method of psychoanalytical therapy is to deepen the historical consciousness of
      the individual ... till he awakens from his own history as from a nightmare' (Brown 1959,
      p. 19).
11   Heraclitus 2001, p. 63.
12   Freud 1961, p. 48.

reality ... Thus we call a belief an illusion when a wish-fulfillment is a prominent factor in its motivation, and in doing so we disregard its relations to reality, just as the illusion itself sets no store by verification.[13]

As an example, Freud mentions 'the assertion made by certain nationalists that the Indo-Germanic race is the only one capable of civilisation'.[14]

A significant difference between the psychoanalytic approach to overcoming this 'illusory' consciousness and the kind of approach presented in Marx's work is that Marx presents the process that mires us in 'illusions' as one that also brings about a historical 'evolution' of the human mind whereby the illusion is overcome along with the life activity that gives rise to it. The idea that psychoanalysis by an external analyst is necessary for this awakening is antithetical to Marx's view that overcoming 'estrangement' is a result of the process of 'estrangement' itself. From his perspective we can dispel our 'mystical consciousness' only through activity which transforms our conditions of life and our subjectivity simultaneously. Thus he insisted that revolutionary theorists are limited to presenting what is actually happening for individuals whose life activity is transforming them to the extent required to comprehend it. But he also maintained that conditions of 'estrangement' foment counter-revolutionary tendencies. Indeed, his writing indicates that he perceived a tendency to become saturated in the various illusions that arise organically out of our conditions of life and resist what he considered the 'reform of consciousness'. A conspicuous example from his work is the prejudice and division observable among sections of the English and Irish proletariat in 1870 which has both a 'material' and a psychological basis.[15]

It must be reemphasised that Marx's social analysis indicates that there are forms of human life which impede the development of the capacity for reas-

---

13   Freud 1961, pp. 48–9.
14   Freud 1961, p. 48.
15   Consider the following from Erica Benner who points to the subjective dimension of this issue as a fundamental component: 'In explaining this rift, Marx began by observing that the economic insecurity engendered by capitalism tended to fuel intra-proletarian resentments ... But why, within a class that was supposed to represent the triumph of shared interests over divisive prejudices, should competition among English workers themselves be any less fierce than competition with their Irish counterparts? Marx suggested that part of the answer lay in a psychological effect of the asymmetrical relations between metropole and colony, which allowed the English worker to regard himself as "a member of the ruling nation." By succumbing to such prejudices, the English worker tacitly endorsed the acts of exploitation which had demeaned Irish national identity and obliged Irish workers to leave the country in search of employment' (Benner 2018, p. 189).

onable political attitudes and activity. This recognition has significant implications for the practice of revolutionary social philosophy. In the words of Adorno et al. in *The Authoritarian Personality*, 'Rational arguments cannot be expected to have deep or lasting effects upon a phenomenon that is irrational in its essential nature'.[16] Indeed, the illusory and at times profoundly deluded character of 'mystical consciousness' undermines insight into social life and any attempt to put social and political problems into 'the form corresponding to [humanity that] has become conscious of [itself]'.[17] And yet any analysis of it on Marx's premises necessarily involves analysing the consciousness of those who struggle in a reactionary way, such as those who are irrationally tied to their oppressors; e.g., the 'the supressed classes' who Freud claimed 'can be emotionally attached to their masters'.[18] Consider Marx's idea of the 'social scum', a host body for the virus of reactionary politics whose 'conditions of life' make them particularly susceptible to manipulation by the ruling class, preparing them 'for the part of a bribed tool of reactionary intrigue'.[19] But the rise of the far-right in the twentieth century and today indicates that the so-called 'dangerous class' is not just limited to the *Lumpenproletariat*, and thus that the concept of 'dangerous' in this context must be expanded. To start, we can consider Marx's broad observation that such individuals are not *thinking*. In an article on a counter-revolutionary trend in 1848 he mentioned how the '*lazzaroni*, lumpenproletariat hired and armed', were 'used against the working and thinking proletarians'.[20] Of course these individuals are still human beings who are inherently rational, but Marx's writing suggests that their cognition suffers from a conspicuous limitation. He was aware of and concerned with distorted political perception, a form of 'delusive prejudice', and he associated 'prejudice' and 'superstition' in particular with the need to be led by others. For instance, Marx claimed the Bonaparte dynasty represented 'the superstition of the peasant; not his judgment, but his prejudice'.[21] This harkens back to the discussion of Kant's view of superstition as a form of prejudice which is associated with a cognitive impairment and the need to be led by others. Adorno et al. made this connection as well, claiming that 'superstition and stereotypy embrace, over

---

16   Adorno et al. 1950, p. 973. Cf. Schiller's claim that 'it must be something in men's psyche that obstructs the acceptance of truth, even when it is so vividly convincing' (Schiller 2016, p. 27).

17   MECW 3, p. 144.

18   Freud 1961, p. 17.

19   MECW 6, p. 494. He described this 'dangerous class' as 'that passively rotting mass, thrown off by the lowest layers of old society' (MECW 6, p. 494).

20   MECW 7, p. 505.

21   MECW 11, p. 188.

and above the mere lack of intelligence in the ordinary sense, certain dispositions in thinking which are closely akin to prejudice', which 'can be understood,
in part at least, as expressions of ego weakness'.[22] In their analysis, 'ego weakness' is 'a concomitant of conventionalism and authoritarianism'.[23] Kleinian
psychoanalysis offers a potential explanation for the mental struggles associated with cognitive distortions and delusive worldviews in extreme conspiratorial politics, such as the QAnon movement, which illuminates the connection
to authoritarianism. Klein claimed that

> Permanent submission to the authority principle, permanent greater or
> less intellectual dependency and limitation, are based on this first and
> most significant experience of authority, on the relationship between the
> parents and the little child. Its effect is strengthened and supported by
> the mass of ethical and moral ideas that are presented duly complete
> to the child and which form just so many barriers to the freedom of his
> thought.[24]

The authors of *The Authoritarian Personality* considered it necessary to comprehend such phenomena and 'take into account the whole structure of the
prejudiced outlook' in order to develop 'countermeasures' to the growth of the
fascist character.[25] In their view, 'resistance to self-insight and resistance to
social facts are contrived, most essentially, of the same stuff', and they claimed
that psychology plays 'its most important role' in the development of techniques for 'overcoming resistance'.[26] The task then involves adapting psycho-
therapeutic techniques from the 'field of individual psychotherapy ... for use
with groups and even for use on a mass scale'.[27] They thought that

> it may be hoped that knowledge of what the potential fascist is like ... will
> make symptomatic treatment more effective. Thus, for example, although
> appeals to [their] reason or to [their] sympathy are likely to be lost on
> [them], appeals to [their] conventionality or to [their] submissiveness
> toward authority might be effective.[28]

---

22   Adorno et al. 1950, p. 236.
23   Adorno et al. 1950, p. 234.
24   Klein 1998, p. 23.
25   Adorno et al. 1950, p. 973.
26   Adorno et al. 1950, p. 976.
27   Ibid.
28   Adorno et al. 1950, p. 973. Mark Fisher claimed that 'people are more likely to be persuaded
      if defensive character armour is not triggered' (Fisher 2018, p. 583).

But according to these authors, 'such activity would in no way reduce [their] conventionality or authoritarianism or [their] fascist potential'.[29] Thus even if we figured out how to perform mass psychotherapy on the foundation of a psychology that can address the potential fascist in their larval stage (such as, for example, some form of mass Dialectical Behavior Therapy to address dichotomous thinking in politics), there is still the general principle, expressed in Marx's work, that it is ultimately life activity (developmental conditions, immediate material circumstances, general social conditions, etc.) that primes the subject for receptivity to such 'treatment' and the effectiveness of revolutionary social theory in general. In the words of Adorno et al.,

> It seems obvious therefore that the modification of the potentially fascist structure cannot be achieved by psychological means alone. The task is comparable to that of eliminating neurosis, or delinquency, or nationalism from the world. These are products of the total organisation of society and are to be changed only as that society is changed.[30]

Despite this issue, psychological theory is arguably a necessary component of the kind of social philosophy that Marx practiced. This is prefigured in the Socratic tradition of philosophy that greatly influenced Marx. Plato, for instance, structured the social order of his Republic around his conception of what he understood to be the proper functioning of the tripartite psyche, whereby the particular character of individuals (rooted in the part of the soul that they are predominantly motivated by) is sublated into social soul-life.[31] Treating human society itself as an ensouled entity enables us to conceptualise how individuals with extreme political attitudes and behaviours exist as an acute expression of broader tendencies that percolate in social life. Such a perspective is not derived from a reification of the activities of individual minds, or a mere aggregation of individuals into an abstract totality, but rather the rational soul of the collective human world, the living totality of the human mind which exists as the sublation of our individual minds (whereby our individual and historically determinate forms of 'estrangement' can be develop-

---

29   Adorno et al. 1950, p. 973.

30   Adorno et al. 1950, p. 975. Cf. Wolfenstein's claim that 'politics cannot be therapy and therapy should not be politics. How, then, to heal political wounds? The Marxist and psychoanalytic-Marxist answer to this question is political transformation' (Wolfenstein 1993, p. 390).

31   Marx's conception of society as a kind of ensouled entity arises in such articulations as 'general intellect' and 'social intelligence' (MECW 29, pp. 92; 95).

mental for the human species).[32] Aristotle's search for 'human good and human happiness' led to an examination of 'virtue' and 'human excellence' which 'belongs not to the body but to the soul', and he makes this a concern of the 'one skilled in politics' who he claims 'must study the soul'.[33] The political relevance of such analysis for Marx's revolutionary social theory is apparent in his depiction of instances when working people develop irrational, counter revolutionary tendencies. A theorist equipped with psychological insight can more effectively play their role as the mouthpiece of the struggle for emancipation because they would be sensitive to the vicissitudes of human subjectivity in a time of crisis, particularly when strain on the social organism leads to political polarisation and the onset of extreme political attitudes and behaviour.

Developing awareness of the effects of capitalism on our minds enriches our understanding of sociopolitical phenomena and more favourably positions us to make effective interventions in the social life process. Mark Fisher, for instance, considered it urgent to re-politicise 'mental illness' as a challenge to 'the deleterious psychic effects of neoliberalism'.[34] He claimed that 'Widespread mental illness is one of the hidden costs of neoliberal capitalism; stress has been privatised'.[35] A chief reason for this, according to him, was mentioned in Chapter Five, namely that 'Neoliberalism instills a perpetual anxiety – there is no security'. This is particularly relevant for the so-called *precariat*, i.e., those workers who experience 'constant conditions of instability and insecurity, short-term employment, [and] casualization'.[36] In such circumstances we tend to take our activity and relations (e.g., competition, exchange, exploitation, etc.) for granted, typically because our lives leave us too desperate, weakened and demoralised to do anything about it. Fisher commented further that 'With precarity increasing and welfare programmes eroding, it's not sur-

---

32   Consider this perspective along the lines of Durkheim's claim that 'individuals by combining form a psychical existence of a new species, which consequently has its own manner of thinking and feeling' (Durkheim 1979, p. 310).

33   Aristotle 2002, pp. 19–20.

34   Fisher 2018, p. 631.

35   Ibid.

36   Consider, for instance, the 'incredible amount of pressure' that Amazon puts on its workers 'to work faster and faster', a practice which they go along with because of 'the fear of being "written up" and losing their jobs, which will thrust them into other low-paid jobs with fewer benefits' (Semuels 2018). As one worker put it: 'The constant trying to chase your rate [of productivity], trying to stay ahead of being written up – it affects you psychologically'. Another worker claimed that 'what makes people not want to quit' Amazon is 'the pay': 'People say, "You can treat met any type of way, since this is the best money we can get out here in Moreno Valley"' (Ibid.).

prising that there should be an increase in depression and anxiety'.[37] The effects of such conditions on working people undermines the revolutionary process and disturbs the attitudes required for the struggle for universal emancipation. From a Kleinian standpoint, excessive anxiety spurred on by deteriorating social conditions and precarity could trigger some individuals toward regressive politics insofar as 'an increase of anxiety will lead to a regression to the defensive mechanisms of earlier stages' of psychical life.[38]

The idea of mentality in Marx's social philosophy is thoroughly social. A key premise of Marx's 'materialist conception of history' is the idea that the 'production of life' is simultaneously a 'natural' and a 'social relationship'.[39] The 'need, the necessity', of 'associating with the individuals around' us to sustain life connotes the fundamentally social nature of human life and consciousness.[40] While Marx focused on the labour process in 'civil society' as a primary nexus of human development and 'estrangement', he also thought that these processes are mediated by other relations and forms of the social practice of production and reproduction. One such nexus that he mentions explicitly in the process of elaborating the premises of his theory of history is within family units, and more specifically in the relations between 'parents and children'. He depicts this as a kind of primary social unit within which individuals develop, which is itself sublated within other social units, and his writing indicates that he had a sensitivity to the character of this relationship within a developmental, psychosocial framework. As he claimed, in 'too many cases' a working person 'is even too ignorant to understand the true interest of [their] child, or the normal conditions of human development'. When this statement is viewed through a Freudian lens, it can be said that Marx has opened a psychosexual dimension of social life, and the roots of his thinking in Aristotelian philosophy is conducive to this perspective insofar as Aristotle conceived of the *oikos* as the primary socioeconomic unit sublated within the polity. Marx's critical appropriation of Hegelian philosophy is also complimentary in this instance. The dialectic of self-consciousness, as it were, also takes place within the household, the site of social reproduction, and not just at the level of broader socioeconomic relations in 'civil society'. Before this dialectic takes place in the labour

---

37   Fisher 2018, p. 667.
38   Klein 1997b, p. 177.
39   MECW 5, p. 43.
40   MECW 5, p. 44. This emphasis on the sociality of our psyche is implicit in Freudian psychoanalysis. As Jacqueline Rose put it, Freud conceptualised the psyche as 'a social space': 'Even when we dream, we are not alone. Our most intimate psychic secrets are always embedded in the others – groups, masses, institutions, and peoples – from which they take their cue' (Rose 2011, pp. 86; 113).

process, the individual's psyche is primed in the relationship between the child and parents or other caregivers. The household, or early developmental context, is one in which the individual experiences their prototypical experience of political relationships, which is more or less beneficial for future liberatory attitudes and revolutionary practice. We may consider that the revolutionary transformation of society begins in the childhood of the generations that will rise to resist exploitation and oppression, and that their experience with authority as children – e.g., caregivers who are more of a friend, relating through love, or more of a foe, relating through disciplinary authoritarianism – will determine their prospects for revolutionary transformation in their later adult life. In other words, the implication is that the difference between individuals' character as politically active adults is that some people experience development in earlier years that is conducive to revolutionary activity in later life while others do not.

In this respect, Marx's social theory overlaps with the psychoanalytic emphasis on conditions of childhood development and the centrality of the individual's relationship to their parents and caregivers. From this perspective, the character of the parents and their parenting style, alongside the nature of domestic life in general, is a key factor in individual development and the formation of individual character. This leads to an organic conception of the society in which the character of individuals and groups is sublated into the broader character of the state and mass social institutions, which then exerts an influence on the formation of individual character in turn. Money-Kyrle described this as 'the influence of the state on the moral character of adults', 'the influence of the moral character of adults on that of children', and 'the influence of the moral character of these children, when they become adults, on the state'.[41] He highlighted the contrast between homes of 'humanists' and 'authoritarians' by describing the former's household as one in which there tended to be 'an unusual degree of both freedom and affection', and the latter's as having a 'strict patriarchal nature ... to which they gratefully attribute their own regard for discipline'.[42] However, Money-Kyrle noted that 'the typical fascist or Nazi was more often the product of a disturbed or broken than of a patriarchal home'.[43] Indeed, Klein's work suggests that such disturbances in character development are more directly rooted in an excessively disciplinary parenting relationship in particular. She claimed that

---

41   Money-Kyrle 1951, p. 108.
42   Money-Kyrle 1951, pp. 12–13.
43   Money-Kyrle 2015, p. 240.

the vital influence of early environment has also the effect that unfavourable aspects of the attitudes of the adult towards the child are detrimental to his development because they stir up in him hatred and rebellion or too great submissiveness. At the same time he internalises this hostile and angry adult attitude. Out of such experiences, an excessively disciplinarian parent, or a parent lacking in understanding and love, by identification influences the character formation of the child.[44]

This is consistent with the findings presented in *The Authoritarian Personality*. The authors claim that one of 'the most important differences as compared with the family of the typical high scorer' on the scale that measures fascistic personality traits 'is that less obedience is expected of the children. Parents are ... less intolerant toward manifestations of socially unaccepted behavior. Instead of condemning they tend to provide more guidance and support'.[45] Thus alongside an excessively disciplinary relationship, Adorno et al. highlight other factors in the conduct of parents and caregivers in relation to their children which contributes to the formation of the 'prejudiced personality', such as insufficient affection and insensitivity to mental and emotional needs. They wrote that

When we consider the childhood situation of the most prejudiced subjects, we find reports of a tendency toward rigid discipline on the part of the parents, with affection which is conditional rather than unconditional, i.e., dependent upon approved behavior on the part of the child.

---

44   Klein 1997, p. 260. For Klein, the most significant factor for 'a stable emotional development' is the 'young infant's relation to the mother and to the food, love and care she provides' (Klein 1997, p. 271). Adorno et al. put forward the claim that, 'Forced into a surface submission to parental authority, the child develops hostility and aggression which are poorly channelled. The displacement of a repressed antagonism toward authority may be one of the sources, and perhaps the principal source, of his antagonism toward outgroups. That is to say, the prejudiced subject's ambivalence toward his parents, with a repression and externalisation of the negative side of this ambivalence, may be a factor in determining his strongly polarised attitudes, such as his uncritical acceptance of the ingroup and violent rejection of the outgroup' (Adorno et al. 1950, p. 482). They claim further that 'ethnocentrists tend to be submissive to ingroup authority, anti-ethnocentrists to be critical or rebellious, and that the family is the first and prototypic ingroup. The individual's relation to parental authority, particularly his disposition to be submissive or critically independent, appears to be a basic personality trend which partially determines his political party preference and his ideology about group relations' (Adorno et al. 1950, p. 192).

45   Adorno et al. 1950, pp. 387–388.

Related to this is a tendency apparent in families of prejudiced subjects to base interrelationships on rather clearly defined roles of dominance and submission, in contradistinction to equalitarian policies. Faithful execution of prescribed roles and the exchange of duties and obligations is, in the families of the prejudiced, often given preference over the exchange of free-flowing affection. The hypothesis may be offered that some of the traits of the prejudiced personality are an outcome of this family situation.[46]

This stands in contrast with the 'families of unprejudiced subjects' in which there is 'on the whole, more affection, or more unconditional affection', whereby such individuals 'received more love and therefore have basically more security in their relationships to their parents'.[47] It is worth underscoring that it is not necessarily a *patriarchal* family that is at the root of extreme political personalities, but authoritarianism (excessively controlling and disciplinary childrearing practices), and thus while markedly patriarchal family life tends to be authoritarian, matriarchal family life can also have similar outcomes. It is thus a question of the general character of the relationships within the developmental context, not simply the nature of sex or gender roles.

Another contributing factor to the development of personalities akin to political insanity which derives from excessively disciplinary and authoritarian parenting relationships and domestic environments is the likelihood that the child will experience excessive frustration which can affect them in ways that are detrimental for their development. Klein elaborates this point by claiming that

> Naturally, frustration which is in reality unnecessary or arbitrary and shows nothing but lack of love and understanding is very detrimental. It is important to realise that the child's development depends on, and to a large extent is formed by, his capacity to find the way to bear inevitable and necessary frustrations and the conflicts of love and hate which are in part caused by them; that is to find his way between his hate which is increased by frustrations, and his love and wish for reparation which bring in their train the sufferings of remorse. The way the child adapts himself to these problems in his mind forms the foundation for all his later social relationships, his adult capacity for love and cultural development.[48]

---

46   Adorno et al. 1950, p. 482.
47   Adorno et al. 1950, p. 357.
48   Klein 1998, p. 316.

Paula Heimann and Susan Isaacs also illustrated the relationship between frustration and regression. They claim that, according to Freud,

> it is frustration that initiates regression. But, in our view, it does so not only by a simple 'damming-up' of libido, but also by evoking hate and aggression and consequent anxiety. The newly evoked hate and aggression reactivate the hardly overcome pre-genital sadism, and this in its turn pulls back the libido to its earlier forms, in order to neutralise the destructive forces once again at work in the mind.[49]

We can thus use the term 'regressive politics' as a way to describe the reactionary individual whose politics are regressive from both a social and psychological standpoint. Their work can also be taken to suggest that it contributes to the psychological development of individuals that is analogous to the kind of mentality met with in extreme political attitudes and behaviour toward social and political out-groups and enemies, including those who function as scapegoats to take blame for economic struggle, corruption, etc.:

> Since frustration acts as a lever for the deflection of hate and destructiveness from the self, it is sought after because an object which inflicts the pain of frustration may be more justifiably hated and annihilated. Thus frustration has its appointed place in the design of primitive defences. But precisely for this reason a frustrating environment, lack of understanding and love are so dangerous for the child. When the environment meets his needs for the deflection of his destructive impulses half-way by coldness, rejection and hostility, a vicious circle is created. The child grows up in the expectation of badness and, when he finds his fears confirmed in the world outside, his own cruel and negativistic impulses are perpetuated and increased.[50]

This adds another layer to the Kleinian view of the 'link between social structure, character and specific experiences of infancy' because of its effect on the 'super-ego'.[51] In particular, Heimann and Issacs claim that 'the hate and aggression aroused by the frustration which starts the regressive process at once evokes the dread of the super-ego, the hating and vengeful internal object; and this in its turn stimulates the need to hate and fight again with all the weapons

---

49   Heimann and Isaacs 1952, p. 176.
50   Heimann and Isaacs 1952, p. 336.
51   Money-Kyrle 1951, p. 106.

of pre-genital sadism'.[52] This is particularly detrimental because the 'severe demands' of a 'harsh super-ego' will 'increase depressive and paranoid anxieties', which contributes significantly to the psychology of a regressive political personality.[53] This is also politically significant because, as Money-Kyrle claimed, the 'influence of the state results ... from the fact that it is nearly always personified as a parental figure' and that it 'is something into which we tend to project our super-egos'.[54]

It must be emphasised that psychological theory on its own is limited for the purpose of comprehending social and political phenomena. As the authors of *The Authoritarian Personality* wrote,

> our findings are strictly limited to the psychological aspects of the more general problem of prejudice. Historical factors or economic forces operating in our society to promote or to diminish ethnic prejudice are clearly beyond the scope of our investigation. In pointing toward the importance of the parent-child relationship in the establishment of prejudice or tolerance we have moved one step in the direction of an explanation. We have not, however, gone into the social and economic processes.[55]

This dimension of human life, the so-called 'material' conditions of existence, is the domain of a social theory which has a developmental framework like the one created by Marx. The link between developmental conditions and political attitudes and behaviour is an issue that requires socioeconomic analysis that accounts for the organic interrelation between social existence and psychological development. There is a direct connection between socioeconomic adversity experienced by parents and caregivers (which disproportionately affects the working class) and adverse conditions of childhood development, such as when children are neglected by their parents because of excessive work obligations (which disproportionately affects certain groups within the working class). Consider, for example, situations when mental and physical exhaustion is compounded by the attendant effects of the stress associated with being of a lower socioeconomic status, such as financial precarity, underemployment and unemployment. In such conditions there is an increased likelihood of domestic authoritarian oppression and abusiveness which stunts

---

52   Heimann and Isaacs 1952, p. 182.
53   Klein 1997, p. 313.
54   Money-Kyrle 1951, p. 108.
55   Adorno et al. 1950, p. 972.

moral development by disrupting emotional function and regulation.[56] This alone does not provide ideological content for an individual's political orientation, but it does nevertheless predispose individuals – in the sense of being psychologically susceptible – to the kind of politics associated with authoritarian oppression. From the perspective of Klein's theory in particular, abuse and mistreatment of children is conducive to the development of a personality that is susceptible to far-right politics because it arouses and reinforces 'paranoid-schizoid' tendencies, heightening the risk for the rise of the morality of fascism in social conditions of crisis and decay in which there is a significant strain on our rational faculties.

The strain is worse for individuals who are more predisposed psychologically because of adverse conditions of development that become compounded by adverse socioeconomic conditions in their adult life. Marx pointed to a correlation between a particularly adverse set of life circumstances faced by some individuals and the form of state that they support in his analysis of the 'lumpenproletariat'. He claimed that Bonaparte 'constitutes himself *chief of the Lumpenproletariat*' and perceived 'in this scum, offal, refuse of all classes the only class upon which he can base himself unconditionally'.[57] At the time, Marx described them as 'vagabonds, discharged soldiers, discharged jailbirds, escaped galley slaves, rogues, mountebanks, *lazzaroni*, pickpockets, tricksters, gamblers, *maquereaus*, brothel keepers, porters, *literati*, organ-grinders, ragpickers, knife grinders, tinkers, beggars'.[58] A conspicuous common characteristic shared by this 'indefinite, disintegrated mass' is that they have been 'thrown hither and thither' by the ebb and flow and socioeconomic life.[59] Such individuals are comparable to some members of the contemporary precariat, whose conditions of life leave them psychologically debilitated from a political standpoint, particularly if they are those who feel no significant stake in society and no meaningful political representation by conventional mainstream

---

56   Parental stress and burnout increases the risk of abuse and maltreatment, especially for those with predisposed characters. Studies indicate that 'Parents who exert an excess of parental control (i.e., authoritarian parents) have children with weaker self-regulatory skill', and that 'Moral reasoning and development subsequent to a history of maltreatment often reflect poor self-regulation and aggressive themes' (Piotrowski, Lapierre and Linebarger 2013, p. 434; Crooks and Wolfe 2007, p. 667). Studies also indicate that physically abusive families are 'significantly more often low income' (Whipple and Webster-Stratton 1991, p. 279). It is relevant in this instance to recall Klein's claim that 'above all we shall reject physical punishment and threats' in childrearing practices (Klein 1998, p. 26).

57   MECW 11, p. 149.

58   Ibid.

59   Ibid.

parties, and who thereby see through the façade of the elite political class but not with actual clarity of the socioeconomic situation. They do not trust individuals at the helm of political power because they are downtrodden, which can become a basis for extreme politics when their psyche is predisposed to react to socioeconomic stresses in a way that exacerbates pre-existing political confusion, such as a predisposition to paranoia.

Such circumstances call for a psychosocial philosophy that can address these issues appropriately. If an attempt is made at bridging psychoanalytic theory and Marx's social philosophy for this purpose, they will necessarily sublate into something more than just another social psychology. The ultimate aim would be comprehension for the sake of devising ways inoculate our society against extreme politics.[60] There is a caveat, however, which relates to the vanguardist fallacy, because it would appeal to those among us who are rational enough to act on the insight it provides. It is futile to make a case for socialist politics or democracy or workers' rights or human needs, and so on, to those who such demands cannot resonate with. But this is no reason to give up resistance to authoritarianism, or the fight to defend the oppressed and exploited. This could take the form of public policy that takes up the mantle of the precarious on the basis of an understanding of the significance of meeting such needs from a deeper psychological perspective. The fight against the far-right is often narrowly conceived as one for the streets with weapons like bats and guns, but much more effective weapons against political insanity involve things like massive anti-poverty programs and a broader movement to refranchise people into society. Preventing the metamorphosis of a larval fascist by improving social conditions is much more desirable than confronting a mature fascistic mass movement. Consider Marx's emphasis on incremental developments in the life circumstances of working people through advancements in public policy like the Ten Hours Act (i.e. the Factories Act of 1847) which is something that would contribute to the mental culture of the working class, among other aspects of life, and has the broader effect of widening the scope of freedom for successive generations. Even if such progress is incremental, it nevertheless works to wash away 'the muck of ages', the trauma of history. Such trauma is reflected in the ethos of capitalism which degrades humanity as it relentlessly debases working-class individuals who reproduce a set of social conditions and

---

60   Money-Kyrle claimed that 'One of the politically most important problems to which analysis can be applied is that of the interdependence between social form and individual character', and it can be utilised to 'give a more detailed answer to the question: what social conditions are likely to be favourable, and what unfavourable, to the development of mature and healthy personality' (Money-Kyrle 1951, pp. 106; 123).

perpetuate a pattern of activities and relations which wear down our capacity for reason. We must keep in mind that this capacity is something that develops from infancy and therefore requires a society with an ethos that is oriented toward nurturing all of its members from the time of their birth. The need to create such a world is highlighted by Margaret and Michael Rustin who maintain that caregivers need care too:

> [Development] in infants depends on intimate relationships between an infant and a mother or other parent-figure who needs to have the security and emotional space to bear the intense and (often negative and anxious) feelings of the infant and to modulate its experience of the outside world in balance with its capacity to handle them for itself ... [E]motional development depends on identification, and is especially furthered where those who support growth are able to understand and mitigate the pains of unavoidable limits and deprivation. This should not lead us to set up idealised and prosecuting specifications of what are 'good' parents or care-givers. The question should rather be, how are caregivers themselves to be cared for, since their own needs being met is the precondition for their being able to meet the needs of children or other dependents.[61]

A society based on this nurturing ethos is that which revolutionary subjects aim to establish for the benefit of themselves and their families with the awareness that it will benefit the generations to come. The ethos of this world free of estrangement would be akin to a society based on 'mutual moral support' as envisioned by Durkheim:

> For they cling to life more resolutely when belonging to a group they love, so as not to betray interests they put before their own. The bond that unites them with the common cause attaches them to life and the lofty goal they envisage prevents their feeling personal troubles so deeply. There is, in short, in a cohesive and animated society a constant interchange of ideas and feelings from all to each and each to all, something like a mutual moral support, which instead of throwing the individual on his own resources, leads him to share in the collective energy and support his own when exhausted.[62]

---

61   Rustin and Rustin 1984, p. 209.
62   Durkheim 1979, pp. 209–10.

The embryonic revolutionary subject must develop the capacities to enable them to establish a movement which consciously seeks to create the world of mutual care required to uplift humanity. Political and economic crises may create an opportunity for change and perhaps even be a catalyst for growth, but they can also be destructive and debilitating if the fabric of society unravels and estrangement intensifies. This appears to be the situation facing us now and it is the reason why we have received the 'call to comprehend'.

Social philosophy can be understood as a kind of therapeutic practice for the social soul, but Marx's work indicates that even if social scientists can comprehend the causes of extremism, staging an intervention or preventative measures on their part is only a moment of the transformative process. As Adorno et al. claimed,

> It would not be difficult ... to propose a program which, even in the present cultural pattern, could produce nonethnocentric personalities. All that is really essential is that children be genuinely loved and treated as individual humans. But all the features of such a program would have the aspect of being more easily said than done.[63]

After all, the educator needs to be educated.[64] The reflex to revert to the vanguardist fallacy must be resisted.[65] The upsurge of regressive politics cannot be attributed to the absence of a left-wing alternative – it happens for the same reason that the political left is absent or negligent, and this needs to be adequately taken account of and comprehended. The reason, in brief, can be located in the forms of subjectivity within the population. After all, there are progressive currents in contemporary society and culture (in grassroots movements, political parties, policy debates, and so forth) alongside the reactionary ones. Rebellion takes on different forms.[66] The problem of differentiating

---

63   Adorno et al. 1950, p. 975.

64   Fromm echoed this problem posed by Marx's social philosophy from the perspective of political psychology: 'I believe psychologists have an important function in studying the characterological differences behind ... various types of political ideologists. But in order to do so properly they must, I fear, ... be revolutionary characters' (Fromm 1963, p. 166).

65   Reich's work provides countless examples of this fallacious way of thinking. Consider, for example, his claim that 'sex-economy must play an essential role in the ordering of social relations. The more extensively and deeply the reactionary structure has taken hold of the toiling masses, the more decisive is the importance of the sex-economic work of educating the masses of the people to assume social responsibility' (Reich 1980, p. 60).

66   Cf. Reich's claims that 'Fascist rebelliousness always accrues where a revolutionary emo-

between the struggles of an emancipatory subject and individuals who drift rightward requires recognising that class categories are limited for the purpose of social analysis. This problem calls for a social philosophy with a robust psychological theory to articulate why some people respond to a given social problem one way or the other, especially if they are of the same class. The unfortunate explanation for the ascendancy of the rightward trend is that those politics genuinely appeal to masses of people who face overwhelming struggles and crippling despair. A social philosophy rooted in the tenets of Marx's thought can benefit from psychological explanations about why anger against politicians who bailed out banks and mega corporations after the financial crisis of 2008 moved right instead of left, or why the prejudiced thinking between English and Irish proletarians is capable of being 'artificially sustained', as Marx claimed. As Reich maintained regarding the Nazi situation, 'it is precisely a question of understanding why the masses *proved to be accessible to deception, befogging, and a psychotic situation.* Without a precise knowledge of what *goes on in the masses*, the problem cannot be solved'.[67] Here, too, we have to resist the vanguard fallacy, and cannot rely on tired explanations such as that the working masses have been let down by labour leadership or that the vanguard of the working class did not rise to the occasion. In a discussion of the shortcomings of revolutionary movements in Germany in 1848, Engels highlighted the necessity of developing a broader understanding of the conditions of the people and how it affects their political movements, instead of relying on the betrayal of leadership as an explanation. He claimed that

> the study of the causes that necessitated both the late outbreak and its defeat ... are not to be sought for in the accidental efforts, talents, faults, errors or treacheries of some of the leaders, but in the general social state and conditions of existence of each of the convulsed nations. That the sudden movements of February and March 1848, were not the work of single individuals, but spontaneous, irresistible manifestations of national wants and necessities, more or less clearly understood, but very distinctly felt by numerous classes in every country, is a fact recognised everywhere; but when you inquire into the cause of the counterrevolutionary successes, there you are met on every hand with the ready reply that it was Mr. This or Citizen That who 'betrayed' the people. Which

---

tion, out of fear of truth, is distorted into illusion', and that fascism 'represents an amalgam between *rebellious* emotions and reactionary social ideas' (Reich 1980, p. xiv).

67   Reich 1980, p. 36.

reply may be very true or not, according to circumstances, but under no circumstances does it explain anything – not even show how it came to pass that the 'people' allowed themselves to be thus betrayed. And what a poor chance stands a political party whose entire stock-in-trade consists in a knowledge of the solitary fact, that citizen So-and-So is not to be trusted.[68]

The power that the far-right has to pull mainstream politics to the right has to be understood as a power they exert psychologically, not just because working people have no progressive socialist choice. If regressive politics is the form that disaffection and resistance to capitalism is taking, we have to 'study' the *peculiar* character' of this to effectively struggle against the many morbid symptoms, as Gramsci put it, in the interregnum of progressive social change, and perform the maieutic 'midwife' role. The function of this role assumes that the reactionary growth we are witnessing is not merely a regressive deviation but a kind of psychosocial birth pang, and that developing clarity about the situation is therapeutic.

From the perspective of Marx's work, success at this endeavour ultimately hinges on the development of the working class's revolutionary subjectivity. The social philosopher of this kind takes account of the irrationality endemic in regressive political movements to comprehend it and offer clarity and an alternative vision for those able to perceive it. As a necessary moment in this process, 'philosophical consciousness itself' must be 'drawn into the torment of the struggle, not only externally but also internally'.[69] For Marx this torment was transformative – it altered his perspective. He thereby achieved the awareness necessary for breathing life into his radical social philosophy. This was evident in 1843, for instance, when he wrote that 'if, nevertheless, I do not despair ... that is only because it is precisely the desperate situation which fills me with hope'.[70] Marx glimpsed freedom in the workers' revolutionary activity in Paris in 1844, proving to him that the struggle was transformative after witnessing what he considered new needs among workers and the genesis of an embryonic revolutionary subject. Thus he did not despair in 1870 when he saw the English and Irish workers divided by nationalistic and religious prejudices because he knew that there is a tendency toward emancipation that remains even if it struggles to stay afloat under the immense pressure of reactionary

---

68   MECW 11, p. 6.
69   MECW 3, p. 142.
70   MECW 3, p. 141.

waves in an ocean of social decay and political dismemberment. This tendency is present for us to see in the various progressive movements and the people who are motivated by radical love and revolutionary courage, who stand with the oppressed and proclaim through their words and action '*Solidarity forever!*' Acts of solidarity, as a form of radical recognition, are restorative and transform our perception of what is possible, providing us with glimmers of hope that have the potential to sustain our struggle for emancipation. The reality of freedom is revealed by the struggle itself. And while freedom is not inevitable, it is a real possibility nonetheless. After all, Marx framed the problem of 'estranged labour' into the question of how such 'estrangement', and 'estrangement' in general, is 'rooted in the nature of human development'.[71] To address this question requires an understanding of the psychosocial dynamic of our 'estrangement'.

> And meanwhile we spawn senses and sensations, drown in delusions
> And the river, sated with blood and mud and bile
> We suck it up bursting in air, we suck it like blood from a puncture by a
>   rust-eaten needle
> We walk crippled, our feet leaden, bound by ropes of greed, the cable of
>   defective pleasure and desire to succeed
> Charlatans multiply, they breathe the land of the brave around me, I
>   scream as if in dreams, dumb ...[72]

---

71   MECW 3, p. 281.
72   Efthymiades 2016, p. 27.

Bibliography

Adorno, Theodor W., and Else Frenkel-Brunswik, Daniel J. Levinson, R. Nevitt Sanford 1950, *The Authoritarian Personality*, New York: Harper and Brothers.

Alford, C.F. 1989, *Melanie Klein and Critical Social Theory*, New Haven: Yale University Press.

Alighieri, Dante 1985, *The Divine Comedy, Purgatory*, Volume 2, translated by Mark Musa, New York: Penguin Books.

Anderson, Kevin B. 2010, *Marx at the Margins: On Nationalism, Ethnicity, and Non-Western Societies*, Chicago: University of Chicago Press.

Aristotle 1998, *Politics*, translated by C.D.C. Reeve, Indianapolis: Hackett Publishing Company.

Aristotle 2002, *Nicomachean Ethics*, translated by Joe Sachs, Newbury: Focus Publishing.

Aristotle 2004, *Aristotle's On the Soul and On Memory and Recollection*, translated by Joe Sachs, Santa Fe: Green Lion Press.

Aristotle 2011, *Eudemian Ethics*, translated by Anthony Kenny, Oxford: Oxford University Press.

Arthur, Christopher J. 2014, 'Marx, Hegel and the Value-Form', in *Marx's Capital and Hegel's Logic: A Reexamination*, edited by Fred Moseley and Tony Smith, Leiden: Brill Academic Publishers.

Associated Press 2006, 'Penis pump judge gets 4-year jail term', *USA Today*, August 18, 2006: http://usatoday30.usatoday.com/news/nation/2006-08-18-judge-sentenced_x .htm.

Avineri, Shlomo 1968, *The Social & Political Thought of Karl Marx*, Cambridge: Cambridge University Press.

Barry, Ellen 2016, 'Young Rural Women in India Chase Big-City Dreams', *The New York Times*, September 24: http://www.nytimes.com/2016/09/25/world/asia/bangalore-i ndia-women-factories.html.

Benner, Erica 2018 [1995], *Really Existing Nationalisms*, London: Verso.

Bensaïd, Daniel 2002, *Marx for Our Times, Adventures and Misadventures of a Critique*, translated by Gregory Elliott, London: Verso.

Brenner, Robert 2017, 'Introducing Catalyst', *Catalyst*, 1, 1: https://catalyst-journal.com/ vol1/no1/editorial-robert-brenner

Brentano, Franz 2015, *Psychology from an Empirical Standpoint*, London: Routledge.

Brown, Norman O. 1959, *Life Against Death: The Psychoanalytical Meaning of History*, Middletown: Wesleyan University Press.

Burns, Tony 2005, 'Whose Aristotle? Which Marx? Ethics, Law and Justice in Aristotle and in Marx', *Imprints*, 8, 2: 125–155.

Caligaris, Gaston and Guido Starosta 2014, 'Which "Rational Kernel"? Which "Mystical Shell"? A Contribution to the Debate on the Connection between Hegel's *Logic* and Marx's *Capital*', in *Marx's Capital and Hegel's Logic: A Reexamination*, edited by Fred Moseley and Tony Smith, Leiden: Brill Academic Publishers.

Canadian Press 2016, 'Get used to the "job churn" of short-term employment and career changes, Bill Morneau says', *National Post*, October 22: http://nationalpost .com/news/canada/get-used-to-the-job-churn-of-short-term-employment-and-car eer-changes-bill-morneau-says

Carlyle, Thomas 2002, *The French Revolution: A History*, New York: The Modern Library.

Chattopadhyay, Paresh 2006, 'Passage to Socialism: The Dialectic of Progress in Marx', *Historical Materialism*, 14, 3: 45–84.

Cohen, Gerald A. 1988, *History, Labour, and Freedom: Themes from Marx*, Oxford: Clarendon Press.

Crooks, Claire V. and David A. Wolfe 2007, 'Child Abuse and Neglect', in *Assessment of Childhood Disorders*, edited by E.J. Mash & R.A. Barkley, New York: The Guilford Press.

Dixit, Pranav and Ryan Mac 2018, 'How WhatsApp Destroyed a Village', *Buzzfeed News*, September 9: https://www.buzzfeednews.com/article/pranavdixit/whatsapp-destr oyed-village-lynchings-rainpada-india.

Draper, Hal 1971, 'The Principle of Self-Emancipation in Marx and Engels', *Socialist Register*, 8: 81–109.

Draper, Hal 1977, *Karl Marx's Theory of Revolution: State and Bureaucracy*, Volume 1, New York: Monthly Review Press.

Draper, Hal 1978, *Karl Marx's Theory of Revolution: The Politics of Social Classes*, Volume 1, New York: Monthly Review Press.

Durkheim, Emile 1979 [1951], *Suicide: A Study in Sociology*, translated by John A. Spaulding and George Simpson, New York: The Free Press.

Efthymiades, Yiannis 2016, 'O Say Can You See', in *Austerity Measures: The New Greek Poetry*, edited by Karen van Dyck, London: Penguin Books.

Engels, Friedrich MECW 25, *Marx-Engels Collected Works*, Volume 25, London: Lawrence & Wishart.

Engels, Friedrich MECW 50, *Marx-Engels Collected Works*, Volume 50, London: Lawrence & Wishart.

Engels, Friedrich and Karl Marx, MECW 5, *Marx-Engels Collected Works*, Volume 5, Lawrence & Wishart.

Engels, Friedrich and Karl Marx, MECW 6, *Marx-Engels Collected Works*, Volume 6, London: Lawrence & Wishart.

Engels, Friedrich and Karl Marx, MECW 8, *Marx-Engels Collected Works*, Volume 8, London: Lawrence & Wishart.

Engels, Friedrich and Karl Marx, MECW 11, *Marx-Engels Collected Works*, Volume 11, London: Lawrence & Wishart.

Engels, Friedrich and Karl Marx, MECW 24, *Marx-Engels Collected Works*, Volume 24, London: Lawrence & Wishart.

Engels, Friedrich and Karl Marx, MECW 26, *Marx-Engels Collected Works*, Volume 26, London: Lawrence & Wishart.

Fisher, Mark 2009, *Capitalist Realism, Is There No Alternative?*, Winchester: Zero Books.

Fisher, Mark 2018, *K-Punk: The Collected and Unpublished Writings of Mark Fisher (2004–2016)*, London: Repeater Books.

Fraser, Ian 1997, 'Two of a Kind: Hegel, Marx, Dialectic and Form', *Capital & Class*, 21, 1: 81–106.

Freud, Sigmund 1939, *Moses and Monotheism*, New York: Vintage Books.

Freud, Sigmund 1959, *Group Psychology and the Analysis of the Ego*, translated by James Strachey, New York: W.W. Norton & Company, Inc.

Freud, Sigmund 1961, *The Future of an Illusion*, Garden City: Doubleday & Company, Inc.

Freud, Sigmund 1966, 'A Project for Scientific Psychology', in *The Standard Edition of the Complete Psychological Works of Sigmund Freud*, Volume 1, edited by James Strachey, London: Hogarth Press.

Freud, Sigmund 1966b, *Introductory Lectures on Psycho-Analysis*, translated by James Strachey, New York: W.W. Norton & Company, Inc.

Freud, Sigmund 1969, *An Outline of Psycho-Analysis*, translated by James Strachey, New York: W.W. Norton & Company, Inc.

Freud, Sigmund 1991, *On Metapsychology: The Theory of Psychoanalysis*, translated by James Strachey, London: Penguin Books.

Freud, Sigmund n.d. 'Why War?': https://www.transcend.org/tms/wp-content/uploads/2017/06/Why-War-Freud.pdf

Fromm, Erich 1947, *Man For Himself, An Inquiry into the Psychology of Ethics*, Greenwich: Fawcett Publications, Inc.

Fromm, Erich 1962, *Beyond the Chains of illusion, My Encounter with Marx & Freud*, London: Abacus.

Fromm, Erich 1963, *The Dogma of Christ and Other Essays on Religion, Psychology and Culture*, New York: Owl Book.

Fromm, Erich 1970, *The Crisis of Psycho-Analysis, Essays on Freud, Marx, and Social Psychology*, Greenwich: Fawcett Publications.

Geras, Norman 1983, *Marx & Human Nature, Refutation of a Legend*, London: Verso.

Geras, Norman 1984, 'The controversy about Marx and justice', *Philosophica*, 33, 1: 33–86.

Hardimon, Michael O. 1992, 'The Project of Reconciliation: Hegel's Social Philosophy', *Philosophy & Public Affairs*, 21, 2: 165–195.

Hegel, Georg W.F. 1956, *The Philosophy of History*, Mineola: Dover Publications Inc.

Hegel, Georg W.F. 1961, *On Christianity: Early Theological Writings*, translated by T.M. Knox and Richard Kroner, New York: Harper & Brothers.

Hegel, Georg W.F. 1968, *Hegel's Lectures on The History of Philosophy*, Volume 1, London: Routledge.

Hegel, Georg W.F. 1969, *Science of Logic*, New York: Humanities Press.

Hegel, Georg W.F. 1971, *Philosophy of Mind*, Oxford: Clarendon Press.

Hegel, Georg W.F. 1977, *The Phenomenology of Spirit*, Oxford: Oxford University Press.

Hegel, Georg W.F. 1991, *Elements of the Philosophy of Right*, Cambridge: Cambridge University Press.

Hegel, Georg W.F. 1991b, *The Encyclopaedia Logic*, Indianapolis: Hackett Publishing Company Inc.

Hegel, Georg W.F. 2007b, *Lectures on the Proofs of the Existence of God*, edited and translated by Peter C. Hodgson, Oxford: Oxford University Press.

Heimann, Paula and Susan Isaacs 1952, 'Regression', in *Developments In Psycho-Analysis*, edited by Melanie Klein, Paula Heimann, Susan Isaacs and Joan Riviere, London: The Hogarth Press Ltd.

Heine, Heinrich 1982, *Poetry and Prose*, The German Library, Volume 32, New York: The Continuum Publishing Company.

Heraclitus 2001, *Fragments*, translated by Brooks Haxton, London: Penguin Books.

Hinshelwood, Robert Douglas 1983, 'Projective identification and Marx's concept of Man', *International Review of Psycho-Analysis*, 10: 221–226.

Hofstadter, Richard 1964, 'The Paranoid Style in American Politics', *Harpers Magazine*, November: https://harpers.org/archive/1964/11/the-paranoid-style-in-american-politics/

Hunt, Tristram 2009, *Marx's General: The Revolutionary Life of Friedrich Engels*, New York: Metropolitan Books.

Husserl, Edmund 1970, *The Crisis of the European Sciences and Transcendental Phenomenology*, Evanston: Northwestern University Press.

Husserl, Edmund 1999, 'Phenomenological Psychology and Transcendental Phenomenology', in *The Essential Husserl: Basic Writings in Transcendental Phenomenology*, edited by Donn Welton, Indianapolis: Indiana University Press.

Kant, Immanuel 2006, *Toward Perpetual Peace and Other Writings on Politics, Peace, and History*, New Haven: Yale University Press.

Kant, Immanuel 2007, *Critique of Judgement*, translated by James Creed Meredith, Oxford: Oxford University Press.

Klein, Melanie 1997, *Envy and Gratitude*, London: Vintage Books.

Klein, Melanie 1997b, *The Psycho-Analysis of Children*, London: Vintage Books.

Klein, Melanie 1998, *Love, Guilt and Reparation and other works 1921–1945*. London: Vintage Books.

Kouvelakis, Stathis 2003, *Philosophy and Revolution*, London: Verso.

Kosík, Karel 1969, 'Reason and History', *Telos*, 3: 64–71.

Lapavitsas, Costas and Stathis Kouvelakis 2019, 'The Radical Left: The Time for its Re-founding', blog, July 11, Verso Books: https://www.versobooks.com/en-ca/blogs/news/4373-the-radical-left-the-time-for-its-re-founding

Lenin, Vladimir I. 1943, *Essential Works of Lenin: 'What Is to Be Done?' and Other Writings*, edited by Henry M. Christman, New York: Dover Publications, Inc.

Levine, Norman 2012, *Marx's Discourse with Hegel*, London: Palgrave Macmillan.

Löwy, Michael 2005, *The Theory of Revolution in the Young Marx*, Chicago: Haymarket Books.

Löwith, Karl 1949, *Meaning in History*, Chicago: University of Chicago Press.

Lukács, Georg 1971, *History and Class Consciousness*, Cambridge: The MIT Press.

Marcuse, Herbert 1962, *Eros and Civilization: A Philosophical Inquiry into Freud*, New York: Vintage Books.

Marcuse, Herbert 1969, *An Essay on Liberation*, Boston: Beacon Press.

Marković, Mihailo 1974, *From Affluence to Praxis: Philosophy and Social Criticism*, Michigan: Ann Arbor Paperback.

Marx, Karl MECW 1, *Marx-Engels Collected Works*, Volume 1, London: Lawrence & Wishart.

Marx, Karl MECW 3, *Marx-Engels Collected Works*, Volume 3, London: Lawrence & Wishart.

Marx, Karl MECW 4, *Marx-Engels Collected Works*, Volume 4, London: Lawrence & Wishart.

Marx, Karl MECW 7, *Marx-Engels Collected Works*, Volume 7, London: Lawrence & Wishart.

Marx, Karl MECW 10, *Marx-Engels Collected Works*, Volume 10, London: Lawrence & Wishart.

Marx, Karl MECW 12, *Marx-Engels Collected Works*, Volume 12, London: Lawrence & Wishart.

Marx, Karl MECW 14, *Marx-Engels Collected Works*, Volume 14, London: Lawrence & Wishart.

Marx, Karl MECW 19, *Marx-Engels Collected Works*, Volume 19, London: Lawrence & Wishart.

Marx, Karl MECW 20, *Marx-Engels Collected Works*, Volume 20, London: Lawrence & Wishart.

Marx, Karl MECW 21, *Marx-Engels Collected Works*, Volume 21, London: Lawrence & Wishart.

Marx, Karl MECW 22, *Marx-Engels Collected Works*, Volume 22, London: Lawrence & Wishart.

Marx, Karl MECW 23, *Marx-Engels Collected Works*, Volume 23, London: Lawrence & Wishart.

Marx, Karl MECW 24, *Marx-Engels Collected Works*, Volume 24, London: Lawrence & Wishart.

Marx, Karl MECW 26, *Marx-Engels Collected Works*, Volume 26, London: Lawrence & Wishart.

Marx, Karl MECW 28, *Marx-Engels Collected Works*, Volume 28, London: Lawrence & Wishart.

Marx, Karl MECW 29, *Marx-Engels Collected Works*, Volume 29, London: Lawrence & Wishart.

Marx, Karl MECW 31, *Marx-Engels Collected Works*, Volume 31, London: Lawrence & Wishart.

Marx, Karl MECW 32, *Marx-Engels Collected Works*, Volume 32, London: Lawrence & Wishart.

Marx, Karl MECW 34, *Marx-Engels Collected Works*, Volume 34, London: Lawrence & Wishart.

Marx, Karl MECW 35, *Marx-Engels Collected Works*, Volume 35, London: Lawrence & Wishart.

Marx, Karl MECW 37, *Marx-Engels Collected Works*, Volume 37, London: Lawrence & Wishart.

Marx, Karl MECW 39, *Marx-Engels Collected Works*, Volume 39, London: Lawrence & Wishart.

Marx, Karl MECW 40, *Marx-Engels Collected Works*, Volume 40, London: Lawrence & Wishart.

Marx, Karl MECW 41, *Marx-Engels Collected Works*, Volume 41, London: Lawrence & Wishart.

Marx, Karl MECW 42, *Marx-Engels Collected Works*, Volume 42, London: Lawrence & Wishart.

Marx, Karl MECW 43, *Marx-Engels Collected Works*, Volume 43, London: Lawrence & Wishart.

McCarney, Joseph 1987, 'Hegel, Marx and Dialectic', in *Hegel and Modern Philosophy*, edited by David Lamb, London: Croom Helm.

McCarney, Joseph 1990, *Social Theory and the Crisis of Marxism*, London: Verso.

McCarney, Joseph 1991, 'The True Realm of Freedom: Marxist Philosophy after Communism', *New Left Review*, 189: 19–38.

McCarney, Joseph 2000, 'Hegel's Legacy', in *The Hegel-Marx Connection*, edited by Tony Burns and Ian Fraser, London: Macmillan Press Ltd.

McIvor, David W. 2016, 'The Cunning of Recognition: Melanie Klein and Contemporary Critical Theory', *Contemporary Political Theory*, 15, 3: 243–263.

McLellan, David 1973, *Karl Marx: His Life and Thought*, New York: Harper and Row.

McNally, David 2006, *Another World Is Possible: Globalization & Anti-Capitalism*, Winnipeg: Arbeiter Ring Publishing.

Meikle, Scott 1985, *Essentialism in the Thought of Karl Marx*, London: Duckworth.

Merleau-Ponty, Maurice 1964, *Sense and Non-Sense*, Evanston: Northwestern University Press.

Mészáros, Istvan 2011, *Social Structure and Forms of Consciousness: Dialectic of Structure and History*, Volume 2, New York: Monthly Review Press.

Miller, Richard W. 1981, 'Marx and Aristotle: A Kind of Consequentialism', in *Marxism and Morality*, edited by Kai Nielsen and Steven C. Patten. Guelph: Canadian Association for Publishing in Philosophy.

Money-Kyrle, Roger E. 1944, 'Towards a Common Aim – A Psycho-analytical Contribution to Ethics', *British Journal of Medical Psychology*, 20: 105–117.

Money-Kyrle, Roger E. 1944b, 'Some Aspects of Political Ethics from the Psycho-Analytical Point of View', *The International Journal of Psycho-Analysis*, 25: 166–171.

Money-Kyrle, Roger E. 1951, *Psychoanalysis and Politics: A Contribution to the Psychology of Politics and Morals*, New York: W.W. Norton & Company.

Money-Kyrle, Roger E. 1952, 'Psycho-Analysis and Ethics', *The International Journal of Psycho-Analysis*, 33: 225–234.

Money-Kyrle, Roger E. 2015, *The Collected Papers of Roger Money-Kyrle*, London: Karnac Books Ltd.

Moseley, Fred and Smith, Tony 2014, 'Introduction', in *Marx's Capital and Hegel's Logic: A Reexamination*, edited by Fred Moseley and Tony Smith, Leiden: Brill Academic Publishers.

Nietzsche, Friedrich 1996, *Thus Spoke Zarathustra*, translated by Walter Kaufmann, London: Penguin Books.

Novalis 2000, *Hymns to the Night*: https://logopoeia.com/novalis/hymns.html

Ollman, Bertell 1978, *Social and Sexual Revolution: Essays on Marx and Reich*. Montreal: Black Rose Books.

Ollman, Bertell 2003, *Dance of the Dialectic: Steps in Marx's Method*, Chicago: University of Illinois Press.

Paci, Enzo 1972, *The Function of the Sciences and the Meaning of Man*. Evanston: Northwestern University Press.

Piotrowski, Jessica Taylor and Matthew A. Lapierre, Deborah L. Linebarger 2013, 'Investigating correlates of self-regulation in early childhood with a representative sample of English-speaking American families', *Journal of Child and Family Studies*, 22, 3: 423–436.

Plato 1997, *Plato: Complete Works*, Indianapolis: Hackett Publishing Company.

Pomeroy, Anne Fairchild 2004, *Marx and Whitehead: Process, Dialectics, and the Critique of Capitalism*, Albany: State University of New York Press.

Reich, Wilhelm 1980, *The Mass Psychology of Fascism*, New York: Farrar, Straus and Giroux.

Reich, Wilhelm 2012, *Sex-Pol: Essays, 1929–1934*. London: Verso.

Rose, Jacqueline 2011, *The Jacqueline Rose Reader*, edited by Justin Clemens and Ben Naparstek, Durham: Duke University Press.

Rousseau, Jean-Jacques 1984 [1775], *A Discourse on Inequality*. London: Penguin Books.

Rustin, Michael 1982, 'A Socialist Consideration of Kleinian Psychoanalysis', *New Left Review* 131: 71–96.

Rustin, Margaret and Michael Rustin 1984, 'Relational Preconditions of Socialism', in *Capitalism and Infancy: Essays on Psychoanalysis and Politics*, edited by Barry Richards, London: Free Association Books.

Sayers, Sean 1987, 'The Actual and the Rational', in *Hegel and Modern Philosophy*, edited by David Lamb, London: Routledge.

Sayers, Sean 1998, *Marxism and Human Nature*, London: Routledge.

Sayers, Sean 2011, *Marx & Alienation, Essays on Hegelian Themes*, New York: Palgrave MacMillan.

Sayers, Sean 2019, 'Marx and Teleology', *Science & Society*, 83, 1: 37–63.

Schiller, Friedrich 2016, *On the Aesthetic Education of Man* and *Letters to Prince Frederick Christian von Augusenburg*, translated by Keith Tribe. London: Penguin Books.

Schipper, Arthur 2016, 'Review of *Dialectics in World Politics* edited by Shannon Brincat', *Marx & Philosophy Review of Books*: https://marxandphilosophy.org.uk/reviews/8124_dialectics-in-world-politics-review-by-arthur-schipper/.

Seferis, George 2016, *Novel and Other Poems*, translated by Roderick Beaton, Athens: Aiora Press.

Semuels, Alana 2018, 'What Amazon Does to Poor Cities', *The Atlantic*, February 1: https://www.theatlantic.com/business/archive/2018/02/amazon-warehouses-poor-cities/552020/

Shelley, Percy Bysshe 1956, *Shelley: Selected Poetry*, London: Penguin Books.

Skillen, Anthony 1981, 'Workers' Interests and the Proletarian Ethic; Conflicting Strains in Marxian Anti-moralism', in *Marxism and Morality*, edited by Kai Nielsen and Steven C. Patten, Guelph: Canadian Association for Publishing in Philosophy.

Starosta, Guido 2005, 'Commodity Fetishism and Revolutionary Subjectivity: A Symposium on John Holloway's *Change the World without Taking Power*. Editorial Introduction', *Historical Materialism*, 13, 4: 161–168.

Starosta, Guido 2013, 'The System of Machinery and Determinations of Revolutionary Subjectivity in the *Grundrisse* and *Capital*', in *In Marx's Laboratory: Critical Interpretations of the Grundrisse*, edited by Riccardo Bellofiore, Guido Starosta, and Peter D. Thomas, Leiden: Brill Academic Publishers.

Starosta, Guido 2016, *Marx's* Capital, *Method and Revolutionary Subjectivity*, Leiden: Brill Academic Publishers.

Sterne, Laurence 2009, *The Life and Opinions of Tristram Shandy, Gentleman*, Oxford: Oxford University Press.

Struhl, Karsten J. 2016, 'Marx and Human Nature: The Historical, the Trans-Historical, and Human Flourishing', *Science & Society*, 80, 1: 78–104.

Tabak, Mehmet 2012, *Dialectics of Human Nature in Marx's Philosophy*, New York: Palgrave MacMillan.

Taylor, A.E. 1952, *Socrates*, New York: Doubleday.

Whipple, Ellen E. and Carolyn Webster-Stratton 1991, 'The role of parental stress in physically abusive families', *Child Abuse and Neglect*, 15: 279–291.

Whitehead, Alfred N. 1925, *Science and the Modern World*, New York: The Free Press.

Whitehead, Alfred N. 1929, *Function of Reason*. Boston: Beacon Press.

Whitehead, Alfred N. 1967, *Adventures of Ideas*, New York: The Free Press.

Whitehead, Alfred N. 1968, *Modes of Thought*, New York: The Free Press.

Whitman, Walt 1975, *The Complete Poems*, edited by Francis Murphy, London: Penguin Education.

Wilson, H.T. 1991, *Marx's Critical/Dialectical Procedure*, London: Routledge.

Winslow, Ted 2015, '"Internal relations" and Marx's "materialist conception of history,"' *Capital & Class*, 39, 1: 95–110.

Wood, Allen 2004, *Karl Marx*, London: Routledge.

Wood, Ellen Meiksins 2008, 'Historical Materialism in "Forms Which Precede Capitalist Production,"' in *Karl Marx's Grundrisse: Foundations of the Critique of Political Economy 150 Years Later*, edited by Marcello Musto, London: Routledge.

Wolfenstein, Eugene Victor 1967, *The Revolutionary Personality: Lenin, Trotsky, Gandhi*, Princeton: Princeton University Press.

Wolfenstein, Eugene Victor 1993, *Psychoanalytic-Marxism: Groundwork*, London: The Guilford Press.

Index

www.ingramcontent.com/pod-product-compliance
Lightning Source LLC
Chambersburg PA
CBHW061732120626
46550CB00005B/1780